The American Assembly, *Columbia University*

THE CONGRESS AND
AMERICA'S FUTURE

Second Edition

Prentice-Hall, Inc., *Englewood Cliffs, N. J.*
A SPECTRUM BOOK

Library of Congress Cataloging in Publication Data

AMERICAN ASSEMBLY
  The Congress and America's future.

  (A Spectrum Book)
  Essays designed as background reading for the 26th American Assembly at
Arden House, Oct. 29 to Nov. 1, 1964, and for other sessions of the American
Assembly, are now rev. and updated.
  Includes bibliographical references.
    1. United States. Congress—Addresses, essays, lectures. I. Truman, David Bick-
nell, ed. II. Title.
JK1061.A73 1973   328.73'07   72–10005
ISBN 0–13–167585–0
ISBN 0–13–167577–X (pbk)

Printed in the United States of America.

10   9   8   7   6   5   4   3   2

PRENTICE-HALL INTERNATIONAL, INC. (*London*)
PRENTICE-HALL OF AUSTRALIA, PTY. LTD. (*Sydney*)
PRENTICE-HALL OF CANADA, LTD. (*Toronto*)
PRENTICE-HALL OF INDIA PRIVATE LIMITED (*New Delhi*)
PRENTICE-HALL OF JAPAN, INC. (*Tokyo*)

Table of Contents

Preface to the Second Edition

In 1964 the Twenty-sixth American Assembly met at Arden House, Harriman, New York, to consider what steps might be taken to assure the continued vitality and effectiveness of the Congress of the United States. Discussions at the Assembly were based on a series of chapters written by a group of authorities under the editorial supervision of Dr. David B. Truman. The chapters were published in 1965 by Prentice-Hall under the title *The Congress and America's Future* and immediately found wide readership among students of government and the general public. The volume also provided background reading for American Assemblies on congressional reform held with the cooperation of Tulane University, Occidental College, University of Oregon, U.S. Air Force Academy, George Washington University, Brigham Young University, and Ball State University—all on a generous grant from The Ford Foundation.

Demand for the volume continued, for the authors had dealt candidly and critically with the troubles of our national legislature and pointed to needed improvements in its capacity to handle the complex problems of a modern industrial state. With time it became apparent that as the organizational problems of Congress persisted so did the need for the book. It is presented herewith—revised and updated by Dr. Truman and all of the original writers —in the light of national and world parliamentary developments since the days of the first edition.

A large measure of thanks is due The Laurel Foundation for making this second edition possible. But neither the Foundation nor The American Assembly should be associated with the views herein, which belong to the authors themselves.

Clifford C. Nelson
President
The American Assembly

David B. Truman, Editor

Introduction

Criticism of the Congress is a hardy perennial of American life. But in the past fifteen years the pattern and volume of criticism directed at the Congress have taken on a character unlike anything since the close of the first decade of this century. To the familiar objections of individuals and groups whose desires have not met with legislative approval have been added a growing number of criticisms from responsible senators and representatives, from journalists and scholars, and from a growing set of publics which alternately see the Congress as unresponsive to national needs and as having abdicated or otherwise lost critically important power to the Presidency and to the executive branch. The concerns and the proposals emanating from these sources are not consistent in detail nor are they uniformly well considered. But most of them display a common element of worry that, unless ways are found to alter the functioning of the Congress, the fortunes of the nation may be inadequately guarded or seriously diminished.

Concern about the Congress, though stimulated by periodic crises and disillusionments, has its ultimate roots in three rather distinct sets of circumstances. Examination of these essays and reflections on the Congress will be more productive if these are kept in mind.

In the first place, the trials of our national legislature are in part a reflection of the "parliamentary crisis" that has affected the West for at least five decades. The twentieth century, it is often noted, has been hard on legislatures. Compelled in some fashion to deal with the complexities of increasingly urbanized, rapidly industrialized, and

DAVID B. TRUMAN *is president and professor of political science at Mount Holyoke College. He is the author of numerous works on the functions and processes of government, including* The Governmental Process *and* The Congressional Party.

irrevocably interdependent societies, they have found themselves alternating in varying degrees between two equally dangerous and distasteful situations: yielding the initiative as well as the implementing responsibilities to bureaucrats whose actions might be imperfectly mediated by political officials, or attempting to retain one or both of these functions at the expense of delay, indecision, and instability. The conferences of the Inter-Parliamentary Union, which have included delegates from the Congress of the United States, have been concerned with these problems since the close of World War I. The charges of "rubber stamp" against the Congresses of Franklin Roosevelt's first administration have been matched by criticisms from within and without the National Assembly of the Fifth French Republic, from critics of West Germany's "chancellor democracy," and even from within the British Parliament; the delays and debilitating compromises of other American Congresses have had at least their equivalents in the Third and Fourth French Republics, in Italy, and in most of the governments of northwestern Europe. Even the recently current charges of presidential usurpation in the United States have had their equivalents, at least in milder form, in other representative systems. To this awkward alternation has been added the inevitable increase in executive power that comes from the continued dominance of questions of foreign policy.

Some critics in American society and in other countries of the West would like to wish out of existence the industrial and technological changes that are at the roots of this "parliamentary crisis" and return to a simpler day. Such sentiments, though entirely understandable, are more than unrealistic. They are, as the European experience in the inter-war decades demonstrates, a seedbed for movements that would subvert and destroy the values underlying representative and constitutional systems. Solutions must be sought to the "parliamentary crisis," if these sentiments are not to produce such movements, by means that will acknowledge the irreversibility of the twentieth century's precipitating changes and will simultaneously preserve the essential values of the system—the stabilizing and legitimating processes of autonomous criticism and consent.

Secondly, concern over the performance of the Congress derives in part from two constitutional and closely related political features of the American system: the constitutional separation of the Congress and the President and the diffusing effects of federalism. The former is not strictly a separation of powers but, as Richard Neustadt has phrased it, "separated institutions sharing powers." [1] This arrangement, a source of tension and rivalry since the earliest days of the Republic, has complicated congressional adaptation to the twentieth century. The rhetoric of separation, as Neustadt argues in his essay (chapter 5),

[1] Richard E. Neustadt, *Presidential Power* (New York: Wiley, 1960), pp. 33, 39, 186ff.

helps to perpetuate in the Congress the illusion that it must and should be the principal source of policy initiatives, of grand designs for national programs, an illusion pregnant with frustration. At the same time, separation has played no small part in keeping the Congress more vital, more a political force to be reckoned with, than perhaps any national legislature in the world. This vitality, misdirected though it may sometimes be, is an asset not to be lightly overlooked in the search for function and organization appropriate to contemporary problems.

The handicapping effects of separation are complicated and reinforced by the federal character not only of the constitutional order but equally and consequently of the political order and especially of the major parties. This means not only that local or sectional interests are represented on Capitol Hill, but also that the most serious risks confronting the member of Congress are local. Except as these can be combined, as occasionally they are, with central demands in the Congress itself or in the White House, they tend to insulate the representative or senator from any policy constraint, from any political sanction, whose reach is not primarily local. To the strains of separation are thus added the diversity and incongruity of political risk that are induced by a federalized governmental and political structure. The political risks of senators and representatives, as Douglas Price's analysis demonstrates (chapter 2), may not be quite what they once were or what they appear to be, but the thrust of localism has not been altered.

In many respects, of course, this pull of localism is as it should be. Diverse interests within a continental country are often geographically defined, and they need to have access to the national legislature if that body is to be, in any reasonable sense, a representative one. Criticism arises when it appears that congressional stakes in national action are too weak to provide sufficient support for a national power to govern. Again, the problem is more complex because it is not one of clear and mutually exclusive alternatives but one of balance, of relative weights.

The third and most obvious source of concern about the Congress is those structural and procedural practices—including such matters as the seniority rule, "extended debate" in the Senate, and the powers of the House Committee on Rules—that appear to weaken the power to govern, to subject national objectives to local priorities, and to grant inequitable power advantages to interests and to persons strategically situated to exploit these practices. Most discussions of congressional "reform" focus on these items, or a fraction of them, without substantial reference to the two more fundamental sources of dissatisfaction and as if the criticized practices were awkward bits of machinery wholly without deeper origins or justifying function. Yet, as Richard

F. Fenno, Jr. and Ralph K. Huitt both point out in their discussions of the separate and quite distinct influence structures in the House and Senate (respectively chapters 3 and 4), these arrangements are parts of two coherent and well-developed systems. "The Congress" is in a very real sense a fiction, but each of the houses is an integral fact. To modify any of these conspicuous practices would be to alter fundamentally the internal power structure of each chamber. It would also, as Price's essay indicates, in many instances presuppose or at least precipitate fundamental alterations in the pattern of most contemporary congressional careers. This might be desirable, yet it might also take more effective power than is required to produce particular substantive results from the existing arrangements.

Despite the implications of some criticisms of the Congress, it is not precisely the institution it was at the turn of the century. But how is it different? Samuel P. Huntington (chapter 1) argues that the Congress has experienced a steady insulation from nationalizing changes and sources of power in the society at the same time that power within the legislature has become increasingly dispersed. These trends are serious and perhaps represent insuperable obstacles to congressional achievement of the institutional adaptations called for by the problems and patterns of the contemporory scene, by the American version of the "parliamentary crisis."

The crucial test of the Congress and of the federal government as a whole will not be in abstract terms, however, but rather in the quality of its policy output in matters of basic consequence for the nation's welfare. In order to assess a part of that output, in chapters 6 and 7 Harvey C. Mansfield and Holbert N. Carroll examine the role and the effect of the Congress in two broad areas of continuing basic importance, economic policy and national security policy. Both are concerned with the problem of limiting or eliminating the fragmentation of power and perspective that characterizes congressional operation. Their assessment of the House and Senate records in these two crucial areas does not, however, support a wholesale indictment of congressional performance. But it does lead much of the analysis outside the Congress and toward the White House. It underscores the possibility, argued by Neustadt (chapter 5), that in the days ahead the convergent but nonidentical interests of Presidents and members of Congress will require a greatly increased measure of collaboration between these two sets of elective politicians, if their distinctive skills are to control the demands of a consolidating officialdom.

The tempo of debate over these matters and particularly over the Congress and its functioning has fluctuated over the years, and the perspectives of the critics have shifted with changes in the policy context. The debate continues, however, and no sign of its diminution or disappearance is evident.

The essays in this book were planned to make a constructive contribution to the debate on causes and prescriptions, but they are not intended to promote any one of the many alternative proposals for reorganizing the Congress. Nor are they designed to champion a particular line of criticism. Rather they attempt a further analysis of the problems of the Congress by seeing its life and work in context, by identifying its characteristic ways and the reasons for them, and by examining the nature of its product in two areas crucial to the future of the nation. No single group of essays can pretend to have exhausted the subject of congressional reform. The authors of these papers are gratified by the widespread use of the collection and by the resulting request that they be updated and revised to reflect changes in the past decade. How they view the fact that, despite some changes in detail, nothing has changed in ten years that would alter their fundamental analysis the editor does not presume to inquire.

Samuel P. Huntington

1

Congressional Responses
to the Twentieth Century

Congress is a perennial source of anguish to both its friends and its foes. The critics point to its legislative failure. The function of a legislature, they argue, is to legislate and Congress either, does not legislate or legislates too little and too late. The intensity of their criticism varies inversely with the degree and dispatch with which Congress approves the President's legislative proposals. When in 1963 the Eighty-eighth Congress seemed to stymie the Kennedy legislative program, criticism rapidly mounted. "What kind of legislative body is it," asked Walter Lippmann, neatly summing up the prevailing exasperation, "that will not or cannot legislate?" When in 1964 the same Eighty-eighth Congress passed the civil rights, tax, and other bills, criticism of Congress correspondingly subsided. Reacting differently to this familiar pattern, the friends of Congress lamented its acquiescence to presidential dictate. Since 1933, they said, the authority of the executive branch—President, administration, and bureaucracy— has waxed, while that of Congress has waned. They warned of the constitutional perils stemming from the permanent subordination of one branch of government to another. In foreign and military policy, as well as domestic affairs, Congress is damned when it acquiesces in presidential leadership (Tonkin Gulf Resolution, 1964) and also when it attempts to seize the initiative (Mansfield Resolution, 1971).

SAMUEL P. HUNTINGTON *is Frank G. Thomson Professor of Government at Harvard University. He is the author of many books and articles on military policy and political development, including* Political Order in Changing Societies *and, as co-editor and contributor,* Authoritarian Politics in Modern Society: The Dynamics of Established One-Party Systems *(with Clement Henry Moore).*

At the same time that it is an obstructive ogre to its enemies, Congress is also the declining despair of its friends. Can both images be true? In large part, they are. The dilemma of Congress, indeed, can be measured by the extent to which congressional assertion coincides with congressional obstruction.

This paradox has been at the root of the "problem" of Congress since the early days of the New Deal. Vis-à-vis the executive, Congress in an autonomous, legislative body. But apparently Congress can defend its autonomy only by refusing to legislate, and it can legislate only by surrendering its autonomy. In the past, there has been a familiar pattern: Congress balks, criticism rises, the clamoring voices of reformers fill the air with demands for the "modernization" of the "antiquated procedures" of an "eighteenth century" Congress so it can deal with "twentieth century realities." The demands for reform serve as counters in the legislative game to get the President's measures through Congress. Independence thus provokes criticism; acquiescence brings approbation. If Congress legislates, it subordinates itself to the President; if it refuses to legislate, it alienates itself from public opinion. Congress can assert its power or it can pass laws; but it cannot do both.

Legislative Power and Institutional Crisis

The roots of this legislative dilemma lie in the changes in American society during the twentieth century. The twentieth century has seen: rapid urbanization and the beginnings of a postindustrial, technological society; the nationalization of social and economic problems and the concomitant growth of national organizations to deal with these problems; the increasing bureaucratization of social, economic, and governmental organizations; and the sustained high-level international involvement of the United States in world politics. These developments have generated new forces in American politics and initiated major changes in the distribution of power in American society. In particular, the twentieth century has witnessed the tremendous expansion of the responsibilities of the national government and the size of the national bureaucracy. In 1901, the national government had 351,798 employees or less than 1½ percent of the national labor force. In 1971 it had 5,637,000 employees, constituting almost 7 percent of the labor force. The expansion of the national government has been paralleled by the emergence of other large, national, bureaucratic organizations: manufacturing corporations, banks, insurance companies, labor unions, trade associations, farm organizations, newspaper chains, radio-TV networks. Each organization may have relatively specialized and concrete interests, but typically it functions on a national basis. Its headquarters are in New York or Washington; its operations are scattered across a dozen or more states. The emergence of these organizations truly constitutes, in Kenneth Boulding's expressive phrase, an "organizational revolution." The existence of this private "Establishment," more than anything else, distinguishes twentieth-century America from nineteenth-century America. The leaders of these organizations are the notables of American society: they are the prime wielders of social and economic power.

ADAPTATION CRISES

These momentous social changes have confronted Congress with an institutional "adaptation crisis." Such a crisis occurs when changes in the environment of a governmental institution force the institution either to alter its functions, affiliation, and modes of behavior, or to face decline, decay, and isolation. Crises usually occur when an institution loses its previous sources of support or fails to adapt itself to the rise of new social forces. Such a crisis, for instance, affected the Presidency in the second and third decades of the nineteenth century. Under the leadership of Henry Clay the focal center of power in the national government was in the House of Representatives; the congressional caucus dictated presidential nominations; popular interest in and support for the Presidency were minimal. The "Executive," Justice Story remarked in 1818, "has no longer a commanding influence. The House of Representatives has absorbed all the popular feelings and all the effective power of the country." The Presidency was on the verge of becoming a weak, secondary instrumental organ of government. It was rescued from this fate by the Jacksonian movement, which democratized the Presidency, broadened its basis of popular support, and restored it as the center of vitality and leadership in the national government. The House of Commons was faced with a somewhat similar crisis during the agitation preceding the first Reform Bill of 1832. New social groups were developing in England which were demanding admission to the political arena and the opportunity to share in political leadership. Broadening the constituency of the House of Commons and reforming the system of election enabled the House to revitalize itself and to continue as the principal locus of power in the British government.

In both these cases a governmental institution got a new lease on life, new vigor, new power, by embodying within itself dynamic, new social forces. When an institution fails to make such an alignment, it must either restrict its own authority or submit to limitations upon its authority imposed from outside. In 1910, when the House of Lords refused to approve Lloyd George's budget, it was first compelled by governmental pressure, popular opinion, and the threat of the creation of new peers to acquiesce in the budget and then through a similar process to acquiesce in the curtailment of its own power to obstruct legislation approved by the Commons. In this case the effort to block legislation approved by the dominant forces in the political community resulted in a permanent diminution of the authority of the offending institution. A somewhat similar crisis developed with respect to the Supreme Court in the 1930s. Here again a less popular body attempted to veto the actions of more popular bodies. In three years the Court invalidated twelve acts of Congress. Inevitably this precipitated vigorous criticism and demands for reform, culminating in Roosevelt's court reorganization proposal in February of 1937. The alternatives confronting the Court were relatively clear-cut: it could "reform" or be "reformed." In "the switch in time that saved nine," it chose the former course, signaling its change by approving the National Labor Relations Act in April 1937 and the Social Security Act in May. With this switch, support for the reorganization of the Court drained away. The result was, in the words of Justice Jackson, "a failure of the reform forces and a victory of the reform."

CONGRESS'S RESPONSE

Each of these four institutional crises arose from the failure of a governmental institution to adjust to social change and the rise of new viewpoints, new needs, and new political forces. Congress's legislative dilemma and loss of power stem from the nature of its overall institutional response to the changes in American society. This response involves three major aspects of Congress as an institution: its affiliations, its structure, and its functions. During the twentieth century Congress gradually insulated itself from the new political forces which social change had generated and which were, in turn, generating more change. Hence the leadership of Congress lacked the incentive to take the legislative initiative in handling emerging national problems. Within Congress power became dispersed among many officials, committees, and subcommittees. Hence the central leadership of Congress lacked the ability to establish national legislative priorities. As a result, the legislative function of Congress declined in importance, while the growth of the federal bureaucracy made the administrative overseeing function of Congress more important. These three tendencies—toward insulation, dispersion, and oversight—have dominated the evolution of Congress during the twentieth century.

Affiliations: Insulation from Power

CONGRESSIONAL EVOLUTION

Perhaps the single most important trend in congressional evolution for the bulk of this century was the growing insulation of Congress from other social groups and political institutions. In 1900 no gap existed between congressmen and the other leaders of American society and politics. Half a century later the changes in American society, on the one hand, and the institutional evolution of Congress, on the other, had produced a marked gap between congressional leaders and the bureaucratically oriented leadership of the executive branch and of the establishment. The growth of this gap can be seen in seven aspects of congressional evolution.

(*1*) *Increasing Tenure of Office*—In the nineteenth century few congressmen stayed in Congress very long. During the twentieth century the average tenure of congressmen has inexorably lengthened. In 1900 only 9 percent of the members of the House of Representatives had served five terms or more and less than 1 percent had served ten terms or more. In 1957, 45 percent of the House had served five terms or more and 14 percent ten terms or more. In 1897, for each representative who had served ten terms or more in the House, there were 34 representatives who had served two terms or less. In 1971 the ratio was down almost to equality, with 1.2 members who had served two terms or less for each ten-termer.[1] In the middle of the nineteenth century, only about half the representatives in any one Congress had served in a previous Congress, and only about one-third of the senators had been elected to the Senate more than once. By the second half of the twentieth century, close to 90 percent of the House were veterans, and almost two-thirds of the senators were beyond their first term. The biennial infusion of new blood had reached an all-time low.

(*2*) *The Increasingly Important Role of Seniority*—Increasing tenure of congressmen is closely linked to increasingly rigid adherence to the practices of seniority. The longer men stay in Congress, the more likely they are to see virtue in seniority. Conversely, the more important seniority is, the greater is the constituent appeal of men who have been long in office. The rigid system of seniority in *both* houses of Congress is a product of the twentieth century.

In the nineteenth century seniority was far more significant in the Senate than in the House. Since the middle of that century apparently only in five instances—the last in 1925—has the chairmanship of a Senate committee been denied to the most senior member of the committee. In the House, on the other hand, the Speaker early received the power to appoint committees and to designate their chair-

---

[1] George B. Galloway, *History of the United States House of Representatives* (House Document 246, Eighty-seventh Congress, First Session, 1962), p. 31; T. Richard Witmer, "The Aging of the House," *Political Science Quarterly*, 79 (Dec. 1964), pp. 526–541. See Nelson Polsby, "The Institutionalization of the U.S. House of Representatives," *American Political Science Review*, 62 (March 1968), pp. 144–68, for documentation in historical detail for the House of Representatives of several of the trends posited here and analysis of them according to criteria of institutionalization (autonomy, coherence, complexity) which I elaborated in "Political Development and Political Decay," *World Politics*, 17 (April 1965), pp. 386–430.

Table I
Veteran Congressmen in Congress

Congress	Date	Representatives elected to House more than once	Senators elected to Senate more than once
42nd	1871	53%	32%
50th	1887	63	45
64th	1915	74	47
74th	1935	77	54
87th	1961	87	66
92nd	1971	88	65

Source: Figures for representatives for 1871–1915 are from Robert Luce, *Legislative Assemblies* (Boston: Houghton Mifflin Company, 1924), p. 365. Other figures were calculated independently. I am indebted to Emily Lieberman for assistance in updating these and other statistics in this essay.

men. During the nineteenth century Speakers made much of this power. Committee appointment and the selection of chairmen were involved political processes, in which the Speaker carefully balanced factors of seniority, geography, expertise, and policy viewpoint in making his choices. Not infrequently prolonged bargaining would result as the Speaker traded committee positions for legislative commitments. Commenting on James G. Blaine's efforts at committee construction in the early 1870s, one member of his family wrote that Blaine "left for New York on Wednesday. He had cotton and wool manufacturers to meet in Boston, and, over and above all, pressure to resist or permit. As fast as he gets his committees arranged, just so fast some after-consideration comes up which overtopples the whole list like a row of bricks." [2] Only with the drastic curtailment of the powers of the Speaker in 1910 and 1911 did the seniority system in the House assume the inflexible pattern which it has today. Only twice in the years after the 1910 revolt—once in 1915 and once in 1921—was seniority neglected in the choice of committee chairmen.

In the 1960s seniority came under increasing criticism within Congress and some small steps away from it were taken. In 1965 the House Democratic caucus stripped two southern congressmen of their committee seniority for supporting Barry Goldwater in 1964. One of them, John Bell Williams of Mississippi, had been a member of the

[2] Gail Hamilton, *Life of James G. Blaine*, p. 263, quoted in DeAlva S. Alexander, *History and Procedure of the House of Representatives* (Boston: Houghton Mifflin, 1916), p. 69. On the development of the House seniority system, see Michael Abram and Joseph Cooper, "The Rise of Seniority in the House of Representatives," *Polity*, 1 (Fall 1968), pp. 52–85, and Nelson Polsby, Miriam Gallaher, and Barry Spencer Rundquist, "The Growth of the Seniority System in the U.S. House of Representatives," *American Political Science Review*, 63 (Sept. 1969), pp. 787–807. For the operation of the system, see, in general, Barbara Hinckley, *The Seniority System in Congress* (Bloomington: Ind. Univ. Press, 1971).

House since 1947 and was the second-ranking Democrat on the Committee on Interstate and Foreign Commerce. In 1967 a select House committee recommended punishing Representative Adam Clayton Powell by, among other things, taking away his seniority and hence his position as chairman of the Committee on Education and Labor. The House, however, instead voted to deny Mr. Powell a seat in the Ninetieth Congress. In 1971 the House Republican and Democratic caucuses decreed that the selection of committee chairmen should be subject to caucus approval; the Democratic caucus then approved as chairmen those who would have been chairmen by seniority. Nor was a serious effort made to change the seniority system in the Legislative Reorganization Act of 1970. These events suggest that the system will remain but that deviations from it (at least in the House) will occasionally occur and will be accepted as legitimate.

(*3*) *Extended Tenure: a Prerequisite for Leadership*—Before 1896 Speakers, at the time of their first election, averaged only 7 years' tenure in the House. Since 1896 Speakers have averaged 23 years of House service at their first election. In 1811 and in 1859 Henry Clay and William Pennington were elected Speaker when they first entered the House. In 1807 Thomas Jefferson arranged for the election of his friend, William C. Nicholas, to the House and then for his immediate selection by the party caucus as floor leader. Such an intrusion of leadership from the outside would now be unthinkable. Today the Speaker and other leaders of the House and, to a lesser degree, the leaders of the Senate are legislative veterans of long standing. In 1971 46 House leaders averaged over 23 years' service in the House while 40 leading senators averaged 17 years of senatorial service. The top House leaders (Speaker, floor leaders, chairmen and ranking minority members of Ways and Means, Appropriations, and Rules Committees) averaged 26 years in the House and 8 in leadership positions in 1971. Top Senate leaders (President *pro tem.*, floor leaders, chairmen, and ranking minority members of Finance, Foreign Relations, and Appropriations Committees) averaged 23 years of service in the Senate and 11 in leadership positions. Increasing tenure means increasing age. In the nineteenth century the leaders of Congress were often in their thirties. Clay was 34 when he became Speaker in 1811; Hunter, 30 when he became Speaker in 1839; White, 36 at his accession to the Speakership in 1841; and Ore, 35 when he became Speaker in 1857. In contrast, Rayburn was 58 when he became Speaker, Martin 63, McCormack 71, and Albert 62. In 1971 the top leaders of the House averaged 63 years, those of the Senate 69 years.

(*4*) *Leadership within Congress: a One-way Street*—Normally in American life becoming a leader in one institution opens up leadership possibilities in other institutions: corporation presidents head civic agencies or become cabinet officers; foundation and university executives move into government; leading lawyers and bankers take over industrial corporations. The greater one's prestige, authority, and accomplishments within one organization, the easier it is to move to other and better posts in other organizations. Such, however, is not the case with Congress. Leadership in the House of Representatives leads nowhere except to leadership in the House of Representatives. To a lesser degree, the same has been true of the Senate. The successful House or Senate leader has to identify himself completely with his institution, its mores, traditions, and ways of behavior. "The very ingredients which make you a powerful House leader," one representative has commented, "are the ones which keep you from being a public leader." [3] Representatives typically confront a "fourth-term crisis": if they wish to run for higher office—for governor or senator— they must usually do so by the beginning of their fourth term in the House. If they stay in the House for four or more terms, they in effect choose to make a career in the House and to forswear the other electoral possibilities of American politics. Leadership in the Senate is not as exclusive a commitment as it is in the House. But despite such notable exceptions as Taft and Johnson, the most influential men in the Senate have typically been those who have looked with disdain upon the prospect of being anything but a United States Senator. Even someone with the high talent and broad ambition of Lyndon Johnson could not escape this exclusive embrace during his years as majority leader. In the words of Theodore H. White, the Senate, for Johnson, was "faith, calling, club, habit, relaxation, devotion, hobby, and love." Over the years it became "almost a monomania with him, his private life itself." [4] Such "monomania" is normally the prerequisite for Senate leadership. It is also normally an insurmountable barrier, psychologically and politically, to effective leadership outside the Senate.

(5) *The Decline of Personnel Interchange Between Congress and the Administration*—Movement of leaders in recent years between the great national institutions of the establishment and the top positions in the administration has been frequent, easy, and natural. This pattern of lateral entry distinguishes the American executive branch from the governments of most other modern societies. The circulation of individuals between leadership positions in governmental and private institutions eases the strains between political and private leadership and performs a unifying function comparable

[3] Quoted in Charles L. Clapp, *The Congressman: His Work as He Sees It* (Washington: Brookings Institution, 1963), p. 21.
[4] Theodore H. White, *The Making of the President, 1960* (New York: Atheneum Press, 1961), p. 132.

to that which common class origins perform in Great Britain or
common membership in the Communist party does in the Soviet
Union.

The frequent movement of individuals between administration
and establishment contrasts sharply with the virtual absence of such
movement between Congress and the administration or between
Congress and the establishment. The gap between congressional leadership and administration leadership has increased sharply during
this century. Seniority makes it virtually impossible for administration leaders to become leaders of Congress and makes it unlikely that
leaders of Congress will want to become leaders of the administration.
The separation of powers has become the insulation of leaders. Between 1861 and 1896, 37 percent of the people appointed to posts in
the President's cabinet had served in the House or Senate. Between
1897 and 1940, 19 percent of the Cabinet positions were filled by
former congressmen or senators. Between 1941 and 1963, only 15
percent of the cabinet posts were so filled. Former congressmen received only 4 percent of over 1,000 appointments of political executives made during the Roosevelt, Truman, Eisenhower, and Kennedy
administrations.[5] In 1963, apart from the President and Vice-President,
only one of the top 75 leaders of the Kennedy administration (Secretary of the Interior Udall) had served in Congress. The Nixon administration was somewhat more hospitable to legislators, but in 1971
only 4 of its 75 top leaders (apart from the President) had congressional experience.

Movement from the administration to leadership positions in
Congress is almost equally rare. In 1971 only one of 84 congressional
leaders (Senator Anderson) had previously served in the President's
cabinet. Those members of the administration who do move on to
Congress are typically those who have come to the administration from
state and local politics rather than from the great national institutions. Few congressmen and even fewer congressional leaders move
from Congress to positions of leadership in national private organizations, and relatively few leaders of these organizations move on to
Congress. Successful men who have come to the top in business, law,
or education naturally hesitate to shift to another world in which
they would have to start all over again at the bottom. In some cases,
establishment leaders also consider legislative office simply beneath
them.

(6) *The Social Origins and Careers of Congressmen*—Congressmen

[5] See Pendleton Herring, *Presidential Leadership* (New York: Farrar and Rinehart, 1940), pp. 164–65 for figures for 1861–1940; figures for 1940–1963 have been
calculated on same basis as Herring's figures; see also Dean E. Mann, "The Selection of Federal Political Executives," *American Political Science Review*, 58 (March
1964), p. 97.

are much more likely to come from rural and small-town backgrounds than are administration and establishment leaders. A majority of the senators holding office between 1947 and 1957 were born in rural areas. Of the 1959 senators 64 percent were raised in rural areas or in small towns, and only 19 percent in metropolitan centers. In contrast, 52 percent of the presidents of the largest industrial corporations grew up in metropolitan centers, as did a large proportion of the political executives appointed during the Roosevelt, Truman, Eisenhower, and Kennedy administrations. The contrast in origins is reflected in fathers' occupations. In the 1950s, the proportion of farmer fathers among senators (32 percent) was more than twice as high as it was among administration leaders (13 percent) and business leaders (9 to 15 percent).[6]

Of perhaps greater significance is the difference in geographical mobility between congressmen and private and public executives. Forty-one percent of the 1959 senators, but only 12 percent of the 1959 corporation presidents, were currently residing in their original hometowns. Seventy percent of the presidents had moved 100 miles or more from their hometowns but only 29 percent of the senators had done so.[7] In 1971 over two-fifths of the leaders of Congress but only 13 percent of administration leaders were still living in their places of birth. Seventy-five percent of the congressional leaders were living in their states of birth, while 62 percent of the administration leaders had moved out of their states of birth. Fifty-nine percent of administration leaders had moved from one region of the country to another, but only 16 percent of congressional leaders had similar mobility.

During the course of this century the career patterns of congressmen and of executive leaders have diverged. At an earlier period both

[6] See Andrew Hacker, "The Elected and the Anointed," *American Political Science Review*, 55 (Sept. 1961), pp. 540–41; Mann, *ibid.*, 58 (March 1964), pp. 92–93; Donald R. Matthews, *U.S. Senators and Their World* (Chapel Hill: Univ. of N.C. Press, 1960), pp. 14–17; W. Lloyd Warner *et al.*, *The American Federal Executive* (New Haven: Yale Univ. Press, 1963), pp. 11, 56–58, 333; W. Lloyd Warner and James C. Abegglen, *Occupational Mobility in American Business and Industry* (Minneapolis: Univ. of Minn. Press, 1955), p. 38; Suzanne Keller, "The Social Origins and Career Patterns of Three Generations of American Business Leaders" (Ph.D. dissertation, Columbia Univ., 1953), cited in Wendell Bell, Richard J. Hill, and Charles R. Wright, *Public Leadership* (San Francisco: Chandler Press, 1961), p. 106. Leroy N. Rieselbach has noted that congressmen in the 1950s and 1960s were not more rural or small-town in their birthplaces than the population of the country as a whole in 1900 and 1910. "Congressmen as 'Small Town Boys': A Research Note," *Midwest Journal of Political Science*, 14 (May 1970), pp. 321–30. His argument, however, involves a quite different question from that argued here which concerns not the representativeness of congressmen compared to the general population, but rather the similarity or difference in background of congressional and other elites.

[7] Hacker, *op. cit.*, p. 544. For further analysis of the limited geographical mobility of representatives, see Roger H. Davidson, *The Role of the Congressman* (New York: Pegasus, 1969), pp. 54–59.

Table II

GEOGRAPHICAL MOBILITY OF NATIONAL LEADERS

	Congressional Leaders		Administration Leaders		Political Executives	Business Leaders
	(*1963*) N-81	(*1971*) N-86	(*1963*) N-74	(*1971*) N-75	(*1959*) N-1865	(*1952*) N-8300
None	37%	43%	11%	13%	}14%	}40%
Intrastate	40	35	19	25		
Interstate, intraregion	5	8	9	3	10	15
Interregion	19	14	61	52	73	45
International	0	0	0	7	3	0

Sources: "Political Executives," Warner *et al, op. cit.*, p. 332; business leaders, Warner and Abegglen, *op. cit.*, p. 82; congressional and administration leaders, independent calculation. Geographical mobility is measured by comparing birthplace with current residence. For administration leaders, current residence was considered to be last residence before assuming administration position. The nine regions employed in this analysis are defined in Warner *et al.*, *op. cit.*, pp. 42–43.

leaderships had extensive experience in local and state politics. In 1903 about one-half of executive leaders and three-quarters of congressional leaders had held office in state or local government. In 1971 the congressional pattern had not changed significantly, with 71 percent of the congressional leaders having held state or local office. The proportion of executive leaders with this experience, however, had dropped drastically. The proportion of administration leaders who had held state or local office was still less than half that of congressional leaders, although it had gone up to 31 percent from 17 percent in 1963. When coupled with the data presented earlier on the larger number of former congressmen in the Nixon administration than in the Kennedy administration, these figures suggest a slight shift in recruitment toward local politics and away from the national establishment for the former as compared to the latter.

In recent years, congressional leaders have also more often been professional politicians than they were earlier: in 1903 only 5 percent of the congressional leaders had no major occupation outside politics, while in 1963, 22 percent of the congressional leaders had spent almost all their lives in electoral politics. Roughly 90 percent of the members of Congress in recent years, it has been estimated, "have served apprenticeship in some segment of our political life." [8]

The typical congressman may have gone away to college, but he then returned to his home state to pursue an electoral career, working his way up through local office, the state legislature, and eventually to Congress. The typical political executive, on the other hand, like

[8] Davidson, *Role of the Congressman,* p. 54.

Table III

Experience of National Political Leaders
in State and Local Government

Offices Held	Congressional Leaders			Administration Leaders		
	1903	*1963*	*1971*	*1903*	*1963*	*1971*
Any state or local office	75%	64%	71%	49%	17%	31%
Elective local office	55	46	37	22	5	4
State legislature	47	30	42	17	3	9
Appointive state office	12	10	16	20	7	12
Governor	16	9	5	5	4	7

the typical corporation executive, went away to college and then did not return home but instead pursued a career in a metropolitan center or worked in one or more national organizations with frequent changes of residence. As a result, political executives have become divorced from state and local politics, just as the congressional leaders have become isolated from national organizations. Congressional leaders, in short, come up through a "local politics" line while executives move up through a "national organization" line.

The differences in geographical mobility and career patterns between congressional and administration leaders reflect two different styles of life which cut across the usual occupational groupings. Businessmen, lawyers, and bankers are found in both Congress and the administration. But those in Congress are more likely to be small businessmen, small-town lawyers, and small-town bankers. Among the 66 lawyers in the Senate in 1963, for instance, only 2—Joseph Clark and Clifford Case—had been "prominent corporation counsel[s]" before going into politics.[9] Administration leaders, in contrast, are far more likely to be affiliated with large national industrial corporations, with Wall Street or State Street law firms, and with New York banks.

(7) *The Provincialism of Congressmen*—The absence of mobility between Congress and the executive branch and the differing backgrounds of the leaders of the two branches of government stimulate different policy attitudes. Congressmen have tended to be oriented toward local needs and small-town ways of thought. The leaders of the administration and of the great private national institutions are more likely to think in national terms. Analyzing consensus-building on foreign aid, James N. Rosenau concluded that congressmen typically had "segmental" orientations while other national leaders had "continental" orientations. The segmentally oriented leaders

---

[9] Andrew Hacker, "Are There Too Many Lawyers in Congress?" *New York Times Magazine,* January 5, 1964, p. 74.

"give highest priority to the subnational units which they head or represent" and are "not prepared to admit a discrepancy between" the national welfare and "their subnational concerns." The congressman is part of a local consensus of local politicians, local businessmen, local bankers, local trade union leaders, and local newspaper editors who constitute the opinion-making elite of their districts. As Senator Richard Neuberger noted: "If there is one maxim which seems to prevail among many members of our national legislature, it is that local matters must come first and global problems a poor second— that is, if the member of Congress is to survive politically." As a result, the members of Congress are "isolated" from other national leaders. At gatherings of national leaders, "members of Congress seem more conspicuous by their absence than by their presence." One piece of evidence is fairly conclusive: of 623 national opinion-makers who attended ten American Assembly sessions between 1956 and 1960, only 9 (1.4 percent) were members of Congress! [10]

The differences in attitude between segmentally oriented congressmen and the other, continentally oriented national leaders are particularly marked in those areas of foreign policy (such as foreign aid) which involve the commitment of tangible resources for intangible ends. But they have also existed in domestic policy. The approaches of senators and corporation presidents to economic issues, Andrew Hacker found, were rooted in "disparate images of society." Senators were provincially oriented; corporation presidents "metropolitan" in their thinking. Senators might be sympathetic to business, but they thought of business in small-town, small-business terms. They might attempt to accommodate themselves to the needs of the national corporations, but basically they were "faced with a power they do not really understand and with demands about whose legitimacy they are uneasy." As a result, Hacker suggests, "serious tensions exist between our major political and economic institutions. . . . There is, at base, a real lack of understanding and a failure of communication between the two elites." [11]

"Segmental" or "provincial" attitudes are undoubtedly stronger in the House than they are in the Senate. But they have also existed in the Senate. Despite the increased unity of the country caused by mass communications and the growth of "national as distinguished from local or sectional industry," the Senate in the 1950s was, according to an admiring portraitist, "if anything progressively less national in its approach to most affairs" and "increasingly engaged upon the protection of what is primarily local or sectional in economic life." [12]

[10] James N. Rosenau, *National Leadership and Foreign Policy* (Princeton: Princeton Univ. Press, 1963, pp. 30–31, 347–350.
[11] Hacker, *op. cit.*, pp. 547–49.
[12] William S. White, *Citadel* (New York: Harper & Bros., 1956), p. 136.

For both House and Senate these local patterns are being challenged and in some degree undermined by the nationalizing impact of the media and the geographical extension of party competition.[13] Yet within Congress old ideas, old values, and old beliefs linger on. The structure of Congress encourages their perpetuation. The newcomer to Congress is repeatedly warned that "to get along he must go along." To go along means to adjust to the prevailing mores and attitudes. The more the young congressman desires a career in the House or Senate, the more readily he makes these adjustments. The country at large has become urban, suburban, and metropolitan. Its economic, social, educational, and technological activities are increasingly performed by huge national bureaucratic organizations. In the 1960s these developments were only beginning to make themselves felt in Congress, as gradually younger and more adventurous congressmen took the initiative in challenging the old ways. On Capitol Hill the nineteenth-century ethos of the small town, the independent farmer, and the small businessman slowly wanes behind the institutional defenses which developed in this century to insulate Congress from the new America.

DEFECTS IN REPRESENTATION

In the twentieth century the executive branch grew in power vis-à-vis Congress for precisely the same reason that the House of Representatives grew in power vis-à-vis the executive in the second and third decades of the nineteenth century. It became more powerful because it had become more representative. Congress lost power because it had two defects as a representative body. One, relatively minor and in part easily remedied, dealt with the representation of people as individuals; the other, more serious and perhaps beyond remedy, concerned the representation of organized groups and interests.

Congress was originally designed to represent individuals in the House and governmental units—the states—in the Senate. In the course of time the significance of the states as organized interests declined, and popular election of senators was introduced. In effect, both senators and representatives now represent relatively arbitrarily-defined territorial collections of individuals. This system of individual representation has suffered from two inequities. First, of course, is the constitutional equal representation of states in the Senate irrespective of population. Second, in the House, congressional districts have varied widely in size and may also be gerrymandered to benefit one party or group of voters. For much of this century the net effect of these practices was to place the urban and the suburban voter at a disadvantage vis-à-vis the rural and small-town voter. The correction of this im-

[13] See John S. Saloma III, *Congress and the New Politics* (Boston: Little, Brown, 1969), pp. 68–69.

balance moved rapidly ahead, however, following the Supreme Court decisions (*Baker* v. *Carr*, 1962; *Wesberry* v. *Sanders*, 1964) mandating equal size for districts. As a result of the Court action, there was a net shift of between 10 and 19 districts from predominantly rural to predominantly urban during the 1960s.[14] The application of the new standards to the 1970 census population, it has been estimated, should result in 291 metropolitan districts in 1972 compared to 254 in 1962. Of these 129 would be suburban districts compared to 92 such districts in 1962. Central city representation, on the other hand, will drop to 100 congressmen from 106 in 1962 and a peak of 110 in 1966.[15] As Milton Cummings notes:

> In all this there is a very considerable irony. The battle for greater urban representation in the House in the 1950s and 1960s was often accompanied by rhetoric stressing the need to help the central cities, who, it was asserted, were penalized by rural overrepresentation. Now that the one-man/one-vote doctrine is being implemented, however, it is the suburbs, not the central cities, that stand to gain the most.[16]

The overall membership of the House will thus be increasingly metropolitan and suburban. Adherence to seniority, however, means that the leadership of the House will remain southern rural and northern urban for some years to come.

The second and more significant deficiency of Congress as a representative body concerns its insulation from the interests which have emerged in the twentieth century's "organizational revolution." How can national institutions be represented in a locally-elected legislature? In the absence of any easy answer to this question, the administration has tended to emerge as the natural point of access to the government for these national organizations and the place where their interests and viewpoints are brought into the policy-making process. In effect, the American system of government is moving toward a three-way system of representation. Particular territorial interests are represented in Congress; particular functional interests are represented in the administration; and the national interest is represented territorially and functionally in the Presidency.

Every four years the American people choose a President, but they

---

[14] Authorities vary on the exact impact of the Court decisions on the rural-urban balance in Congress, but they generally agree that it was less than had been anticipated. See Saloma, *Congress and the New Politics*, pp. 77–87; Andrew Hacker, *Congressional Districting: The Issue of Equal Representation* (Washington: Brookings Institution, rev. ed., 1964).

[15] Richard Lehne, "Shape of the Future," *National Civic Review*, 58 (Sept. 1969), pp. 351–55.

[16] Milton C. Cummings, Jr., "Reapportionment in the 1970's: Its Effects on Congress," in Nelson W. Polsby, ed., *Reapportionment in the 1970's* (Berkeley: Univ. of Cal. Press, 1971), p. 222.

elect an administration. In this century the administration has acquired many of the traditional characteristics of a representative body that Congress has tended to lose. The Jacksonian principle of "rotation in office" and the classic concept of the Cincinnatus-like statesman are far more relevant now to the administration than they are to Congress. Administration officials, unlike congressmen, are more frequently mobile amateurs in government than career professionals in politics. The patterns of power in Congress are rigid. The patterns of power in the administration are flexible. The administration is thus a far more sensitive register of changing currents of opinion than is Congress. A continuous adjustment of power and authority takes place within each administration; major changes in the distribution of power take place at every change of administration. The Eisenhower administration represented one combination of men, interests, and experience, the Kennedy-Johnson administration another, and the Nixon administration yet a third. Each time a new President takes office, the executive branch is invigorated in the same way that the House of Representatives was invigorated by Henry Clay and his western congressmen in 1811. A thousand new officials descend on Washington, coming fresh from the people, representing the diverse forces behind the new President, and bringing with them new demands, new ideas, and new power. Here truly is representative government along classic lines and of a sort which Congress has not known for decades. One key to the "decline" of Congress lies in the defects of Congress as a representative body.

Structure: The Dispersion of Power in Congress

The influence of Congress in our political system thus varies directly with its ties to the more dynamic and dominant groups in society. The power of Congress also varies directly, however, with the centralization of power in Congress. The corollary of these propositions is likewise true: centralization of authority within Congress usually goes with close connections between congressional leadership and major external forces and groups. The power of the House of Representatives was at a peak in the second decade of the nineteenth century, when power was centralized in the Speaker and when Henry Clay and his associates represented the dynamic new forces of trans-Appalachian nationalism. Another peak in the power of the House came during Reconstruction, when power was centralized in Speaker Colfax and the Joint Committee on Reconstruction as spokesmen for triumphant northern radicalism. A third peak in the power of the House came between 1890 and 1910, when the authority of the Speaker reached its height and Speakers Reed and Cannon reflected the newly established forces of nationalist conservatism. The peak in Senate power came during the post-Reconstruction period of the 1870s and 1880s. Within Congress, power was centralized in the senatorial leaders who represented the booming forces of the rising industrial capitalism and the new party machines. These were the years, as Wilfred Binkley put it, of "the Hegemony of the Senate."

SPECIALIZATION WITHOUT CENTRALIZATION

Since its first years, the twentieth century has seen no comparable centralization of power in Congress. Instead, the dominant tendency has been toward the dispersion of power. This leaves Congress only partially equipped to deal with the problems of modern society. In general, the complex modern environment requires in social and political institutions *both* a high degree of specialization and a high degree of centralized authority to coordinate and to integrate the activities of the specialized units. Specialization of function and centralization of authority have been the dominant trends of twentieth-century institutional development. Congress, however, has adjusted only half-way. Through its committees and subcommittees it has provided effectively for specialization, much more effectively, indeed, than the national legislature of any other country. But it has failed to combine increasing specialization of function with increasing centralization of authority. Instead the central leadership in Congress has been weakened, and as a result Congress lacks the central authority to integrate its specialized bodies. In a "rational" bureaucracy authority varies inversely with specialization. Within Congress authority usually varies directly with specialization.

The authority of the specialist is a distinctive feature of congressional behavior. "Specialization" is a key norm in both House and Senate. The man who makes a career in the House, one congressman has observed, "is primarily a worker, a specialist, and a craftsman—someone who will concentrate his energies in a particular field and gain prestige and influence in that." "The members who are most successful," another congressman concurred, "are those who pick a specialty or an area and become real experts in it." [17] The emphasis on specialization as a norm, of course, complements the importance of the committee as an institution. It also leads to a great stress on reciprocity. In a bureaucracy, specialized units compete with each other for the support of less specialized officials. In Congress, however, reciprocity among specialists replaces coordination by generalists. When a committee bill comes to the floor, the non-specialists in that subject acquiesce in its passage with the unspoken but complete understanding that they will receive similar treatment. "The traditional deference to the authority of one of its committees overwhelms the main body," one congressman has observed. "The whole fabric of

[17] Clapp, *op. cit.*, pp. 23–24.

Congress is based on committee expertise. . . ." Similarly, in the Senate "a large number of highly specialized experts generally accept each other's work without much criticism." [18] Reciprocity thus substitutes for centralization and confirms the diffusion of power among the committees.

HISTORY OF DISPERSION

The current phase of dispersed power in Congress dates from the second decade of this century. The turning point in the House came with the revolt against Speaker Cannon in 1910, the removal of the Speaker from the Rules Committee, and the loss by the Speaker of his power to appoint standing committees. For a brief period, from 1911 to 1915, much of the Speaker's former power was assumed by Oscar Underwood in his capacities as majority floor leader and chairman of the Ways and Means Committee. In 1915, however, Underwood was elected to the Senate, and the dispersion of power which had begun with the overthrow of the Speaker rapidly accelerated.

During the first years of the Wilson administration, authority in the Senate was concentrated in the floor leader, John Worth Kern, a junior senator first elected to the Senate in 1910. Under his leadership the seniority system was bypassed, and the Senate played an active and creative role in the remarkable legislative achievements of the Sixty-third Congress. Conceivably the long-entrenched position of seniority could have been broken at this point. "If the rule of 'seniority' was not destroyed in 1913," says Claude G. Bowers, "it was so badly shattered that it easily could have been given the finishing stroke." [19] Kern, however, was defeated for re-election in 1916, seniority was restored to its earlier position of eminence, and the power which Kern had temporarily centralized was again dispersed. Except for a brief reversal in the 1930s, this process of dispersion has intensified over the years. This is, it has been argued, the natural tendency of the Senate, with centralizing moves usually requiring some outside stimulus. In the late 1960s "important institutional positions" were "being dispersed ever more widely. . . ." As a result, "Virtually all senators acquire substantial legislative influence." The pattern is not even one of "decentralization"; it is one of "individualism." [20]

Thus since 1910 in the House and since 1915 in the Senate the overall tendency has been toward the weakening of central leadership and the strengthening of the committees. Most of the "reforms" which have been made in the procedures of Congress have contributed to

[18] Clem Miller, *Member of the House* (New York: Scribner's, 1962), p. 51; Randall B. Ripley, *Power in the Senate* (New York: St. Martin's Press, 1969), p. 172.

[19] Claude G. Bowers, *The Life of John Worth Kern* (Indianapolis: Hollenback Press, 1918), p. 840.

[20] Ripley, *Power in the Senate,* pp. 15–16, 53, 77, 185.

this end. "Since 1910," observed the historian of the House in 1962, "the leadership of the House has been in commission. . . . The net effect of the various changes of the last 35 years in the power structure of the House of Representatives has been to diffuse the leadership, and to disperse its risks, among a numerous body of leaders." [21] The Budget and Accounting Act of 1921 strengthened the appropriations committees by giving them exclusive authority to report appropriations, but its primary effects were felt in the executive branch with the creation of the Bureau of the Budget. During the 1920s power was further dispersed among the Speaker, floor leaders, Rules, Appropriations, Ways and Means chairmen, and caucus chairman. In the following decade political development also contributed to the diffusion of influence when the conservative majority on the Rules Committee broke with the administration in 1937.

The dispersion of power to the committees of Congress was intensified by the Legislative Reorganization Act of 1946. In essence, this act was a "committee reorganization act" making the committees stronger and more effective. The reduction in the number of standing committees from 81 to 34 increased the importance of the committee chairmanships. Committee consolidation led to the proliferation of subcommittees, now estimated to number about 250. Thus the functions of integration and coordination which, if performed at all, would previously have been performed by the central leadership of the two houses, were now devolved on the leadership of the standing committees. Before the reorganization, for instance, committee jurisdictions frequently overlapped, and the presiding officers of the House and Senate could often influence the fate of a bill by exercising their discretion in referring it to committee. While jurisdictional uncertainties were not totally eliminated by the act, the discretion of the presiding officers was drastically curtailed. The committee chairman, on the other hand, could often influence the fate of legislation by manipulating the subcommittee structure of the committee and by exercising his discretion in referring bills to subcommittees. Similarly, the intention of the framers of the Reorganization Act to reduce, if not to eliminate, the use of special committees had the effect of restricting the freedom of action of the central leadership in the two houses at the same time that it confirmed the authority of the standing committees in their respective jurisdictions. The Reorganization Act also bolstered the committees by significantly expanding their staffs and by specifically authorizing them to exercise legislative overseeing functions with respect to the administrative agencies in their field of responsibility.

The act included few provisions strengthening the central leadership of Congress. Those which it did include in general did not operate successfully. A proposal for party policy committees in each house

[21] Galloway, *op. cit.*, pp. 95, 98, 128.

was defeated in the House of Representatives. The Senate subsequently authorized party policy committees in the Senate, but they did not become active or influential enough to affect the legislative process significantly. The act's provision for a Joint Committee on the Budget which would set an appropriation ceiling by February 15 of each year was implemented twice and then abandoned. In 1950 the appropriations committees reported a consolidated supply bill which cut the presidential estimates by $2 billion and was approved by Congress two months before the approval of the individual supply bills of 1949. Specialized interests within Congress, however, objected strenuously to this procedure, and it has not been attempted again. The net effect of the Reorganization Act was thus to further the dispersion of power, to strengthen and to institutionalize committee authority, and to circumscribe still more the influence of the central leadership. The Legislative Reorganization Act of 1970, a far more modest measure than that of 1946, reinforced these tendencies. It did not deal with seniority and none of its provisions was designed to strengthen central leadership. To the extent that it was implemented, its effects were, indeed, to disperse power still further within committees by reducing the prerogatives of the chairmen.

In the years after the 1946 reorganization, the issues which earlier had divided the central leadership and committee chairmen reappeared in each committee in struggles between committee chairmen and subcommittees. The chairmen attempted to maintain their own control and flexibility over the number, nature, staff, membership, and leadership of their subcommittees. Several of the most assertive chairmen either prevented the creation of subcommittees or created numbered subcommittees without distinct legislative jurisdictions, thereby reserving to themselves the assignment of legislation to the subcommittees. Those who wished to limit the power of the chairman, on the other hand, often invoked seniority as the rule to be followed in designating subcommittee chairmen. In 1961 31 of the 36 standing committees of the House and Senate had subcommittees and in 24 the subcommittees had fixed jurisdictions and significant autonomy, thus playing a major role in the legislative process. In many committees the subcommittees go their independent way, jealously guarding their autonomy and prerogatives against other subcommittees and their own committee chairman. "Given an active subcommittee chairman working in a specialized field with a staff of his own," one congressional staff member observes, "the parent committee can do no more than change the grammar of a subcommittee report." [22] In the Senate after World War II the predominant influence in legislation shifted from committee chairmen to subcommittee chairmen and individual

[22] George Goodwin, Jr., "Subcommittees: The Miniature Legislatures of Congress," *American Political Science Review*, 56 (Sept. 1962), pp. 596–601.

senators. Specialization of function and dispersion of power, which once worked to the benefit of the committee chairmen, now work against them.

POSITION OF CENTRAL LEADERS

The Speaker and the majority floor leaders are the most powerful men in Congress, but their power is not markedly greater than that of many other congressional leaders. In 1959, for instance, thirteen of nineteen committee chairmen broke with the Speaker to support the Landrum-Griffin bill. "This graphically illustrated the locus of power in the House," one congressman commented. "The Speaker, unable to deliver votes, was revealed in outline against the chairmen. This fact was not lost on Democratic Members." [23] The power base of the central leaders has tended to atrophy, caught between the expansion of presidential authority and influence, on the one hand, and the institutionalization of committee authority, on the other.

At times individual central leaders have built up impressive networks of personal influence. These, however, have been individual, not institutional, phenomena. The ascendancy of Rayburn and Johnson during the 1950s, for instance, tended to obscure the difference between personal influence and institutional authority. With the departure of the Texas coalition their personal networks collapsed. "Rayburn's personal power and prestige," observed Representative Richard Bolling, "made the institution *appear* to work. When Rayburn died, the thing just fell apart." [24] Similarly, Johnson's effectiveness as Senate leader, in the words of one of his assistants, was "overwhelmingly a matter of personal influence. By all accounts, Johnson was the most personal among recent leaders in his approach. For years it was said that he talked to every Democratic senator every day. Persuasion ranged from the awesome pyrotechnics known as 'Treatment A' to the apparently casual but always purposeful exchange as he roamed the floor and the cloakroom." [25] When Johnson's successor was accused of failing to provide the necessary leadership to the Senate, he defended himself on the grounds that he was Mansfield and not Johnson. His definition of the leader's role was largely negative: "I am neither a circus ringmaster, the master of ceremonies of a Senate nightclub, a tamer of Senate lions, or a wheeler and dealer. . . ." [26] The majority leadership role was uninstitutionalized and the kindly, gentlemanly, easygoing qualities which Mansfield had had as Senator from Montana were not

[23] Miller, *op. cit.*, p. 110.
[24] Quoted in Stewart Alsop, "The Failure of Congress," *Saturday Evening Post*, 236 (December 7, 1963), p. 24.
[25] Ralph K. Huitt, "Democratic Party Leadership in the Senate," *American Political Science Review*, 55 (June 1961), p. 338.
[26] *Congressional Record* (Nov. 27, 1963), pp. 21, 758 (daily ed.).

changed when he became majority leader. The power of the President has been institutionalized; the powers of the congressional committees and their chairmen have been institutionalized; but the power of the central leaders of Congress remains personal, *ad hoc,* and transitory.

In the House the dispersion of power has weakened the central leadership and strengthened committee and subcommittee chairmen. The latter, products of the seniority system, are normally legislative veterans of long standing. In the Senate, on the other hand, the more widespread dispersion of power within a smaller body has produced a more egalitarian situation in which freshmen senators are often able to take the initiative on important issues of particular concern to them or on which they have developed special expertise. The dispersion of power in the Senate, in short, has tended to open up that body to new and outside influences while in the House it has had the reverse effect.

In both houses, however, the dispersion of power makes obstruction easy and the development of a coherent legislative program difficult. Congress cannot play a positive role in the legislative process so long as it lacks a structure of power which makes positive leadership possible. During the last decades of the nineteenth century, for instance, the Speakers of the House centralized power, exercised personal leadership, and played an innovative role in policy. In subsequent years, in contrast, the Speakers "lost or gave away powers" and what initiative there was in policy came from the executive branch.[27] So long as the Speaker remains, in Bolling's words, "a weak King surrounded by strong Dukes," the House cannot organize itself to lead: "A strong Speaker is crucial to the House. He is the indispensable man for its legislative and political health, education, and welfare." [28] The same is true of the majority leader in the Senate. Perpetuation there of the dispersion of power, on the other hand, means that there is "no general plan for bringing bills to the floor in a given order or at a given time"; the legislative process as a whole becomes "highly segmented"; and the prospects for organized institutional reform are very low.[29]

Function: The Shift to Oversight

LOSS OF INITIATIVE

The insulation of Congress from external social forces and the dispersion of power within Congress have stimulated significant changes

[27] Randall B. Ripley, *Party Leaders in the House of Representatives* (Washington: Brookings Institution, 1967), pp. 16–17.
[28] Richard Bolling, *Power in the House: A History of the Leadership of the House of Representatives* (New York: E. P. Dutton, 1968), p. 29.
[29] Ripley, *Power in the Senate*, pp. 13–14.

in the functions of Congress. The congressional role in legislation has largely been reduced to delay and amendment; congressional activity in overseeing administration has expanded and diversified. During the nineteenth century Congress frequently took the legislative initiative in dealing with major national problems. Even when the original proposal came from the President, Congress usually played an active and positive role in reshaping the proposal into law. "The predominant and controlling force, the centre and source of all motive and of all regulative power," Woodrow Wilson observed in 1885, "is Congress. . . . The legislature is the aggressive spirit." [30] Since 1933, however, the initiative in formulating legislation, in assigning legislative priorities, in arousing support for legislation, and in determining the final content of the legislation enacted has clearly shifted to the executive branch. All three elements of the executive branch—President, administration, and bureaucracy—have gained legislative functions at the expense of Congress. Today's "aggressive spirit" is clearly the executive branch.

In 1908, it is reported, the Senate, in high dudgeon at the effrontery of the Secretary of the Interior, returned to him the draft of a bill which he had proposed, resolving to refuse any further communications from executive officers unless they were transmitted by the President himself.[31] Now, however, congressmen expect the executive departments to present them with bills. Eighty percent of the bills enacted into law, one congressman has estimated, originate in the executive branch. Indeed, in most instances congressmen do not admit a responsibility to take legislative action except in response to executive requests. Congress, as one senator has complained, "has surrendered its rightful place in the leadership in the lawmaking process to the White House. No longer is Congress the source of major legislation. It now merely filters legislative proposals from the President, straining out some and reluctantly letting others pass through. These days no one expects Congress to devise the important bills." [32] The President now determines the legislative agenda of Congress almost as thoroughly as the British cabinet sets the legislative agenda of Parliament. The institutionalization of this role was one of the more significant developments in presidential-congressional relations after World War II.[33]

[30] Woodrow Wilson, *Congressional Government* (Boston: Houghton Mifflin, 1885), pp. 11, 36.

[31] George B. Galloway, *The Legislative Process in Congress* (New York: Crowell, 1955), p. 9.

[32] Abraham Ribicoff, "Doesn't Congress Have Ideas of Its Own?" *Saturday Evening Post*, 237 (March 21, 1964), p. 6.

[33] Richard E. Neustadt, "Presidency and Legislation: Planning the President's Program," *American Political Science Review*, 49 (Dec. 1955), pp. 980–1021.

LOSS OF POLICY CONTROL

Congress has conceded not only the initiative in originating legislation but—and perhaps inevitably as the result of losing the initiative —it has also lost the dominant influence it once had in shaping the final content of legislation. Between 1882 and 1909 Congress had a preponderant influence in shaping the content of 16 (55 percent) out of 29 major laws enacted during those years. It had a preponderant influence over 17 (46 percent) of 37 major laws passed between 1910 and 1932. During the constitutional revolution of the New Deal, however, its influence declined markedly: only 2 (8 percent) of 24 major laws passed between 1933 and 1940 were primarily the work of Congress.[34] Certainly its record after World War II was little better.

The loss of congressional control over the substance of policy was most marked, of course, in the area of national defense and foreign policy. At one time Congress did not hesitate to legislate the size and weapons of the armed forces. During the 1940s and 1950s this power— to raise and support armies, to provide and maintain a navy—came to rest firmly in the hands of the executive. Is Congress, one congressional committee asked plaintively in 1962, to play simply "the passive role of supine acquiescence" in executive programs or is it to be "an active participant in the determination of the direction of our defense policy?" The committee, however, already knew the answer:

> To any student of government, it is eminently clear that the role of the Congress in determining national policy, defense or otherwise, has deteriorated over the years. More and more the role of Congress has come to be that of a sometimes querulous but essentially kindly uncle who complains while furiously puffing on his pipe but who finally, as everyone expects, gives in and hands over the allowance, grants the permission, or raises his hand in blessing, and then returns to the rocking chair for another year of somnolence broken only by an occasional anxious glance down the avenue and a muttered doubt as to whether he had done the right thing.[35]

CONGRESSIONAL REASSERTION

This image of Congress accurately summarizes its role in foreign and military policy from the mid-1940s to the mid-1960s. In the late 1960s, however, the winds of change began to blow and congressional groups attempted to reassert their historical role in these areas of policy. The critics of United States involvement in Indochina, particularly those

[34] Lawrence H. Chamberlain, *The President, Congress, and Legislation* (New York: Columbia Univ. Press, 1946), pp. 450–52.
[35] House Report 1406, Eighty-seventh Congress, Second Session (1962), p. 7.

in the Senate Foreign Relations Committee, as well as those more generally concerned about the extent of the United States role in world affairs, moved to challenge Presidential leadership on foreign policy in two key areas. One concerned the size and equipment of the armed forces. In 1969 the Senate came only one vote short of cancelling funds for the administration's anti-ballistic missile system and did compel or induce several significant changes in the nature of that program. In 1971 Congress wrote a limitation on the size of the army which compelled the administration to cut back United States military strength more rapidly than it would have preferred. Congress is now likely to veto major weapons systems and to impose restrictions on the overall size of the armed forces in ways which it never did for twenty years after World War II. The "day is over," as one defense-minded congressman has stated, when a "member of Congress would hesitate to vote against anything proposed by the Joint Chiefs of Staff because he might be subject to the charge of being soft on communism." [36]

The second area in which Congress has seemed to assert a new role concerns the commitment and use of military force. This area, however, is further removed than men and weapons from the traditional control of Congress. As of the spring of 1972, Congress's bark in this field was much more noticeable than its bite; congressional resentment at Presidential power was outrunning congressional reassertion of legislative power. In two instances in 1969 and 1970, Congress legislated prohibitions on the use of funds to support United States ground combat forces in Laos, Thailand, and Cambodia—after the executive branch had stated it had no intention of introducing such forces or was in the process of withdrawing them. Although comparable limitations were proposed on the use of United States forces in Vietnam, these were not approved when the administration opposed them. On a broader front, Congress did move cautiously to redefine in general terms the conditions under which the President could involve United States military forces in armed conflict, the Senate approving such legislation in the spring of 1972. These manifestations of Congress's unhappiness with the profligate commitment of United States troops abroad without its approval undoubtedly introduced greater caution into executive behavior. The actions of Congress during the Johnson and Nixon administrations also indicated, however, a desire to avoid a constitutional showdown with the executive on these issues.

These presidential–congressional differences over foreign policy illustrate one way in which Congress can play a more positive or innovating policy role. Congressional assertion, we have argued, is normally manifested through congressional obstruction. If, however,

[36] Representative George H. Mahon, *Washington Post*, Dec. 27, 1969, quoted in Francis O. Wilcox, *Congress, The Executive, and Foreign Policy* (New York: Harper & Row, 1971), p. 135.

the President and executive agencies continue to pursue overall foreign policy objectives which have become obsolete or dated, congressional efforts to obstruct or to veto these policies can lay the basis for policy innovations. In the 1940s and 1950s, the executive had the initiative in foreign policy, and Congress consequently had either to acquiesce or to obstruct. In the late 1960s and early 1970s, the executive was often less concerned with initiation in foreign policy than with the maintenance of past policies (most dramatically and concretely revealed, for instance, in the insistence of both the Johnson and Nixon administrations on the maintenance of United States military strength in Europe). Unable to produce new policies itself, Congress could by objecting to the continuation of old policies, facilitate the innovation of new ones. In this sense, congressional "negativism" might lead to policy "positivism."

OVERSEEING ADMINISTRATION

The overall decline in the legislative role of Congress in the twentieth century has been accompanied by an increase in its administrative role. The modern state differs from the liberal state of the eighteenth and nineteenth centuries in terms of the greater control it exercises over society and the increase in the size, functions, and importance of its bureaucracy. Needed in the modern state are means to control, check, supplement, stimulate, and ameliorate this bureaucracy. The institutions and techniques available for this task vary from country to country: the Scandinavian countries have their *Ombudsmen;* Communist countries use party bureaucracy to check state bureaucracy. In the United States, Congress has come to play a major, if not the major, role in this regard. Indeed, many of the innovations in Congress in recent years have strengthened its control over the administrative processes of the executive branch. Congressional committees responded with alacrity to the mandate of the 1946 Reorganization Act that they "exercise continuous watchfulness" over the administration of laws. Congressional investigations of the bureaucracy have multiplied: each Congress during the period between 1950 and 1962 conducted more investigations than were conducted by *all* the Congresses during the nineteenth century.[37] Other mechanisms of committee control, such as the legislative veto and committee clearance of administrative decisions, have been increasingly employed. "Not legislation but control of administration," as Galloway remarks, "is becoming the primary function of the modern Congress."[38] In discharging this function, congressmen uncover waste and abuse, push particular projects and innovations, highlight

[37] Galloway, *op. cit.*, p. 166.
[38] *Ibid.*, pp. 56–57.

inconsistencies, correct injustices, and compel exposition and defense of bureaucratic decisions.

CONSTITUENCY SERVICE

In performing these activities, Congress is acting where it is most competent to act: it is dealing with particulars, not general policies. Unlike legislating, these concerns are perfectly compatible with the current patterns of insulation and dispersion. Committee specialization and committee power enhance rather than detract from the effectiveness of the committees as administrative overseers. In addition, as the great organized interests of society come to be represented more directly in the bureaucracy and administration, the role of Congress as representative of individual citizens becomes all the more important. The congressman more often serves their interests by representing them in the administrative process than in the legislative process. The time and energy put into this type of representation undoubtedly varies widely from one congressman to another. "The most pressing day-to-day demands for the time of Senators and Congressmen," according to Hubert Humphrey, "are not directly linked to legislative tasks. They come from constituents." [39] Sixteen percent of one sample of House members listed the "Errand Boy" function as their primary activity; 59 percent listed it as second to their legislative work. Another group of House members was reported to spend 25 to 30 percent of their time and 50 percent of the time of their Washington staffs on constituency service. One freshman representative, however, estimated that half of his own time and two-thirds of that of his staff were devoted to constituent service. Senatorial staffs apparently spend about twice as much time on constituency service and oversight as they do on legislative matters.[40] In performing these services congressmen are both representing their constituents where they need to be represented and checking up on and ameliorating the impact of the federal bureaucracy. Constituent service and legislative oversight are, in some measure, two sides of the same coin. Both are functions which no other public agency is as well qualified as Congress to perform. Responding to needs unmet elsewhere, Congress plays an increasingly important role as the representative of the interests of unorganized individuals and as the stimulant, monitor, corrector, and overseer of a growing federal bureaucracy.

[39] Hubert H. Humphrey, "To Move Congress Out of Its Ruts," *New York Times Magazine* (April 7, 1963), p. 39.
[40] See Davidson, *Role of the Congressman*, pp. 97–107; Saloma, *Congress and the New Politics*, pp. 183–89; Clarence D. Long, "Observations of a Freshman in Congress," *New York Times Magazine* (December 1, 1963), p. 73; Ripley, *Power in the Senate*, pp. 189–95.

Adaptation or Reform

Insulation makes Congress unwilling to initiate laws. Dispersion makes Congress unable to aggregate individual bills into a coherent legislative program. Constituent service and administrative overseeing eat into the time and energy which congressmen give legislative matters. Congress is thus left in its legislative dilemma where the assertion of power is almost equivalent to the obstruction of action. What then are the possibilities for institutional adaptation or institutional reform?

LIVING WITH THE DILEMMA

Conceivably neither adaptation nor reform is necessary. The present distribution of power and functions could continue indefinitely. Instead of escaping from its dilemma, Congress could learn to live with it. In each of the four institutional crises mentioned earlier, the issue of institutional adaptation came to a head over one issue: the presidential election of 1824, the House of Commons Reform Bill of 1832, the Lloyd George budget of 1910, and the Supreme Court reorganization plan of 1937. The adaptation crisis of Congress differs in that to date a constitutional crisis between the executive branch and Congress has been avoided. Congress has procrastinated, obstructed, and watered down executive proposals, but it has also come close to the point where it no longer dares openly to veto them. Thus the challenge which Congress poses to the executive branch is less blatant and dramatic, but in many ways more complex, ambiguous, and irritating, than the challenge which the Lords posed to Asquith or the Supreme Court to Roosevelt. If Congress uses its powers to delay and to amend with prudence and circumspection, there is no necessary reason why it should not retain them for the indefinite future. In this case, the legislative process in the national government would continually appear to be on the verge of stalemate and breakdown which never quite materialize. The supporters of Congress would continue to bemoan its decline at the same time that its critics would continue to denounce its obstructionism. The system would work so long as Congress stretched but did not exhaust the patience of the executive branch and public. If Congress, however, did veto a major administration action, like overseas commitment of military forces, the issue would be joined, the country would be thrown into a constitutional crisis, and the executive branch would mobilize its forces for a showdown over the relative authority of Congress and President.

REFORM VERSUS ADAPTATION: RESTRUCTURING POWER

The resumption by Congress of an active, positive role in the legislative process would require a drastic restructuring of power relationships, including reversal of the tendencies toward insulation, dispersion, and oversight. Fundamental "reforms" would thus be required. In the past, two general types of proposals have been advanced for the structural reform of Congress. Ironically, however, neither set of proposals is likely, if enacted, to achieve the results which its principal proponents desire. One set of reformers, "democratizers" like Senator Clark, have attacked the power of the Senate "Establishment" or "Inner Club" and urged an equalizing of power among congressmen so that a majority of each house can work its will. These reformers stand four-square in the Norris tradition. During the past two decades the Senate has, however, in considerable measure moved precisely in the direction which these reformers advocate. The senatorial "Establishment" has lost its firm hold on proceedings; power has been dispersed; the potential sources of both legislative initiative and legislative veto have multiplied; and, as a result, the prospects of the Senate's generating and approving anything resembling a coherent legislative program have greatly diminished.

The "party reformers" such as Professor James M. Burns, on the other hand, place their reliance on presidential leadership and urge the strengthening of the party organization in Congress to insure support by his own party for the President's measures. In actuality, however, the centralization of power within Congress in party committees and leadership bodies would also increase the power of Congress. It would tend to reconstitute Congress as an effective legislative body, deprive the President of his monopoly of the "national interest," and force him to come to terms with the centralized congressional leadership, much as Theodore Roosevelt had to come to terms with Speaker Cannon. Instead of strengthening presidential leadership, the proposals of the party reformers would weaken it.

The dispersion of power in Congress has created a situation in which the internal problem of Congress is not dictatorship but oligarchy. The only effective alternative to oligarchy is centralized authority. Oligarchies, however, are unlikely to reform themselves. In most political systems centralized power is a necessary although not sufficient condition for reform and adaptation to environmental change. At present the central leaders of Congress are, with rare exceptions, products of and closely identified with the committee oligarchy. Reform of Congress would depend upon the central leaders' breaking with the oligarchy, mobilizing majorities from younger and less influential congressmen, and employing these majorities to expand and to institutionalize their own power.

Centralization of power within Congress would also, in some measure, help solve the problem of insulation. Some of Congress's insulation has been defensive in nature, a compensation for its declining role in the legislative process as well as a cause of that decline. Seniority, which is largely responsible for the insulation, is a symptom of more basic institutional needs and fears. Greater authority for the central leaders of Congress would necessarily involve a modification of the seniority system. Conversely, in the absence of strong central leadership, recourse to seniority is virtually inevitable. Election of committee chairmen by the committees themselves, by party caucuses, or by each house would stimulate antagonisms among members and multiply the opportunities for outside forces from the executive branch or from interest groups to influence the proceedings.

Selection by seniority is, in effect, selection by heredity: power goes not to the oldest son of the king but the oldest child of the institution. It protects Congress against divisive and external influences. It does this, however, through a purely arbitrary method which offers no assurance that the distribution of authority in the Congress will bear any relation to the distribution of opinion in the country, in the rest of the government, or within Congress itself. It purchases institutional integrity at a high price in terms of institutional isolation. The nineteenth-century assignment of committee positions and chairmanships by the Speaker, on the other hand, permitted flexibility and a balancing of viewpoints from within and without the House. External influences, however nefarious (as the earlier remark about Blaine suggests they might be at times), all came to bear on the Speaker, and yet the authority which he possessed enabled him to play a creative political role in balancing these external influences against the claims and viewpoints arising from within the House and against his own personal and policy preferences. The process by which the Speaker selected committee chairmen was not too different from the process by which a President selects a cabinet, and it resembled rather closely the process by which a British Prime Minister appoints a ministry from among his colleagues in Parliament. The resumption of this power by the Speaker in the House and its acquisition by the majority leader in the Senate would restore to Congress a more positive role in the legislative process and strengthen it vis-à-vis the executive branch. Paradoxically, however, the most ardent congressional critics of executive power are also the most strenuous opponents of centralized power in Congress.

Congressional insulation may also be weakened in other ways. The decline in mobility between congressional leadership positions and administration leadership positions has been counterbalanced, in some measure, by the rise of the Senate as a source of Presidents. This is due to several causes. The almost insoluble problems confronting state governments tarnish the glamor and limit the tenure of their governors. The nationalization of communications has helped senators play a role in the news media which is exceeded only by the President. In addition, senators, unlike governors, can usually claim some familiarity with the overriding problems of domestic and foreign policy.

Senatorial insulation may also be weakened to the extent that individuals who have made their reputations on the national scene find it feasible and desirable to run for the Senate. It is normally assumed that too much attention to national problems and too much neglect of state and constituency issues complicate election or reelection to the Senate. Lucas, McFarland, George, and Connally are cited as cases in point. Given the nationalization of communications, however, a political leader may be able to develop greater appeal in a local area by action on the national level than by action on the local level. It is effective testimonial to the extent to which the President dominates the national scene and the national scene dominates the news that in 1964 Robert Kennedy would probably have been the strongest possible Democratic candidate for the Senate in any one of a dozen northeastern industrial states.

Recruitment of senators from the national scene rather than from local politics would significantly narrow the gap between Congress and the other elements of national leadership. The "local politics" ladder to the Senate would be replaced or supplemented by a "national politics" line in which mobile individuals might move from the establishment to the administration to the Senate. This would be one important step toward breaking congressional insulation. The end of insulation, however, would only occur if at a later date these same individuals could freely move back from the Senate to the administration. Mobility between Congress and the administration similar to that which now exists between the establishment and the administration would bring about drastic changes in American politics, not the least of which would be a great increase in the attractiveness of running for Congress. Opening up this possibility, however, depends upon the modification of seniority, and that, in turn, depends upon the centralization of power in Congress.

ADAPTATION AND REFORM: REDEFINING FUNCTION

A politically easier, although psychologically more difficult, way out of Congress's dilemma involves not the reversal but the intensification of the recent trends of congressional evolution. Congress has a legislative dilemma because opinion conceives of it as a legislature. If it gave up the effort to play a major role in the legislative process, it could, quite conceivably, play a much more positive and influential role in the political system as a whole. Representative assemblies have not always been legislatures. They had their origins in medieval times as courts and as councils. An assembly need not legislate to exist and to be important. Indeed, some would argue that assemblies should not legislate. "[A] numerous assembly," John Stuart Mill contended, "is as little fitted for the direct business of legislation as for that of administration." [41] Representative assemblies acquired their legislative functions in the seventeenth and eighteenth centuries; there is no necessary reason why liberty, democracy, or constitutional government depends upon their exercising those functions in the twentieth century. Legislation has become much too complex politically to be effectively handled by a representative assembly. The primary work of legislation must be done, and increasingly is being done, by the three "houses" of the executive branch: the bureaucracy, the administration, and the President.

Far more important than the preservation of Congress as a legislative institution is the preservation of Congress as an autonomous institution. When the performance of one function becomes "dysfunctional" to the workings of an institution, the sensible course is to abandon it for other functions. In the 1930s the Supreme Court was forced to surrender its function of disallowing national and state social legislation. Since then it has wielded its veto on federal legislation only rarely and with the greatest of discretion. This loss of power, however, was more than compensated for by its new role in protecting civil rights and civil liberties against state action. This is a role which neither its supporters nor its opponents in the 1930s would have thought possible. In effect, the Court used the great conservative weapon of the 1930s to promote the great liberal ends of the 1960s. Such is the way skillful leaders and great institutions adapt to changing circumstances.

The redefinition of Congress's functions away from legislation might involve, in the first instance, a restriction of the power of Congress to delay indefinitely presidential legislative requests. Constitutionally, Congress would still retain its authority to approve legislation. Practically, Congress could, as Walter Lippmann and others have suggested, bind itself to approve or disapprove urgent presidential proposals within a time limit of say, three or six months. If thus compelled to choose openly, Congress, it may be supposed, would almost invariably approve presidential requests. Its veto power would become a reserve power like that of the Supreme Court if not like that of the British Crown. On these "urgent" measures it would perform a legitimizing function rather than a legislative function. At the same time, the

[41] John Stuart Mill, "On Representative Government," *Utilitarianism, Liberty, and Representative Government* (London: J. M. Dent), p. 235.

requirement that Congress pass or reject presidential requests would also presumably induce executive leaders to consult with congressional leaders in drafting such legislation. Congress would also, of course, continue to amend and to vote freely on "nonurgent" executive requests.

Explicit acceptance of the idea that legislation was not its primary function would, in large part, simply be recognition of the direction which change has already been taking. It would legitimize and expand the functions of constituent service and administrative oversight which have become so important in recent decades. However isolated it might be from the dominant social forces in society, Congress could still capitalize on its position as the represenative of the unorganized interests of individuals. It would become a proponent of popular demands against the bureaucracy rather than the opponent of popular demands for legislation. It would thus continue to play a major although different role in the constitutional system of checks and balances.

A few years ago a survey of the functioning of legislative bodies in 41 countries concluded that parliaments were in general losing their initiative and power in legislation. At the same time, however, they were gaining power in the "control of government activity." [42] Most legislatures, however, are much less autonomous and powerful than Congress. Congress has lost less power over legislation and gained more power over administration than other parliaments. It is precisely this fact which gives rise to its legislative dilemma. If Congress can generate the leadership and the will to make the drastic reforms required to reverse the trends toward insulation, dispersion, and overseeing, it could still resume a positive role in the legislative process. If this is impossible, an alternative path is to eschew the legislative effort and to adapt itself to discharge effectively those functions of constituent service and bureaucratic control which insulation and dispersion do enable it to play in the national government.

[42] Inter-Parliamentary Union, *Parliaments: A Comparative Study on Structure and Functioning of Representative Institutions in Forty-One Countries* (New York: Praeger, 1963), p. 398.

H. Douglas Price

2

The Electoral Arena

The conditions of entry into a legislative body and of survival through successive terms are a major factor in the behavior of aspirants and incumbents. In turn the career perspectives and ambitions of House and Senate members go a long way toward giving structure to those bodies. Looked at the other way, proposals for changes in the structure or procedure of Congress are likely to have a direct impact on the careers of individual members. Some types of changes in the institution are likely only when changes are made in the risks and rewards of the legislative career, either in Congress or in the constituencies. An understanding of the risks of the electoral arena is vital for an understanding of Congress.

Two basic and divergent trends have shaped the pattern of Congressional careers in the twentieth century. The first has been the *democratization of the Senate,* brought about by the adoption of direct election of senators, the spread of the direct primary, and the growth of effective two-party competition in the great majority of states.[1] In the late nineteenth and early twentieth centuries the Senate was a bastion of conservatism, something of a "rich man's club," and highly resistant to liberal or progressive sentiment. Since World War II the Senate has been the more liberal half of the Congress on most issues and has been highly responsive to the legislative demands of various marginal voting groups. In turn, this trend plus a high degree of

HUGH DOUGLAS PRICE *is professor of political science at Harvard University. He is the author of* The Negro and Southern Politics *and of "Race, Religion, and the Rules Committee," in* The Uses of Power, *edited by Alan F. Westin. His current work is* Causal Models of American Politics *(forthcoming).*

[1] The best account of the late nineteenth century Senate is David Rothman, *Politics and Power: The U.S. Senate, 1869–1901* (Cambridge: Harvard University Press, 1967).

chamber decentralization and good opportunity for media coverage have made the Senate a major breeding ground for presidential candidates.

By contrast, the House in the twentieth century has become more conservative and less subject to competition in the great majority of congressional districts. Thus a second major trend, resulting from the combined effects of safe districts plus the seniority system, has been the *professionalization of the House career*.[2] The "activist political minorities" which are so important for the statewide politics of the Senate (and the Presidency) are important for only a few House districts. At least three-quarters of all House districts are relatively "safe" year after year.[3] This lack of effective party competition at the congressional district level has made reelection to the House generally possible. And the twentieth-century emphasis on the seniority system—which was *not* the standard practice in the nineteenth century—has made repeated reelection desirable and indeed necessary for the member who wants to have an impact on what the House does.

The Formal Rules of the Game

STRUCTURAL DIFFERENCES BETWEEN HOUSES

The structural differences between the House and Senate can be dealt with briefly. The six-year term for senators removes them somewhat from the pressure of imminent reelection campaigns. The two-year term for representatives means that a member from a relatively competitive district is almost perpetually campaigning. House members from "safe" districts, however, may face serious challenge even less frequently than does the typical senator. The reality is thus one of frequent elections but with little serious competition in the case of most members of the House; for the Senate it is infrequent election but a much higher probability of serious opposition.

The equal representation of states in the Senate makes that body technically unrepresentative of sheer population, but there are very few issues which tend to pit small states as such against the states with a large population. And most major sections of the country include states with both large and small populations. The most concentrated sectional over-representation in the Senate is of the Rocky Mountain West (including the Southwest). The eight mountain states elect sixteen senators, but on a population basis are entitled to only 17 of

[2] H. D. Price, "The Congressional Career: Then and Now" (1964 working paper for The American Assembly), reprinted in Nelson Polsby, ed., *Congressional Behavior* (New York: Random House, 1971). For a more teleological view see Polsby, "The Institutionalization of the U.S. House of Representatives," *ibid*.

[3] For an extensive survey of American experience see Milton C. Cummings, *Congressmen and the Electorate* (New York: Free Press, 1966).

the 435 House members (which tells a lot about why the Senate has been more responsive than the House to silver miners and sheep herders). The apportionment of House seats among the states has, since 1929, been put on an automatic basis. But the drawing of individual district lines within a state has long been a problem. Incumbent representatives often oppose upsetting established district lines, and state legislatures controlled by one party have opposed changes that might improve the electoral chances of the other party. States gaining an additional House seat have frequently resorted to electing the additional member at large. Opportunities for such vagaries were finally narrowed, however, by the Supreme Court's reapportionment decisions.[4] These still leave some room for judicious gerrymandering, but only within the confines of districts with substantially equal population. Most state legislatures have done a remarkable job of shoring up the electoral base of most incumbents of both parties, and thus of narrowing even further the number of close competitive districts.

PROCESSES OF REPRESENTATION

A consequence of the electoral process is that local constituencies—states for the Senate, districts for the House—are provided "representation" through at least *three* separate processes. First, there is a kind of automatic representation which is roughly achieved by taking almost any individual from a given state or local district. Senator Eastland of Mississippi and Harlem's Congressman Rangel take sharply contrasting stands on civil rights and integration, and the chances are that most white Mississippi residents and almost any Harlem Negro would do likewise. On such basic issues a legislator himself is likely to share the basic views of his effective constituency and to be in no need of a poll on the subject.

A second process of representation occurs through the election system itself. On issues where the local constituency is not so overwhelmingly in agreement, or where a legislator gets widely out of line with the grass-roots view, then the electoral process provides a means for a popular test. Theoretically, at least, an incumbent may be defeated by an opponent of the opposite party or in a primary contest. This possibility of dumping one man and replacing him with another remains the ultimate sanction in a democratic system, but it is something of a blunderbuss weapon. Elections are infrequent, at times set by law rather than by the rise and fall of popular issues, and there may be a great many issues but only two candidates.

The *possibility* of opposition, however, remains a powerful factor

[4] For a recent summary see Nelson Polsby, ed., *Reapportionment: The Results of a Decade* (Berkeley: Univ. of Cal. Press, 1971).

in attuning the incumbent to the third process of representation. This is the more subtle process by which constituents can express opinions and exert influence in such a manner that the politically sophisticated legislator can, if he desires, make an estimate of the amount of local backing (in terms of influence, not of counting noses) and adapt his position accordingly. Thus the incumbent can often adjust to changes in the make-up of his constituency, to shifts in the national climate, or to new and urgent demands from individuals or groups that are important to him or to his district.[5] To the extent that the representative can, and is willing to, perform this third type of delicate representation, then the probability of the electorate resorting to the second type (throwing the rascal out) is reduced. But the possibility of defeat remains, and in the case of a major electoral landslide it often falls equally on the just and the unjust.

Each of these processes of representation depends upon a variety of institutional arrangements. Operation of the first form is guaranteed through residence requirements. The sharp contrast between the American emphasis on local residence and the British practice of assigning parliamentary candidates to seats anywhere in the country has often been noted. In point of fact, however, the American practice is largely *informal;* the Constitution requires only that a member "when elected, be an inhabitant of that state" in which he is chosen. As the nomination of Pierre Salinger for the Senate in California and the election of Robert Kennedy in New York show, this is a nominal requirement. But the *informal* emphasis on a "local man," who knows, appreciates, and is responsive to the local scene, is still the norm. The customary length of local residence necessary for political acceptance, however, may vary from several generations (in parts of the South) to barely a decade (in southern California or peninsular Florida).

The other two paths of representation, via physical replacement or by bringing about a change of opinion (or at least of vote) by the same incumbent rest upon the use, or possibility of use, of the electoral system. Here again we find a major contrast between the twentieth century Congress and that of the nineteenth century. Up to the turn of the century the likelihood of electoral turnover was quite high: more states and districts were competitive; party slates were voted on as a whole, with little opportunity for differentiation; and few alternative channels of opinion—such as interest groups— were active in Washington. Since 1900 fewer House districts have been competitive; ballot forms have been changed so as to encourage voting

[5] The first systematic effort to distinguish between alternative "paths" or processes of representation is Warren E. Miller and Donald E. Stokes, "Constituency Influence in Congress," *American Political Science Review* (March 1963), reprinted in Angus Campbell et al., *Elections and the Political Order* (New York: Wiley, 1966).

"for the man rather than the party"; and a myriad of groups seek to sway a legislator's *vote* rather than wait and try to replace *him*.

The overall pattern of the legislative career is structured by three successive choice points. First, though often ignored, is the willingness of a member to serve out his elected term and seek reelection. Throughout the nineteenth century the greater part of turnover in House members and Senators was *not* due to electoral defeat, but to voluntary retirement after a term or two, or even resignation without completing one's term.[6] In the twentieth century the attractions of the legislative career have reduced such departures drastically. The second and third winnowing processes, for those desiring to pursue a long-run career, involve renomination by the party and reelection in the November general election. Chronologically the primary election hurdle comes first, but the much greater importance of the general election warrants taking it up first. As we shall see, the primary for most members in most years is a very pale imitation of a contested electoral process.

The General Election: Shared Fates?

What influences the general election vote for House and Senate candidates, and to what extent can *they* hope to affect either the electoral turnout or direction of the vote in their constituency? These are very large questions, for which isolated cases and casual impressions provide conflicting answers. Over the past decade these questions have been pursued on a systematic basis in regard to House elections by Gerald Kramer,[7] and in a different way by Donald E. Stokes.[8] Both have provided notable perspectives from which to evaluate the extent to which the various candidates on a party ticket are involved in a "shared fate" and what seem to be the most important factors affecting the outcomes. Kramer concentrates on the extent to which the overall Congressional vote seems to reflect changes in the performance of the economy. Stokes attempts to disentangle the relative effects of all (unspecified) forces attributable to the individual district, then to common statewide trends, and finally to common nationwide trends.

Again it is useful to consider the baseline of nineteenth century

[6] Thus in the early nineteenth century barely one-third of the members of the Senate would bother to run for reelection, with roughly equal numbers resigning, or quitting at the completion of their term. Concurrently almost 90 percent of the departures from the House were due to resignations or refusal to stand for reelection, rather than to electoral defeat.

[7] Kramer, "Short-Term Fluctuations in U.S. Voting Behavior, 1896–1964," *American Political Science Review* (March 1971), 131–43.

[8] Stokes, "Parties and the Nationalization of Electoral Forces," in William N. Chambers and Walter Dean Burnham, *The American Party Systems* (New York: Oxford University Press, 1967), pp. 182–202.

practice. Down to the 1890s each party printed up a slate of its candidates which the voter had only to take in hand and deposit in the ballot box. On rare occasions some voters might "scratch" the name of one or more party candidates, but the tendency was to generate a "straight" party vote with remarkably little difference in the vote for President, governor, House, state legislator, and so on. Beginning in 1889, however, reform movements succeeded in having a few states adopt the Australian practice of printing up a single official ballot listing *all* the alternative candidates for each office.[9] This made it much easier for voters to skip back and forth across party lines. Indeed, as more states adopted the reform, many sought to further discourage "straight" party voting by adopting a ballot organized not into columns of candidates arranged by party, but rather into successive blocs of candidates grouped together under the office for which they were running. The full impact of these changes was not evident at first, but over time they facilitated tendencies for many voters to cross party lines, or to vote only for President, or both. The extent to which candidates were indeed linked together in a shared electoral fate was thus markedly reduced. Over time there were obvious incentives for incumbents to cultivate personal appeals, and for the parties to promote complex "United Nations" slates of balanced religious and nationality groupings (appealing to the increasingly heterogeneous nature of the twentieth century electorate).

Individual candidates for the House and Senate, whether incumbents or challengers, can seek to influence the size and direction of the vote in many ways. Such efforts may spell the difference between victory and defeat but are still limited to making marginal changes in such massive tendencies as for the presidential vote to far exceed the turnout in nonpresidential election years, or for the electorate to react negatively to an incumbent party in the event of a noticeable downturn of the economy. Political folklore suggests that the Republicans do better in periods of prosperity, with the electorate turning to the Democrats in periods of "bad times." By contrast a rational model of electoral behavior would react symmetrically to the parties, punishing either party's candidates for poor performance of the economy.

ECONOMIC INFLUENCES

For the period 1896–1964 (excepting war years and the 1912 three-party election) Gerald Kramer finds impressive evidence that the share of the total two-party vote for candidates of a party does indeed vary quite systematically with the state of the economy. Moreover, his

---

[9] For the impact of this on voting behavior see Jerrold G. Rusk, "The Effect of the Australian Ballot Reform on Split Ticket Voting: 1876–1908," *American Political Science Review* (Dec. 1970), 1220–38.

evidence supports the rational-model view that the parties are indeed treated equally, despite the historic association of the GOP with the post-1929 depression. Historical evidence on party turnover of seats for the post-Reconstruction period (say, 1874–1894) suggests that the same process was at work then, but with a much higher proportion of House seats changing hands than in the twentieth century.

Kramer's analysis, which works from objective economic variables (primarily real income, with neither unemployment nor cost-of-living proving very useful) to the Congressional vote skips over the customary role of voter attitudes. Detailed attitudinal data is simply not available for the pre-World War II period. Kramer's rational-model approach to the Congressional vote can, however, be reconciled with the attitudes-as-predictor approach (associated with the University of Michigan's Survey Research Center) by thinking of his estimates as short-cuts in a somewhat more complex process.

Thus for non-presidential elections one might visualize the process roughly as indicated in figure I. Kramer's estimates simply bypass the unmeasured intervening variable of attitude. The actual causal process might be assumed to operate via the solid arrows (through attitudes) rather than directly across (via the dashed arrow). For the process to work over time democratic theory would suggest inclusion, at the right of the model, of a box for government policy toward the economy, which is influenced—perhaps in anticipation—by the vote and in turn seeks to affect the level of real income. The Nixon administration's adoption of Phase II controls, after a disappointing Republican showing in the 1970 elections, suggests the extent to which both parties have come to accept the logic of some such relationship.

In presidential election years the situation is a bit more complicated. Then electoral turnout increases sharply, especially among independents and voters with weak party loyalties. In this context the specific presidential candidates and their campaign tactics have a substantial impact on the vote for President. Since House and Senate candidates are voted on at the same time and on the same ballot as the President, there is likely to be some presidential "coattail" effect on the vote for Congress. Kramer finds that in mid-term elections some 56 percent of the total variance in the major-party vote could be attributed to the economic variables; in presidential years this drops to 47 percent, but with an additional 16 percent due to effects of the presidential election.[10]

DISTRICT, STATE AND NATIONAL TRENDS

Another way of looking at sources of change in the vote for Congress is to attempt to assess the proportion of the total variation that can be attributed to the individual House district, to statewide trends, and

[10] Kramer, *op. cit.*, p. 140.

Figure I

Shared Fate in Terms of Voting for the House of Representatives:
Kramer-Style Model of Economic Influences on Variations in the House
Vote, 1896–1964

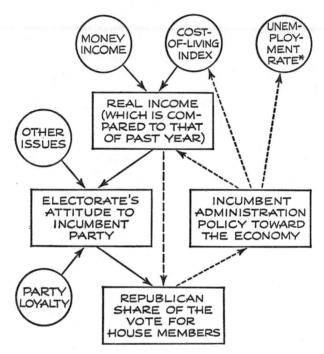

*Note: Unemployment rate is not statistically significant in predicting the House vote.

finally to a nationwide trend (for the Senate the division would be simply between state effects and nationwide trend, unless one wanted to introduce multi-state regions). House districts are neatly "nested" together state by state, and the states are equally neatly nested together within the nation. Donald Stokes has capitalized on this to estimate, within apportionment decades (such as 1952–60), the average relative magnitude of district-level, state-level, and nation-level effects on both turnout and partisan division of the vote. If one is interested in the extent to which Congressional candidates can hope to influence their electoral fate, then the relative size of the district-level effects is a very useful piece of information.

For the decades since Reconstruction table I indicates the relative extent of variation in the partisan division of the vote that Stokes attributes to the local district level. The salience of the local district increases sharply from the 1880s to the 1890s (the decade of greatest ballot change), then remains relatively stable through the 1920s. Under the impact of the depression and Roosevelt's New Deal the role of the local district declines sharply in the 1930s (to the same figure as held for the 1880s). There are further modest declines for the 1940s and 1950s. In regard to extent of electoral turnout Stokes' analysis suggests a much simpler picture: local district influence marks a rather steady decline over most of the entire period, with the sharpest drop between the decade of the 1900s and the 1910s.

Table I

CHANGES IN MAGNITUDE OF LOCAL CONSTITUENCY INFLUENCE ON PARTISAN DIVISION OF THE VOTE FOR HOUSE MEMBERS, BY DECADES
(BASED ON DONALD STOKES' CALCULATION OF VARIANCE COMPONENTS*)

Period Analyzed**	Size of Constituency-Variance Component
1872–80	26.7
1882–90	21.9
1892–1900	32.1
1902–10	28.1
1912–20	33.2
1922–30	36.5
1932–40	21.9
1942–50	18.7
1952–60	14.0
1962–70	(too much reapportionment to permit comparable analysis)

* See Donald E. Stokes, "Parties and the Nationalization of Electoral Forces," in William N. Chambers and Walter Dean Burnham, *The American Party Systems* (New York: Oxford University Press, 1967), pp. 182–202.
** Within each decade each House district is included if (1) it underwent no redistricting within the decade, and (2) each major party nominated a candidate in each election. Thus most of the South is excluded.

Stokes' ingenious analysis sheds light on a problem involving two contrasting trends.[11] On the one hand the local constituency should be of increasing importance because of the weakening of party loyalty and organization, the abandonment of party-supplied ballots, and the use of the primary election with its tendency to encourage members to "paddle their own canoes." On the other hand one might expect the local district to be of less importance vis-à-vis the national scene because of the spread of common living conditions (an urban, industrial way of life) and consequent issues, plus the increased im-

[11] For an extension and critique of the Stokes analysis see the forthcoming article by Richard S. Katz, *American Political Science Review*, 1973.

portance of the Presidency and of such potent national media as
radio (in the 1930s) and, more recently, television.

Perhaps the most important limitation of the Stokes analysis is
that it does not permit one to distinguish between effects in presidential and mid-term elections. The drop in participation in mid-term
elections has developed largely since 1900 and is so regular a feature
of twentieth-century elections that it would be useful to consider
a specific "presidential effect" which is superimposed on the district,
state, and national effects (estimating the "national" effect not due to
the presidential campaign from the various mid-term elections). This
should reduce the size of the presumed national effect quite substantially, especially for mid-term elections, and permit the identification of a specific presidential effect operative only in presidential
election years.

The increased turnout of the electorate in presidential election years
makes the partisan division of the vote in such years substantially
more variable than in mid-term elections. V. O. Key summarized the
reasons for this years ago:

> Explanation of the Administration's loss at midterm must be sought
> not so much by examining the midterm election itself as by looking at
> the preceding presidential election. The presidential campaign mobilizes
> party strength behind the winning presidential candidate and appar-
> ently has the secondary effect of capturing some marginal congressional
> seats, and of holding a few other such seats, for candidates of the Presi-
> dent's party. At the midterm the absence of the supportive power of the
> presidential campaign allows some districts, usually held by the narrowest
> margin, to sag over the line to the opposition.[12]

Key's analysis has been amply vindicated by Survey Research Center
interview data, which Angus Campbell deals with in terms of "surge
and decline" of the presidential and midterm electorates.[13]

In general the midterm elections offer somewhat less of a hazard
to most House and Senate incumbents, since their party membership
usually will match that of the majority of party identifiers in their
constituency. The exceptions are the members who have been swept
in largely because of the added "coattail" effects of a presidential
election. Since they are often from the party in a minority locally
they are likely to face an up-hill struggle to survive in the more
party-oriented midterm election. Hence the customary twentieth century tendency for the party capturing the Presidency to gain some

[12] Key, *Politics, Parties, and Pressure Groups*, 4th ed. (New York: Crowell, 1958),
pp. 615–16.
[13] Campbell, "Surge and Decline: A Study of Electoral Change," *Public Opinion
Quarterly* (Fall 1960), reprinted in Campbell et al., *Elections and the Political
Order*.

added strength in Congress in the presidential election only to lose most of the gains in the following mid-term election.

PARTY IDENTIFICATION

Variations in the vote for House members, and analogously for senators, thus reflect a substantial response of the electorate to the state of the economy, plus a variety of less easily identified factors. A portion of this variation is due to forces operating at the district level, another (usually smaller) portion reflects forces common to each state. But a substantial part of the variation, especially in the case of level of turnout, reflects general nationwide trends. The sources of variation, however, do not operate on an otherwise unstructured electorate. Rather, they work to displace the vote from its underlying partisan division.[14] The extent to which there is a substantial corps of loyal Republican and of loyal Democratic voters in a state or district is of crucial importance. "Safe" states and districts are simply a manifestation of a lopsided distribution of party identifiers. The surplus of party loyalists for one or the other party simply put such states or districts beyond the reach of most short-term forces which affect variation in the vote.

It is well known that a majority of the national electorate have some sort of enduring attachment to one or the other major party. Most voters do not have to stop and "decide" every two years which party they are going to favor; they have a standing decision in favor of one or the other. Much the same thing is true of most congressional districts—and used to be the case with a majority of states. The most marked differences in the incidence of close two-party competition are between the state-level Senate contests and the individual congressional district contests. This in turn is due to the marked increase in the number of competitive states, which reflects the steady erosion of sectionalism in the nation.

Evidence for the change toward greater competition at the state level is available on every side. It is indicated in registration figures, in presidential voting patterns, and in the sharp increase in the number of senators elected by narrow margins. The change in the fundamental geographical basis of partisanship can be seen by comparing the presidential vote of 1900 and 1960: in 1900 there were 18 states in which the Democrats polled less than 40 or more than 60 percent, and only 15 states in which the Democratic percentage of the vote ranged from 45 to 55 percent. In 1960, in contrast, there were 34 states in which the Democratic vote ranged between 45 and

[14] The concept of a pure (normalized) party vote is developed by Phillip E. Converse, in chapter 2 of *Elections and the Political Order*. For its application to Congress see Harvey M. Kabaker, "Estimating the Normal Vote in Congressional Elections," *Midwest Journal of Political Science* (Feb. 1969), 58–83.

55 percent, and only 6 states in which it was under 40 or over 60 percent.

Although the presidential vote is somewhat more volatile than voting for Senate or House members, the same trend is clearly evident in regard to Senate elections. Thus of all senators elected in 1960 and 1962 almost half won by margins of less than 55 percent, and over two-thirds won by less than 60 percent. But the various population and economic trends which are working toward producing two-party competition in virtually every *state* are not producing such competition within the more restricted confines of the individual House *district*. In most post-war elections less than 100 of the 435 House seats have been won by under 55 percent. The "swing" district, like the highly rational "independent" voter, is an exception to the rule and not the usual thing. Electoral turnover has been limited largely to this political "no-man's land." Indeed, Professor Charles O. Jones, in a detailed study of party turnover in the twentieth-century House of Representatives, points out that the number of House districts experiencing change of party control has gradually decreased for half a century.[15]

The "safe" one-party House seats are to be found in every part of the country, including the big, industrialized states which are very closely balanced at the statewide level. Thus in 1962 Pennsylvania voters reelected Senator Joseph Clark with 51.2 percent of the vote. But at the same election the same voters elected 23 of the 27 Pennsylvania congressmen by margins of greater than 10 percent. Much the same thing holds for New York or Illinois or any of the large states. Thus figure II compares the margin of House and Senate victories in the eight most populous states, which elect all told almost half of the House (211 of 435 seats) and which generally dominate the electoral college. There are roughly as many "safe" districts in these eight competitive states as in the eleven states of the South!

That the ordinary tides of political change lap only into relatively competitive states and districts has been amply demonstrated for both House and Senate by V. O. Key.[16] In areas where the minority party lacks a substantial number of partisan supporters, even the most vigorous efforts by the minority party's nominees are generally unavailing. In the absence of a major error by the incumbents, such challengers just do not have the ordinary baseline of partisan support from which to work that a candidate has in a competitive district

[15] Jones, "Inter-Party Competition for Congressional Seats," *Western Political Quarterly* (Sept. 1964), 461–76. By my count the proportion of House districts changing in party control in the decades prior to the 1896 realignment was roughly twice as much as for the decades after 1896.

[16] See the chapter on congressional elections in the fourth or fifth editions of *Politics, Parties, and Pressure Groups*.

Figure II

PARTY COMPETITION IN THE EIGHT MOST POPULOUS STATES: PERCENTAGE DEMO-
CRATIC FOR HOUSE CANDIDATES IN 1962 AND FOR ALL SENATE CANDIDATES,
1958–62 (INCLUDES NEW YORK, CALIFORNIA, PENNSYLVANIA, ILLINOIS, OHIO,
TEXAS, MICHIGAN, AND NEW JERSEY)

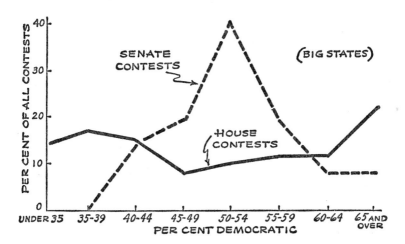

and that is necessary for a chance to win. What needs to be em-
phasized here is both the increasing number of statewide electorates
which *are* becoming susceptible to party change, and the small—and
dwindling—number of competitive House districts. These changes in
the incidence of competition, in turn, have major consequences for
the respective chambers. Close party competition in the House may be
increasingly limited to the handful of "swing" districts plus those
districts where an incumbent has retired or died. Incumbents have
found it increasingly easy to win reelection so long as they make a
good impression back home and do not become involved in scandal
(such as financial irregularities, excessive drinking in public, or highly
publicized marital problems). And for most members, being re-
nominated poses even less of a problem than does the general election.

Making Party Nominations: The Direct Primary

ADOPTION OF PRIMARY

Nomination by primary election is a peculiarly American phenomenon. Just as the delegate convention had replaced the old practice
of nomination by legislative caucus as a more direct and more dem-

ocratic procedure, so the same reasons led to the primary election replacing the convention. The holding of statewide primaries spread rapidly throughout the South during the decade of the 1890s and was adopted by many northern and western states, beginning with Wisconsin in 1903. By 1960 every state had *some* sort of primary election system, although a few still make some statewide nominations by convention. But there has been some tendency since World War II for primary states with complex ethnic or nationality mixes to adopt a pre-primary convention which can endorse a ticket—usually a "balanced" one—in the party primary.

At the turn of the century two major factors combined to generate unusual enthusiasm for the adoption of the primary and for the related issue of direct election of senators. On the one hand, there was widespread and in many cases justifiable dissatisfaction with the manipulation and control of conventions (and state legislatures) by patronage-based bosses and by various special interests. It was a bit optimistic to hope that a shift to nomination by primaries would remove entirely the influence of party bosses or special interests, but it did change the rules of the game. This change reduced the advantages of some types of candidates and some sorts of interests, while improving the position of other candidates and other interests.

The abuses of conventions and of legislative choice of senators were most marked in one-party areas where the general election contest did not constitute a restraining influence. The second factor behind the rapid spread of the primary was the sharp decline in general election competition which occurred in the 1890s. By 1900 so much of the country was one-party Democratic or one-party Republican that if people were to be provided a meaningful vote between rivals it would have to be in the primary. In the South the Negro had been finally removed as a political factor and the Republican party reduced to a nullity. In much of the North the nomination of William Jennings Bryan in 1896 had brought catastrophe to the Democrats. Hence the primary afforded a means of having at least some sort of election contest, and this seemed all the more important since the decline of general election competition severely lessened the restraints on the potential abuses of the largely unregulated convention process. As E. E. Schattschneider has noted, in the period prior to 1896 "the two major parties were able to compete on remarkably even terms throughout the country." As he puts it:

> Thus the crisis of 1896 destroyed the balance of the party system. In 1892 there were thirty-six states in which a competitive party situation existed. By 1904 there remained only six states in which the parties were evenly matched, while there were twenty-nine states in which the parties

were so unbalanced that the situation could no longer be described as competitive.[17]

Under such circumstances the nomination became, for all practical purposes, the decisive step in the electoral contest in most states. By and large the primary has proved to be a poor substitute for general election competition, but in the absence of such competition the primary doubtless has substantial advantages over the convention system. The very flexibility of the primary system, however, seems to have worked so as to further weaken the local minority party. Voters and candidates who might have helped to develop the opposition party instead tended to register and to enter politics in the ranks of the dominant majority. And within the majority party lines were fluid, participation was less than in general elections, and incumbents could usually count on reelection. Except in states with sharp factional cleavage, there was no continuing base of support or group of organizers to advance candidates to challenge the incumbent.[18]

LOCAL EMPHASIS OF PRIMARIES

For congressmen and senators the operation of the primary has tended to emphasize the highly decentralized nature of the American party system. At the nominating stage of the process the national party hardly exists. Rather it provides a label that automatically goes to any and all those local candidates who happen to win in the party's local primaries. The candidate may win solely because of his name or because he vigorously opposes the national party on some major local issue, such as busing in the South. Thus in each state and in most congressional districts the party nomination is up for grabs. Or at least it is when the incumbent is not a candidate for renomination.

The tendency for incumbents to win renomination is a tribute both to the material advantages which accrue to the incumbent and to the skill with which most incumbents work to keep their local fences mended. Charles L. Clapp, summarizing a series of round-table sessions held with both Republican and Democratic members, put the matter this way:

> Although members of Congress are inclined to talk about reelection campaigns in terms of the problems involved, they agree that as incumbents they possess extraordinary advantages over their opponents.

[17] E. E. Schattschneider, "United States: The Functional Approach to Party Government," in Sigmund Neumann, *Modern Political Parties* (Chicago: Univ. of Chicago Press, 1956), p. 203.

[18] The classic account of the difference that the lack of a continuing, organized corps of voters and candidates makes is still chapter 14 of V. O. Key, *Southern Politics* (New York: Knopf, 1949).

There is a tendency to believe that, aside from isolated instances where an overriding issue is present, there is little excuse for defeat.[19]

But many members cultivate their constituencies, even in the non-election year, as if the best way to avoid possible defeat were to scare off any potential competition. And House members have the added decennial threat of changed district boundaries, or even having two incumbents thrown into the same district.

In an analysis of the 1968 primaries for the 302 House seats outside the South and border states Frank Sorauf found that in all but 28 districts the incumbent was running for reelection.[20] Only 87 of the 274 incumbents faced *any* primary competition at all, and there were only 23 instances (less than 10 percent) where the winner's margin was less than two-to-one. For the out-party nomination and where an incumbent had retired, competition was more common but still limited. Even in the major party primaries lacking an incumbent, in more than half there was *no* contest at all. As Sorauf concludes, "the democratic hopes behind the direct primary falter on the lack of competition and low voter turnout." [21]

Sociologists have found it useful to distinguish between educational systems which operate along lines of *sponsored* mobility (such as the British preparatory schools for the upper classes) as contrasted with a more open system of *contest* mobility (such as American public schools and low-tuition state universities). Much the same distinction can be made in regard to party nominating systems—British parties sponsor candidates and assign them constituencies in order to bring them into the national political scene. In American parties the local primary is generally an open contest, to be won by a local candidate campaigning on issues of local concern.

The most difficult problem for a President seeking to influence the outcome of a primary is where an anti-administration incumbent is faced by a challenger. Aided by wartime enthusiasm, Woodrow Wilson was successful in intervening in several Southern primaries in 1918. But Franklin D. Roosevelt was generally unsuccessful in his 1938 "purge" efforts, which were undertaken without much advance planning.[22] Except in unusual circumstances, it would appear that national

---

[19] Charles L. Clapp, *The Congressman: His Work as He Sees It* (Washington: Brookings Institution, 1963), p. 330.
[20] Frank Sorauf, *Party Politics in America,* 2nd ed. (Boston: Little, Brown, 1972), p. 227.
[21] *Ibid.,* p. 226.
[22] On presidential intervention in primaries see Austin Ranney and Willmore Kendall, *Democracy and the American Party System* (New York: Harcourt, Brace and World, 1956), pp. 286–89, and William Riker, *Democracy in the United States* (New York: Macmillan, 1953), pp. 285–93. By contrast, presidential involvement in mid-term elections, in November, has come to be both accepted and expected.

party leaders are more likely to be effective by quietly searching out a strong local candidate or a national figure with a local connection, than by public denunciation of the incumbent. Campaign contributors and assorted technicans (media specialists and political pollsters) can be steered in the direction of a favored contender.

Like the common cold, a primary is seldom fatal but it is almost always an unpleasant disruption. Time, funds, and energy which could otherwise be channeled in other directions have to be diverted to the local scene. Small wonder that most legislators find it advantageous to cultivate the home state or district on a continuous basis, and especially in non-election years, in the hope of deterring primary opposition. In some states and in a good many House districts the same tactic can be used to reduce somewhat the risks of the general election.

Prior political experience and an existing base of support are vital in capturing initial nomination to the House, and a virtual necessity in running for the Senate. Thus House nominations often go to members of a state legislature or of local government, especially in the case of the local majority party. The minority party's nomination, often regarded as a useless honor, is more easily captured by a political neophyte. In turn, the members of the House constitute the single largest source of successful Senate candidates—a point of some dismay to many House leaders. In his study of the 180 members serving in the Senate from 1947 to 1957, D. R. Matthews found that almost half had been elected to *some* public office prior to reaching age 30, and that less than 10 percent came to the Senate without previously holding some public office.[23] He found the most frequent stepping stones to the Senate to be (in decreasing order of importance): House of Representatives, governorship, state or federal administrative office, and law-enforcement posts. In contrast to the nineteenth century, direct movement from state legislature to the Senate occurs for barely one in ten senators.

Nominations are thus generally on a do-it-yourself basis with the incumbent enjoying substantial advantages. Most candidates and most voters do not consider the nomination to be a national matter in which local preferences receive some consideration, but rather as primarily local matters in which any attempt at national intervention, or even outside comment by mass media, may backfire. Thus a popular President (or presidential candidate) may lend great strength to his party's entire ticket in November, but he finds it extraordinarily difficult to influence the primaries that determine the make-up of the remainder of that ticket. One of the few means available is by steering

[23] Donald R. Matthews, *U.S. Senators and Their World* (Chapel Hill: University of North Carolina Press, 1960), pp. 50–55.

major campaign contributors to favored incumbents or—a more risky move—to favored challengers in the party primaries.

Campaign Finance: The High Cost of Candidacy

"It costs too much to run for office." On this incumbents and challengers, Republicans and Democrats all agree. In most parts of the country it does cost a great deal to wage an effective campaign for the House or Senate. Moreover, most of the money has to be raised locally by the candidate and his supporters. The national parties can supply only limited funds plus some research materials and advice to their nominees—and sometimes they may furnish nothing more than a telegram of congratulations.

In a few states, such as heavily industrialized Ohio or Michigan, the state Republican organization may carry out a "united fund" type of drive for the benefit of the entire party ticket. The Democrats, lacking a natural financial base such as the business community, are less likely to be able to carry out such a coordinated fund-raising operation. Except for areas with unusually active labor unions, as in Michigan, or a powerful city organization, as in Chicago, Democratic nominees are likely to have to scrounge for funds on their own. The local emphasis on fund raising thus constitutes another decentralizing feature of the electoral process.

AMOUNTS

Precise accounts of the amounts spent in campaigns are hard to come by. Because of unrealistic state and federal limits, many candidates have made it a point *not* to know in detail how much is being spent in their behalf. But the general order of magnitude is well known. In a large state, expenditure of over a million dollars in a Senate race is regarded as regrettable but necessary. Costs for a House campaign vary widely. An incumbent from a safe district may need only to pay his filing fee, but in a closely contested urban district a figure of from fifty to one hundred thousand dollars is not unusual. Much of course depends upon the amount of use made of television, and whether the House candidate conducts a separate campaign or the party runs a joint one.

The increasing cost of campaigning and the paucity of national party assistance probably work to the advantage of the incumbent, and may mean better access for those local interests which do help foot the bill. In 1962 James A. Michener, the well-known novelist, waged a determined but unsuccessful campaign in a strong Republican district north of Philadelphia. He notes:

> I have come upon quite a few facts I have [*sic*] not known before. The incumbent has an overwhelming advantage . . . He mails letters

free. You pay for yours. For him to send a piece of literature to each family costs about $6,000 paid for by the taxpayers. You cough up your own $6,000 in cash.

He has at his command a staff of about five secretaries and helpers with a total yearly salary of around $45,000 paid for by the taxpayers. You find one girl and pay her yourself.[24]

Every two years a summary and analysis of major campaign contributions is prepared by the Citizens' Research Foundation. The sums reported in presidential election contests are astronomical, and spirited mid-term House or Senate contests often involve breathtaking amounts. Thus in 1970 New York Congressman Richard Ottinger ran for the Senate. He lost, but not for lack of funds or family enthusiasm, the family contributions to his campaign having amounted to some 3.9 million dollars (a figure not too far behind that reported for the family of Governor Nelson Rockefeller). Looking just at unsuccessful bids for Congress in 1970 one runs across the following examples of the direct family contributions to the costs of candidacy:[25]

Candidate	Family Contribution	Election (all 1970)
A. J. Donahue (Conn.)	$699,700	Lost Senate primary
Norton Simon (Calif.)	1,880,000	Lost Senate primary
F. H. Schultz (Fla.)	309,000	Lost Senate primary
H. M. Metzenbaum (Ohio)	507,500	Lost Senate election
Karen Burstein (N.Y.)	104,000	Defeated for House
L. Curtis (Mass.)	27,500	Defeated for House
P. J. Hillings (Calif.)	43,883	Defeated for House
D. J. Houton (Mass.)	30,130	Defeated for House
W. F. McCall, Jr. (Calif.)	40,999	Defeated for House
Jennifer Smith (N.Y.)	183,000	Defeated for House
P. J. Sprague (N.Y.)	240,425	Defeated for House
E. J. Stack (Fla.)	38,450	Defeated for House
W. D. Weeks (Mass.)	64,500	Defeated for House

Clearly money alone does not guarantee success, but it can be a very great advantage.[26]

[24] Quoted in Michael J. Kirwan, *How to Succeed in Politics* (New York: Macfadden Books, 1964), p. 20. For the 1970s, of course, most of these figures would have to be almost doubled.

[25] The 1970 report is summarized in *The New York Times*, April 19, 1972, p. 28.

[26] Successful Senate candidate John Tunney (California) reported family contributions of $123,475. Representative James H. Scheuer reported family contributions of $126,440 in his campaign for reelection. The 1970 championship, both for total expenditure and for family contribution, went to Nelson Rockefeller for his successful reelection campaign as governor. According to the foundation analysis it cost around $8 million, with some $5 million coming from various Rockefellers.

SOURCES

Since around 1900 both state and federal governments have made sporadic efforts at limiting, or at least making public, amounts and sources of campaign spending. Direct contributions by corporations or by labor unions have been prohibited, but efforts at limiting total amount of spending or total individual contributions have had so many loopholes as to be useless (in fact, their chief effect has probably been to reduce public awareness of the facts, which have been muddied by the need for multiple letterhead committees which receive multiple checks from an individual or family).[27] Finally, in 1972 Congress passed a new Federal Election Campaign Practices Act which plugs many of the loopholes; imposes limits on what a candidate and his family can contribute and on total spending for radio, television, and other communications media; and seeks to establish an extensive system for reporting contributions and expenditures.[28] Only time and experience will prove whether the new measure will survive possible amendment, probable court tests, and administrative difficulties of compliance.

When measured against the magnitude of the task, the very limited amounts that can be made available to candidates (usually with emphasis on incumbents) by the Republican and Democratic campaign committees of the House and Senate pale into relative insignificance. Even these amounts are doled out in each party by independent House and Senate campaign committees, thus reenforcing the natural decentralizing tendencies of the American electoral system. Organized labor usually picks up part of the tab for many Democrats—plus an occasional liberal Republican. But probably the most potent centralizing tendency would be the adoption of a system of federal underwriting of at least some of the costs, especially of presidential contests. Senator Russell Long's proposal to permit each taxpayer to earmark a one-dollar tax deduction to be channeled to the party of his choice was adopted by Congress, but then repealed before it could go into effect. The 1972 law includes such a provision, but only to take effect *after* the 1972 election (for which the Republicans saw themselves as being in a much better financial position than the debt-ridden, out-of-power Democrats). And the overall difficulty of adequately yet equitably financing Congressional elections is increased by the substantial—and growing—range of resources available to incumbent members of both House and Senate. Not least of these is the member's activities on behalf of individual constituents.

[27] A classic case in the mobilization of wealth, even in a state with a rather strict campaign finance law, was John F. Kennedy's successful 1952 campaign for the Senate. See H. D. Price, "Campaign Finance in Massachusetts in 1952," *Public Policy*, vol. 6 (1955), pp. 25–46.
[28] See *Congressional Quarterly Almanac*, 1971, for the debate, and 1972 for final enactment.

Care and Feeding of Constituents: The Legislator as Ombudsman

A visitor to the House or Senate office buildings is likely to be impressed by the clatter of electric typewriters, the whir of mimeograph machines, and the stacks of outgoing mail. Most of this blur of activity has little or nothing to do with pending legislation or public policy, but a great deal to do with the reelection possibilities of the members of the House and Senate. Prompt attention to mail, careful follow-up on individual "case" work, and maximum cultivation of district (or state) contacts and media add to the secret weapons by which the modern incumbent hopes to remain in office.

INDIVIDUAL CASEWORK

Several Scandinavian countries have a special official, the *Ombudsman,* who receives complaints and tries to help the average citizen in his contacts with the bureaucracy. But a general complaint bureau is one agency which the New Deal did not get around to establishing. In its stead the United States has 535 legislators who serve—with amazing effectiveness—as "ombudsmen" for their local constituents. As various federal agencies came to have more and more complicated contacts with individual citizens, it was inevitable that some bureaucratic errors would be made and that many people would not know what to do about a missing Social Security check or getting an emergency furlough for a serviceman overseas. The simple solution was to "write your congressman" and hope he could help. Within a generation the flow of requests for help or advice has grown from a tiny trickle into a massive daily tide of mail. And in the process modern senators and congressmen have come to perform functions—and enjoy a continued tenure—undreamed of by their nineteenth-century predecessors.

In most congressional offices there are secretaries who specialize in the various types of "case work" and know the appropriate liaison personnel in the various downtown departments. On the Senate side the volume of work for a single senator may be so great that various secretaries will deal exclusively with cases involving veterans' affairs, or Social Security, or the Department of Defense. This provides a helpful function for the citizen and also can give the legislator some rough idea of some of the problem areas and weak spots of bureaucratic operation. And its political value is beyond question. It was providing assistance in an hour of need which helped cement the immigrant's loyalty to the big-city machines of bygone years. In an updated, white-collar sort of way, today's legislators perform a similar—but much more technical—function. And it is appreciated.

Not all "cases" are small matters. There are "big" problems too, involving disposition of federal land or property, status of urban renewal requests, the location of proposed projects and installations, complex contract negotiations, and all the rest of the contacts between federal agencies and local citizens, local business firms, or even local governmental units. Here again the assistance of the local congressman or senator may be of vital importance. But the dividing line between proper and improper involvement is hard to define, and problems of "conflict of interest" may arise. But in general the level of congressional ethics, despite occasional lapses, seems to be far above that of most state legislatures. And it may not be much below that of the federal bureaucracy or the world of private business.

PROMOTING THE ECONOMY

Since World War II congressmen and senators have also taken on an added role in promoting the growth of the local economy. They are expected to do everything within their power to oppose any move which would destroy local employment or buying power, whether the closing of an ancient naval ropewalk or the curtailing of an obsolescent navy yard. In an age when the federal government is heavily involved in spending not only for defense but for research and for natural resource development, the legislator's local prestige may rise or fall with the curve of federal investment and spending in his state or district. And the member who can land a major plum—such as the NASA Headquarters which went to Houston, Texas—is likely to be regarded as a civic benefactor and local hero.

Finally, a member's name and good works need to be made known to his constituents. Brief radio or television reports may be taped (at cost) and sent to local stations for broadcast, except during campaigns, as a public service. The great majority of members put out some sort of newsletter, and some send out periodic questionnaires. Special letters of congratulations may go to all graduating high school seniors or to newly wed couples. Many members maintain a year-round office in the district or home state. With the increased length of congressional sessions frequent trips home become even more important. Once Congress adjourns, the members from thinly populated areas may cover the local byways in a mobile trailer office, or in a small airplane. As the late Michael J. Kirwan, a chairman of the Democratic Congressional Campaign Committee, once put it: "No Congressman who gets elected and who minds his business should ever be beaten. Everything is there for him to use if he'll only keep his nose to the grindstone and use what is offered." [29]

[29] Kirwan, *op. cit.*, p. 20.

Conclusion: Electoral Change and Institutional Adaptation

What will the impact of the electoral process be on the House and Senate in the years ahead? For the short run "more of the same" is often the safest prediction. But in an important way the question begs the point, since we have no very sure idea of what the future holds for American political parties and electoral behavior. Looking at the broad sweep of American history it is obvious that major changes in the party system or electoral process have usually had very substantial effects on Congress. But it is sobering to notice that most of the more important effects were unintended, and indeed were often not perceived by the major political figures of the day.

The last major change in the electoral base of the House of Representatives came in the 1890s with the triple impact of the emergence of the Solid (lily-white) South, adoption of ballot and registration reforms, and massive voter realignment triggered by the Bryan campaign of 1896. All three changes worked strongly to the advantage of incumbents and rapidly produced a crop of veteran legislators who tended to think in terms of decades rather than years. Members with long service wanted their experience recognized and were unwilling to have all committee posts and chairmanships up for grabs every two years as had been the nineteenth century practice. Discontent over Speaker Joseph Cannon gave the Democrats an added excuse to take the power of committee appointment away from the Speaker when they took over the House in 1911. Subsequently the respective party committees on committees proved unable to resist the demands for respecting seniority of committee service. By roughly 1920 the "modern" House had taken shape: the speakership had been reduced to a marginal role, the Appropriations Committee had been expanded and strengthened, average terms of prior service were higher and percent freshmen members was lower than at any time in the ninteenth century, and both parties were making committee appointments with scrupulous care for seniority. Except for physical change—two new House office buildings—remarkably little has changed over the past 50 years.

The role that the House has carved out for itself since 1920 may not be ideal, but it will not be easy to change. If the depression and New Deal could make no lasting impact on the functioning of the House, one hesitates to predict sweeping changes from a modicum of reapportionment, or from the New Politics.[30] A few members—like Brooklyn's Emanuel Celler—may fall by the wayside, but the overall distribution of party support is such that most House districts will remain

[30] Perhaps the single most likely change for the House is a continued increase in the number of women elected.

relatively "safe" so long as we have Republicans and Democrats. The increased threat of primary opposition may force incumbents into closer attention to casework or more frequent trips home. It seems unlikely that it can convert House members—of whom we have 435—into the modern senatorial mould of televised public-figure, fearless committee-investigator, and activist issue-agitator. For most members of the House the alternative is between anonymous, specialized attention to committee detail and the possible lure of running for the Senate or other high-visibility office.

In contrast to the House, the "greening" of the Senate has been remarkable. Recent political trends have been reflected much more rapidly there, and senators with an eye on the White House (a numerous band) sometimes have to compete in anticipation of potential trends. The change in Senate style is all the more remarkable given the absence of any major formal changes in the position of the Senate in the past half century. To a substantial degree modern senators seem to be making a virtue of the necessity imposed on them by the shift to direct election, in statewide contests, with a direct primary for nominations. This seems to force most senators into the mainstream of American politics in a way that lopsided House elections do not encourage.

The advantages of using the Senate and its committees as a forum for publicizing issues—and senators—is not entirely new. But it reflects a sharp change from pre-World War I days when major investigations were more often relegated to presidential commissions, and congressional committees met with little or no press coverage. The modern pattern began to emerge in the 1920s, with Senator Tom Walsh's investigation of the Teapot Dome scandal as the most spectacular example. This public-oriented style was well suited to Republican Progressives, many of whom migrated to the Senate after failing to bring the House around to their way of thinking. And it was expanded on in the 1930s by men like Robert Wagner, Bob LaFollette, Jr., and Gerald P. Nye. But it was with the arrival of television—first explored by Estes Kefauver and then by Joseph McCarthy—that senators could begin to put it all together.

What results from the combination of close competitive statewide elections, the existence of many real and some imagined public issues, and the availability of mass media to cover as many subcommittees as the senators can make look exciting? From one point of view it is merely senatorial self-interest, in pursuit of publicity to assist in reelection or in a drive for the Presidency. But, as in "The Fable of the Bees," the pursuit of self-interest may be channeled so as to promote the common good. Or, to turn the matter around, in pursuing public issues modern senators have a great deal to gain. The same cannot be said for the current House. There the pursuit of self-interest—and of the public good—is defined in a less spectacular but perhaps no less real way.

Richard F. Fenno, Jr.

3

The Internal Distribution
of Influence: The House

Every action taken in the House of Representatives is shaped by
that body's structure of influence. That structure, in turn, has emerged
as a response to two very basic problems of organization. The first
is the problem of decision-making. That is, who shall be given influence over what, and how should he (or they) exercise that influence?
Influence can be defined simply as a share in the making of House
decisions. The House's first problem, then, involves the distribution
of these shares among its members and, hence, the creation of a
decision-making structure.

The second organization problem is that of holding the decision-
making structure together so that the House can be maintained as an
ongoing institution. This is the problem of maintenance. How, in
other words, should the members be made to work together. so as to
minimize disruptive internal conflicts? The House must be capable
of making decisions, but it must not tear itself apart in the process.
It is in response to these twin problems—decision-making and maintenance—that the House's internal structure of influence has developed.
And it is by focusing on these two problems that the structure can best
be understood.

RICHARD F. FENNO, JR. *is professor of political science at the University of
Rochester. Among his publications are* The Power of the Purse: Appropri-
ations Politics in Congress, The President's Cabinet, National Politics and
Federal Aid to Education *(co-author), and* Congressmen in Committees.

Decision-Making

Shares in the making of House decisions are not distributed equally among the 435 members. Two sets of formal leadership positions have emerged: the decision-making positions, such as those on the committees, which have been established and maintained by the entire membership of the House, and those positions, such as majority leader and minority leader, which have been established and maintained by the members of the two congressional parties. These two structures of influence, the House structure and the party structure, do overlap—the position of the Speaker, for example, fits into both. But they are distinguishable. Those House members who occupy leadership positions in either structure or both possess the greatest potential for influence in the chamber. Some may not be able to capitalize on that potential; and it is wrong to assume that every man occupying a leadership position is, in fact, a leader. On the other hand, few members of the House become very influential without first occupying a formal leadership position in the House or party structures. Decision-making in the chamber must be described primarily in terms of these two interrelated structures.

HOUSE STRUCTURE

In the Ninety-first Congress (1969–70), 20,015 bills and resolutions, public and private, were introduced in the House, each calling for a decision. During the same period, each individual member received thousands of letters, kept hundreds of appointments in his office and attended hundreds of meetings in Washington and at home, nearly all of which produced requests that he take action of some sort. Individually and collectively, House members are called upon to make decisions, sometimes within the space of a few hours, on matters ranging from national security to constituency service. In short, a body of 435 men and women must process a work load that is enormous, enormously complicated, and enormously consequential. And they must do so under conditions in which their most precious resources, time and information, are in chronically short supply. The need for internal organization is obvious.

Committees, Division of Labor, and Specialization—To assist them in making their constituency-related decisions, members hire an office staff and distribute them between Washington and "the district." To meet the more general problems, the House has developed a division of labor—a system of standing committees. To this they have added a few *ad hoc* select committees and, in conjunction with the Senate, a few joint committees. The 21 standing committees plus the Joint Committee on Atomic Energy provide the backbone of the House's decision-making structure. They screen out most of the bills and resolutions introduced in the House—17,424 out of 20,015 in 1969–70. On a small fraction, they hold hearings. In fewer cases still, the committee will send a modified bill out to the floor of the House for final action. With a few important exceptions, the full House accepts the version of the bill produced by the committee. Decisions of the House for the most part are the decisions of its committees.

The authority of the committees in the chamber rests on the belief that the members of a committee devote more time and possess more information on the subjects within their jurisdiction than do the other congressmen. Specialization is believed to produce expertise. For the non-committee member, reliance on the judgment of the experts on the committee is a useful shortcut in making his decisions. For the committee member, the deference of others is a source of influence. A man of whom it can be said that "he does his homework," "he knows what he's talking about," and "he knows more about that executive bureau than they do themselves" is a prestigeful figure in the House. Members pride themselves on producing, through specialization, a home-grown body of legislative experts to guide them in making their decisions and to serve as a counterweight to the experts of the executive branch. Wilbur Mills and John Byrnes on taxes, Wayne Aspinall and John Saylor on natural resources, Edith Green and Albert Quie on higher education, George Mahon on military affairs and Olin Teague on veterans matters are a few such members.

The conditions of committee influence vary. Members are likely to defer to a committee, for example, when the issues are technical and complicated, when large numbers do not feel personally involved, or when committee members are highly unified in support of the committee's proposal. Some or all of these conditions obtain for committees such as Armed Services, Appropriations, and Interior and doubtless help to account for the fact that their recommendations are infrequently altered on the floor. Conversely, members are less likely to defer to the judgment of a committee when the issue is of a broad ideological sort, where national controversy has been stirred, or where the committee is far from unanimous. These latter conditions frequently mark the work of the Committees on Education and Labor, Banking and Currency, and Agriculture. Under such circumstances committee influence may be displaced by the influence of party, of constituency, or of a member's social philosophy. Yet even here the committee can determine the framework for later decision-making, and members not on the committee may still be influenced by the factional alignments within the committee.

Committee claims to expertise stem not only from the individual talents of their leaders, but from the abilities of their professional staffs. One of the goals of the Legislative Reorganization Acts of 1946 and 1970 was to strengthen committee staffs. Within the limits of these laws, and within budgetary limits voted each year by the House, staff selection has long been one of the important prerogatives of the committee chairman. Staff size, partisan composition, professional capacity, and duties will normally reflect his desires. Recently, however, committee chairmen have seen their influence on staff limited somewhat by committee action, by party directive, or by statute. Some committees, like Education and Labor, allow subcommittee chairmen to choose their entire staff; the Democratic caucus has voted to allow all subcommittee chairmen to hire one staff person; and the Legislative Reorganization Act of 1970 directs that no less than one-third of a full committee's budget and two of its professional staff members be allocated to the minority party.

Staff influence varies with the confidence which committee and subcommittee members, and especially their respective chairmen, place in staff abilities and staff judgment. Where the desire to use a staff and confidence in it exist, staff members constitute a linchpin of internal committee decision-making. When these conditions are not present, it does not make much difference what kind of staff a committee has. Such staff influence as does exist in the House exists here— in the committees. One committee, the Joint Committee on Internal Revenue Taxation, functions primarily as the formal "holding company" for an expert staff which dominates decision-making in that field. In only a few cases does any member of a congressman's personal office staff enter the mainstream of legislative decision-making—in marked contrast to the situation in the Senate. Thus, to advocate larger staff in the House is to argue in favor of the division of labor, of subject-matter specialization, and of an increase in the influence of the 21 standing committees.

Committee Leadership and Its Conditions—Acceptance of the division of labor as a necessity by House members makes it likely that committee leaders will have major shares in the making of House decisions. Who, then, are the committee leaders and how do their shares vary? In describing the committee-based leaders, it is easy to mistake form for substance. The most common pitfalls are to assume that invariably the most influential committee leaders are the chairmen and to infer that the vital statistics of these 21 individuals characterize committee leadership. Each committee chairman does have a formidable set of prerogatives—over procedure, agenda, hearings, subcommittee creation, subcommittee membership, subcommittee jurisdiction, staff membership, staff functions—which gives him a potential for influence. His actual influence in the House, however, will depend not only upon the prestige of his committee, but also upon his ability to capitalize on his potential and to control his committee. Consequently, many important committee leaders do not hold the position of chairman. They may be subcommittee chairmen, ranking minority members of committees or subcommittees, and occasionally members who hold no formal committee position.

Because House committees differ tremendously in power and prestige, committees like Ways and Means, Rules, and Appropriations necessarily are more influential than committees like Post Office and Civil Service, House Administration, and District of Columbia. These differentials in influence are demonstrated by the House members themselves when, in seeking to change their committee assignments, they regularly trade the possibility of a chairmanship on a low-influence committee for a low-ranking position on a high-influence committee. Circumstances may, of course, alter the relative importance of committees, but at any point in time influential House leaders must be sought among the most influential House committees.

House leaders must be sought, too, among the subcommittee leaders of important House committees. The Committee on Appropriations, for example, divides its tasks among 13 largely autonomous subcommittees, whose chairmen have as large a share in House decision-making as all but a few full committee chairmen. Thus the chairman of the Appropriations Subcommittee on Foreign Aid exercises more influence over that program than does the chairman of the Foreign Affairs Committee. And the equivalent statement can be made about a half-dozen other Appropriations subcommittee chairmen. When the Reorganization Act of 1946 reduced the number of standing committees from 48 to 19, it stimulated the growth and the importance of subcommittees. This outcome has obscured the realities of committee-based influence. Analyses of committee leadership which exclude the 119 (as of 1972) subcommittees can be but caricatures of the influence patterns in the House. In 1971, House Democrats engineered a major change in the distribution of influence by deciding that no member could serve as chairman of more than one subcommittee. The result was that about 30 members immediately succeeded to subcommittee chairmanships, positions they could not have held under previous rules.

The influence of a committee leader in the House depends not only upon the relative power of his committee, but also upon how each committee or subcommittee makes its decisions. To be influential in the House a committee leader must first be influential in his committee. The patterns vary from autocracy to democracy. A chairman who is the acknowledged expert in his field, whose skill in political maneuver is at least as great as that of his colleagues, and who exploits his prerogatives to the fullest can dominate his committee or subcommittee. But his dominance may well proceed with the acquiescence of a majority of the committee. They may, and usually do, expect him to lead. Since a majority of any committee can make its own rules, it is impossible for a chairman to dictate committee decisions against the wishes of a cohesive and determined majority of its members—at least in the long run. The acquiescence of his subcommittee chairmen will be especially crucial. On the other hand, since timing is of the essence in legislative maneuver, a short-run autocracy may be decisive in shaping House decisions. A successful chairman, however, must retain the support of his committee, and most chairmen are sensitive to pressures which may arise inside the committee for a wider distribution of internal influence. Long-term resistance to such pressures may bring about a revolt inside the committee which permanently weakens the influence of its chairman. Such revolts occurred, for instance, in the Committee on Government Operations in 1953, in the Committee on Education and Labor in 1959 and 1964, and in the Committee on Post Office and Civil Service in 1965. The Legislative Reorganization Act of 1970 attempted to further majority control of committees. But the most significant efforts in this direction have come on a committee-by-committee basis—on occasions when a chairman's views came to differ markedly and persistently from those of a majority of the members.

It is wrong to assume that most chairmen—even if they could—would monopolize decision-making in their committees. In most cases the creation of subcommittees means a sharing of influence inside the committee. Sharing can be kept to a minimum by designating sub-committees (sometimes simply by numbers) but giving them no permanent jurisdiction of any kind—as has been tried by chairmen of the committees on Armed Services. Or the same result can be produced by retaining jurisdiction over certain bills for the full committee, as has been done, for example, by the chairman of the District of Columbia Committee (with home rule) or the chairman of the Foreign Affairs Committee (with foreign aid). But where subcommittees are allowed a maximum of autonomy (Government Operations, Public Works, Appropriations, for example) the chairmen may willingly provide leaders of his subcommittees with a base of influence in the House. In the Committee on Government Operations John Moss's former Subcommittee on Foreign Operations and Government Information, and in the Committee on Public Works John Blatnik's former Subcommittee on Rivers and Harbors come readily to mind. In some cases committee or subcommittee chairmen who work harmoniously with their opposite numbers in the minority party invest the latter with a potential for House influence. The relationship between Judiciary Chairman Emanuel Celler and ranking minority member William McCulloch on civil rights matters is a case in point.

Characteristics of Committee Leaders—The chairmen and ranking minority members of the standing committees attain their formal leadership positions through seniority. A variety of rules exist for determining seniority in the case of simultaneous appointments to a committee, but the rules of advancement from that time on are simple to understand and can be applied automatically. A chairman or ranking minority member who retains his party designation and gets reelected is not removed from his leadership position. In 1971, both parties took steps to make it easier for them to reject a seniority-designated chairman at the opening of each Congress. The Republicans introduced a secret ballot vote on each chairman, with a new designee to be proposed by the Committee on Committees should any fail to receive majority approval. The Democrats countered with a proposal giving ten members the power to put any prospective chairman to a majority vote, with a rejection to be followed by a new Committee on Committees nominee. A 1971 effort to unseat Chairman John McMillan of the District of Columbia Committee failed in the Democratic Caucus by 126–96. Piecemeal exceptions might now occur; but, as the accepted method for selecting committee chairmen, seniority remains intact.

Seniority, however, only partially governs the selection of subcommittee leaders. Oftentimes, these positions are filled by the committee chairman (and by the ranking minority member for his side), and he retains sufficient authority over the subcommittee structure to modify the impact of seniority if he so desires. Once a committee member has been appointed to a subcommittee, he typically rises via seniority to become its chairman or ranking minority member. But the original assignment to subcommittees may not be made in accordance with seniority on the parent committee. It may be made on the basis of constituency interests (as is the case with the crop-oriented Agriculture subcommittees), on the basis of a member's prior experience, or on the basis of the chairman's design for influencing subcommittee decisions. Where the chairman can control subcommittee leadership by his power to determine their jurisdiction and to create or abolish subcommittees, his actions may infuse an important element of flexibility into the rigidities created by strict adherence to seniority. The number of Appropriations subcommittees has varied from nine to fifteen since the Reorganization Act of 1946, and many of these changes resulted in giving or taking away a subcommittee chairmanship without regard for the claims of seniority.

Normal adherence to the rule of seniority means that by and large committee leaders have had long experience in dealing with their subject matter. Committee-based influence in the House operates within subject-matter areas. Along with information and knowledge, the accumulated experience of committee leaders normally produces practical political wisdom on such matters as how to retain the support of a committee, when to compromise on the contents of a bill, when

to take a bill to the floor, how to maneuver in debate, and how to
bargain with the Senate in conference—all in a special subject-matter
area.

Seniority practices also mean that formal committee leaders represent
the traditional areas of party strength. In 1972, twelve of the twenty-
one Democratic chairmen represented districts in the South (eight)
and in the Border States (four). Ten of the twelve (plus four northern-
ers) represented rural areas. Five chairmen came from the urban
North. Of the ranking Republicans, twelve came from the Midwest;
and ten of these represented rural districts. Five others came from
suburban constituencies in the Northeast and Far West. If one includes the formal subcommittee leaders from the Appropriations
Committee, the picture is similar. Eight of thirteen chairmen are
from southern and Border-State districts. Ten of thirteen are from
rural areas. Eight of the thirteen ranking minority members are from
the Midwest. Ten of the thirteen are from rural districts.

What difference does it make to draw committee leaders from safe
constituencies? Clearly such interests as can be identified with these
constituencies are advantaged by the makeup of committee leadership.
The safest general description of those social interests is that they
have tended to be conservative; but this may, of course, change as
urban and suburban constituencies come to provide an increasing
number of safe House seats. In any case, the important question concerns how each particular committee chairman does in fact act on
those matters which come before his particular committee. By itself
the fact that committee leaders come from safe constituencies tells us
only that they will respond to district sentiment that is clear and
intense. In all other instances, however, such men remain freer than
many other members to use their own judgment in legislative matters
without fear of reprisal at the polls. All things being equal, a member
who has flexibility of maneuver in the House will be more influential
there than one whose constituency obligations leave him without
elbow room. In terms of their leadership styles and their reactions to
non-constituency factors, committee leaders defy any simple constitu-
ency-based typology.

The committee structure is a decentralized decision-making system.
A fully accurate description of who it is that benefits from the committee structure almost requires, therefore, a committee-by-committee,
subcommittee-by-subcommittee, and leader-by-leader analysis. Those
who attempt to reform committee operations without making such
an analysis are very likely to miss their mark.

Rules and the Distribution of Influence—What we have called the
House structure of influence (as distinguished from the party structure) results not only from the division of labor by committees but
also from the body of formal rules which superintend decision-making.

One obvious requirement for the House is a body of rules sufficiently restrictive to prevent unlimited delay and to permit the members to take positive action. Such a set of rules must recognize both a majority's right to govern and a minority's right to criticize. Each is necessary if the rules are to be accepted by both. The accomplishment of this kind of balance is best evidenced by the extraordinary devotion to established rules and to procedural regularity which characterize every aspect of House action.

Traditionally, the rules governing action on the House floor have given an advantage to the committee in charge of the bill and, hence, to its recommendations. The quorum necessary to do business has been small, most of the voting on amendments has not been publicly recorded, and the time for debate has been relatively short. Should the committee lose on an amendment, it has been able to call for a second, public roll call vote; but should the committee defeat an amendment, no public second chance has normally been available to the adherents of the amendment. These committee advantages were substantially weakened by a rules change in the Reorganization Act of 1970. The amending process has been made more publicly visible by a change in the "teller" voting. Teller votes, whereby members walk up the center aisle and are counted anonymously, have decided many key amendments—typically in favor of the committee bill. Now, teller votes can be publicly recorded like other roll call votes. More members are now in attendance on the floor, those opposed to the committee bill are now assured of a public vote, and the relative advantage of the committee and its supporters has declined. In 1970, the Appropriations Committee defeated an amendment which would have eliminated all funds for the supersonic transport. The vote, 86–102, came on an anonymous teller vote. A year later, on a recorded teller vote, the committee was overturned on the very same issue, by vote of 217–204—and the SST was stopped. To the degree that committee recommendations tend to be "conservative," the new rules will have a "liberal" impact. To the degree that committee recommendations tend to be "liberal," the recorded teller vote will have a reverse effect.

Increments of influence accrue to those leaders who understand House rules and can put them to use in their behalf. As they exist in the Constitution, in Jefferson's Manual, in the 11 volumes of Hinds's and Cannon's precedents, and in the 42 Rules of the House, the procedures of the chamber represent as technical and complex a body of knowledge as any subject-matter area. Influence inside a committee may carry over to the House floor, but success on the floor requires additional skills. Primary among these are the ability to sense the temper of the House and the ability to use the Rules of the House to advantage. A Wilbur Mills, a Wayne Aspinall, or a Richard Bolling is a procedural specialist, quite apart from any subject-matter competence he may possess.

The official with the greatest potential for influence in the House, especially in matters of procedure, is the Speaker. Although his importance stems primarily from his position as leader of the majority party, he derives considerable influence from his position as the presiding officer of the House. In this capacity, he exercises a series of procedural controls over House activity. And some of these, in turn, provide opportunities to affect the substance of House decisions. He must recognize any member who wishes to speak on the floor; he rules on the appropriateness of parliamentary procedures; he determines the presence of a quorum; he selects the chairman of the Committee of the Whole; he votes in case of a tie; he counts and announces votes; he decides in doubtful cases to which standing committee a bill will be assigned; he appoints special or select committees; he appoints the House members to each conference committee; and he maintains decorum in the chamber. The small element of discretion involved in any of these prerogatives occasionally affects legislation. The refusal, for example, of Speaker Sam Rayburn to entertain dilatory tactics before announcing the 203–202 vote extending the draft in 1941 may have prevented a different outcome.

Because the procedural controls of the Speaker extend fairly broadly across the stages through which legislative proposals must pass before they emerge as law, the scope of his procedural influence is probably more important than its weight at any one point. For most House leaders, however, the various decision-making stages represent boundaries which contain their influence. Committee leaders dominate the initial stage of review, reformulation and recommendation; the Committee on Rules and a few party leaders control the agenda stage; committee leaders, party leaders, and a cluster of other interested members combine to dominate the floor debate and amending stage; a very few committee leaders speak for the House in the conference committee. At each stage a few members normally dominate decision-making. But from stage to stage and from bill to bill, dispersion, not concentration, of influence is the dominant pattern.

The Committee on Rules—No better illustration of these generalizations about influence—its concentration within stages and its dispersion across stages—exists than the Committee on Rules. This committee owes its great influence in the chamber to the fact that it stands athwart the flow of legislation at one stage—the agenda stage. Since bills flow out of the standing committees and onto the various House calendars in considerable profusion, some mechanism is necessary for sending them to the floor in an orderly fashion. For most important bills these agenda decisions are made by the Rules Committee. By "granting a rule" to a bill the committee takes it from a calendar, where action is uncertain, and sends it to the floor, where final action is assured. The rule for a bill specifies the length of the debate and the number and kinds of floor amendments to be allowed, and it may remove from challenge provisions which otherwise would violate standing House rules, such as the prohibition against legislation in an appropriation bill.

Commonly referred to as a toll gate or a traffic cop, the committee obviously functions in the interest of an orderly and efficient flow of business. Just as obviously, however, the Rules Committee functions as a second substantive, policy-making committee for each bill which passes its way. Its fifteen members can exact concessions from the bill's sponsors as their price for granting a rule. Or, as they do on about a dozen bills each year, they can refuse to grant a rule altogether. The committee thus can wield a virtual veto over the decision-making process. The veto power is not absolute. Money bills from the Appropriations Committee do not require a rule. A number of by-passes such as the discharge petition and Calendar Wednesday are available; but they are clumsy and hence are rarely attempted and hardly ever succeed. The members' devotion to procedural regularity contributes an essential underpinning to Rules Committee influence.

Since a House decision is a composite of several formal (and countless informal) decisions, and since at each stage in decision-making a different cluster of House leaders may prevail, supporters of a given bill must build a series of majorities—in the substantive committee, in the Rules Committee, on the floor, and in conference—if they are to be successful. Opponents of a bill, however, need to build but a single majority—at any one stage in the process—to achieve their ends. The Committee on Rules in particular has lent itself to such defensive action. Thus in 1960, when for the first time in history both houses of Congress had passed a federal aid-to-education bill and the Rules Committee refused to grant a rule so that the bill could go to conference, it was the only place in the entire Congress where opponents of federal aid could block a majority vote. But it was enough. The consequence, therefore, of the series of stages when accompanied by a corresponding dispersion of influence is to confer a substantial advantage on those interests in society that wish to preserve the status quo. House rules make it easier to stop a bill than to pass one.

PARTY STRUCTURE

The complex processes of majority-building involve a party structure of influence which is both different from and yet closely interwoven with the House structure of influence. Considered by itself, the House structure of influence is markedly decentralized—substantively in accordance with committee specialization and procedurally in accordance with a sequence of stages. The party groups organize decision-making across committees and across stages, thereby functioning as a centralizing force in the making of House decisions. Specifically, they organize to elect their own members to the formal leadership positions of the House, to superintend the flow of legislation within and across the various stages, and to determine the substance of policy. Generally, they organize to give some element of central direction to the process of majority building.

The Parties as Centralizers—On the record, such centralization as does occur in House decision-making comes about largely as a result of action taken by the party groups. On the other hand, the centralizing capacity of the parties is distinctly limited—so much so that in some ways the net of their activity is to add yet another decentralizing force to that of the House structure. It is a well-established fact that the voting patterns of House members can be explained better by knowing their party affiliation than by knowing anything else about them. On the other hand, it is an equally well-established fact that on many of the most controversial decisions House majorities must be made up of members of both parties. As organizing, centralizing forces inside the House, the parties have inherent strengths and inherent weaknesses.

Their strength rests in the fact that they are the most comprehensive groups in the House and in the fact that for most members the party is a meaningful source of identification, support, and loyalty. For most of its members, a party label stands for some things which they share in common—an emotional attachment, an interest in getting and keeping power, some perceptions of the political world and, perhaps, certain broad policy orientations. But the unitary party label also masks a pluralism of geographic, social, ideological, and organizational sources of identification, support, and loyalty. The roots of this pluralism lie outside the chamber, in the disparity of conditions under which the members are elected and in the decentralized organization of the parties nationally. As electoral organizations, the two parties are coalitions of diverse social interests and party organizations formed to elect governmental officials—especially the president. No national party hierarchy exists to control the nomination and election of House members or to control their decision-making activity once they are elected. Different House members owe their election to different elements in the party coalition, and they can be expected, in the interests of survival, to respond to their own special local sources of support. Each party label therefore papers over disparate factional blocs and conflicting policy viewpoints. Inside the House as well as outside, the parties remain loose coalitions of social interests and local party organizations.

Majority Party Leadership—Since its members constitute an automatic majority in the House, the larger of the two parties has the greater potential for influence. If the members of the majority party could be brought into perfect agreement, they could produce majorities at every stage of decision-making and transform every party decision into a decision of the House. The fact is, of course, that they cannot. But they do come much closer to the goal than does the minority party. Their successes and failures at maintaining their internal unity and at organizing decision-making provide, therefore, the best insights into the strengths and weaknesses of the party groups in the House.

The majority party achieves its maximum degree of unity and, hence, its greatest success, in filling the leadership positions of the House with its own members. Technically, the whole House elects its Speaker, the chairmen of its standing committees, and the members of each committee. But so long as the majority party prefers to vote its own members into these positions in preference to members of the other party, the decisions are made within the majority party and are only ratified on the House floor. On few, if any, other votes can the majority party achieve unanimity.

The leaders selected inside the majority party—in the Democratic caucus or the Republican conference as the case may be—become leaders in the House. The Speaker, of course, is the prime example and represents the complete interweaving of House and party structure. His dual role gives him a centralizing potential far greater than that of any other member. His effectiveness, however, has varied with the formal authority vested in him by the House and the informal authority he could amass through political skill.

The most successful imposition of party influence upon the House has occurred under strong Speakers—men like Thomas Reed and Joseph Cannon. And the basis of their strength lay in the fact that their formal authority extended into critical areas of personnel and procedure. Speaker Cannon, for example, controlled the Rules Committee by sitting as its chairman. He controlled the substantive committees by selecting their chairmen and members—with or without regard to seniority as he saw fit. Given these and other controls, the majority party leader was able to dominate policy-making in the House and become a party leader co-equal with the President. Since 1910, however, the Speaker's formal authority has been modest; and his centralizing influence has been more informal and interstitial than formal and comprehensive. Sam Rayburn's success as Speaker was a triumph of personal skill and only served to obscure the essential modesty of his formal powers.

The majority party elects another leader for the purpose of bringing party influence to bear on the making of House decisions, the majority floor leader. Both he and his counterpart in the minority party remain outside the official House structure. The fact that each of the last nine

Speakers served previously as his party's floor leader suggests not only a close working relationship but also some similarity of personal qualifications. In the post-Cannon era, these qualifications have been those of the negotiator. Prime among them has been the recognized ability to command the trust, respect, and confidence of various party factions to the end that the tasks of informal negotiation among them will be facilitated. Successful Speakers and majority leaders are men who appeal personally to their fellow House members and not men whose main appeal is to party elements outside the House. They have been men whose devotion to the House was considered greater than any devotion to ideological causes. These characteristics improve the likelihood that formal party leaders can influence House decision-making. The Speaker and the majority floor leader constitute the nucleus of that somewhat amorphous group in the majority party known as "the leadership." Such centralization as the majority party is able to bring to House decision-making springs from them.

In barest organizational terms, the job of the majority floor leader is to manage the legislative schedule of the House by programming the day-to-day business on the floor. In so doing, he avails himself of the party whip and his assistants who inform members of the schedule, take polls to assess party sentiment, round up members when a vote is to be taken, and generally channel communications between leaders and followers. In their execution, obviously, these scheduling and communications functions shade into the most crucial kinds of procedural concerns—setting legislative priorities, determining strategies of timing, planning parliamentary maneuver. And these functions, in turn, bring opportunities to affect the substance of decisions. The success of many a bill depends more upon when it is called up than on anything else. The effectiveness of the majority party in centralizing House decision-making depends upon its ability to control the procedural flow of legislation. Such success depends in turn upon the ability of the Speaker, the majority leader, and the whips to pool their resources to this end.

Party Leadership and Committee Personnel—Whether viewed as a control over personnel, procedure, or policy, one fundamental limitation on majority party influence in the House is the inability of its leaders to select committee chairmen. All committee chairmen do, of course, come from the majority party; but the only action which that party takes is to ratify the workings of seniority. More than anything else, this practice perpetuates the separation of House and party structures of influence. The subject-matter committees dominate policy-making in their areas of specialization. The Rules Committee exercises a crucial influence over the flow of legislation. But to the degree that the majority party leaders cannot select the chairmen of these committees, their control over procedure and policy is restricted.

When the leaders of the party and the committee leaders are in basic disagreement, centralized control is impossible. If in such circumstances unity between members of the same party is to be achieved at all, it must be brought about by the subtle processes of negotiation, bargaining, and compromise.

Lacking influence over the selection of committee chairmen, the most important control over committee personnel which remains within the purview of elective party leaders is that of filling committee vacancies. On the Democratic side, committee assignments are made by action of the Democratic members of the Ways and Means Committee. The selection of Democrats for that committee, by the entire caucus, is among the most important decisions made in that party. Accordingly, Democratic Speakers have kept tight control over that process, screened the candidates carefully, and thus influenced all their subsequent deliberations. Committee assignments on the Republican side are made by a committee comprised of one member from each state which has a Republican congressman—with each member having as many votes as there are Republicans in his state's delegation. The party leader is the chairman of the group; he also chooses and then chairs the subcommittee which actually does the work. Thus the Republican leader exercises a direct influence on committee assignments.

These personnel decisions can have important consequences for House decision-making. If there are enough vacancies on a given committee, the impact of committee assignments on committee policy may be immediate—as happened in the filling of six vacancies on the Education and Labor Committee in 1959. In this case, a new majority was created which pushed a new set of rules through the committee, overrode the chairman, and got the first general aid-to-education bill in history through the House. If the policy balance is close, a single appointment may be decisive. Those Democrats who in 1962 defeated Representative Landrum's bid for a seat on the Ways and Means Committee, in caucus and against the wishes of Speaker McCormack, believed that the fate of President Kennedy's trade program, of his tax program, and of the Medicare bill might be at stake in that single assignment. But even if no short-run effect can be foreseen, changes in committee leadership and policy may be affected. So reasoned the Democrats with their five "liberal" appointments to the Foreign Affairs Committee in 1963. It is important to understand that seniority is but one among a large number of criteria that custom prescribes for filling vacancies. Party leaders are not at all bound by it, and the process, therefore, has great potential as a means for impressing party influence on the House.

Typically, a formal party leader does not dictate to his "Committee on Committees." Rather he negotiates with them in making committee assignments. The reason for this is simply that the members of these important committees represent the various elements in the party coalition and, as such, may be important party leaders in their own right. Among the Democrats on the Ways and Means Committee are customarily found representatives of the big-city delegations (New York, Philadelphia, Chicago, Detroit), of key state delegations (California, Texas), and of regional groups (New England, southeastern, and Border states). The membership of the key Republican subcommittee will include representatives from all the large state delegations —New York, Pennsylvania, Ohio, California, and Illinois. The most influential members of these committees are the leaders of party factions. These factions represent important sources of electoral strength and they are the building blocks of the party inside the House as well. In making party decisions, the Speaker and majority leader must always negotiate with the leaders of such coalition elements—thus, in effect, broadening "the leadership" itself into a kind of coalition.

Party Leadership and Policy-Making—Further evidence of the fragmentation of party groups can be found in the attempts by each to organize for the making of policy. Formally the Democratic Caucus can make such decisions and bind all House Democrats to vote as directed. But the exceptions are kept sufficiently broad so that no one is, in effect, under any constraint. Furthermore, so deep has been the cleavage between the northern and the southern factions of the party since the 1930s that the caucus has not often met to discuss policy. To do so, say the leaders, would only heat up factional division and make their task of negotiation among the elements of the coalition more difficult. During the first Nixon administration, the caucus has met a few times—primarily in the context of overall congressional efforts to exert some influence on the Vietnam War. In the spring of 1972, the caucus (Speaker and majority leader included) voted strongly in favor of an end-the-war resolution and directed the Foreign Affairs Committee to report out such a resolution. Whether this action presages a new vigor for the caucus or whether it represents a special confluence of partisan and institutional factors remains to be seen. To the degree that the caucus becomes an arena for the conduct of party business, it will probably enhance the influence of any large segment of the party which finds itself at odds with the formal leaders—of a committee or of the party.

The Republicans have a representative Policy Committee which has been active and whose chairman, at least, is recognized as a member of the Republican "leadership." Typically, however, its main function is one of facilitating communication among various Republican factions—East and Midwest, suburban and rural, young and old, liberal and conservative. Where a policy consensus already exists, the Policy Committee will state the party position. Where disagreement exists, the Policy Committee is powerless to make a statement of party policy —much less enforce one on its members. If dissident party members refuse to be bound by policy pronouncements worked out within the chamber, they are of course far less willing to listen to the counsels of party groups outside Congress, whether the national committees or such *ad hoc* groups as the Democratic Advisory Council and the All-Republican Conference.

Nothing makes clearer the decentralized nature of policy-making by the congressional parties than an examination of certain other policy-oriented groups which exist within (and between) the parties. The most elaborate of these is the Democratic Study Group. These 140 northern and western liberals have concerted their efforts by settling policy positions, by organizing their own whip system to deliver the vote, and by looking even to the financing of House compaigns for like-minded individuals. Conservative southern Democrats also meet occasionally to discuss issues and strategy on matters of regional concern. Across the two parties, linked by the informal communications of their leaders, a coalition of Democrats and Republicans—"the conservative coalition"—has operated off and on since 1938 as an informal policy alliance. Similarly the party delegations from each state meet to discuss and seek unity on policies of interest to them. In the Republican party especially, each "class" of first-term party members forms a group in whose meetings party policy is discussed. Smaller discussion groups—the Marching and Chowder Society, the Wednesday Club—persist as forums in which sympathetic party members can talk shop. And, even more informally, members talk policy at regular coffee hours, during workouts in the gym, at poker games, in visits along the same corridor in the office buildings or between nearby Washington residences. The communication networks of congressmen are infinitely complex and, in the absence of two party hierarchies capable of making policy, all of these less formal sources of consultation become consequential for policy-making.

Such policy leadership as comes to the party group comes most importantly from the President. To the members of his party in the House, his program provides a unifying, centralizing influence. It reduces the necessity for any active policy-making organ for his party. To the members of the other party, presidential initiatives furnish targets to shoot at. Activity is stirred among the minority party's policy-making organs in an attempt to put together some coherent opposition. But, on the evidence, factionalism in the party which cannot claim the President remains more pronounced than in the party which can. The optimum conditions for policy leadership by the majority party in Congress occur when the President is of the same party. Under other conditions fragmentation is harder to check. Even under the best circumstances, however, the limitations on the

President, not in proposing but in disposing of his program, must be recognized. Since he does not control the electoral fortunes or the House careers of most of his own party members, he may not be able to give them what they most want or discipline them if they fail to follow him. He too, therefore, is normally cast in the role of a negotiator with the elements of his party coalition and, when necessary, with elements of the other party coalition.

Majority Building by the Majority Party—The decisions with which the party groups are concerned thus are made by processes of negotiation and bargaining. Through these processes party leaders try to build and maintain the majorities they need to control House personnel, House procedure, and House policy. In the era since Speaker Cannon, the success of the majority party leaders has depended more on a mixed bag of resources than on any massive concentration of formal authority. Typically, in any effort at any stage, "the leadership" of either party can depend on a hard core of support within the party, based on a sympathy of views and overlaid with a sense of party loyalty. Members have, as well, an ingrained respect for the constituted authority of their party leader. All things being equal, party members feel more comfortable when they find it possible to be "with" the party leadership rather than against it. The negotiations of "the leadership" center on making this support possible for a majority of members.

A successful leader of the majority party will put his experience and his political intuition to work in assessing what is possible for key individuals on the committees and in factional blocs. At any point in time, he must make a judgment as to the "temper of the House," what its dominant sentiments are, and what things it can or cannot accept. And the same is true for committees, for blocs, or for individuals. In making these assessments and then negotiating for support the effective Speaker avails himself of his own good personal relations with members, his reputation for fairness, for integrity, for trustworthiness, and for political judgment. He extends his own capacities by using the talents of those friends and protégés whom he locates in every House group. Through them he maintains a line into every committee, every bloc, and every informal group. With them, "the Speaker's boys," he shares his party leadership and, in return, secures a broader base of support than he might otherwise get. Through personal friendship—such as that which existed between Sam Rayburn and Joseph Martin—he maintains a line into the opposition party. Through these networks he identifies the views of others and calculates what concessions he can make before the costs exceed the benefits. He learns whether he can build a majority with his own party or must rely upon negotiations with the other party as well. He decides how partisan a tone he wishes to give to the contest. By adding up support in terms of large blocs, he can determine whether the policy he supports has a fighting chance. If it does not, he is likely to wait, for he will not willingly commit his prestige in a losing cause.

If the large bases of support have been secured and the task of majority building boils down to persuading a few waverers, the knowledge which the party leaders possess of individual idiosyncrasies plus the availability of rewards and punishments may then come into play. The leaders do, after all, influence committee assignments. Through the Congressional Campaign Committee they influence the distribution of campaign money, often in small amounts but badly needed nonetheless. Through the Congressional Patronage Committee they influence the distribution of a few jobs. Through their procedural controls they may influence the disposition of bills on the Private Bill Calendar and the Consent Calendar, and bills passed by a suspension of the rules. Through their contact with the President they may be able to influence the disposition of a "pet project" of a given member—a dam, a post office, a research laboratory, a federal building. By manipulating rewards and punishments like these, the leaders can bargain for increments of support—in the committees or on the floor.

Majority party leaders negotiate in order to overcome the decentralizing tendencies of party factionalism and the committee system. It follows, then, that the sternest challenge to the centralizing capacities of "the leadership" arises when they confront a dissident party faction in control of an important committee. And, since "the leadership" is normally trying to construct a majority on behalf of some positive action, the greatest test of all occurs when an entrenched party faction uses the advantages of the rules to defend the *status quo*. In recent years the classic contests of this sort have occurred between the leadership of the majority Democratic party and the bipartisan coalition of southern Democrats and Republicans operating from the bastion of the Committee on Rules.

Since the mid-1930s the party leadership has had to fight for its view that the Rules Committee is an arm of the majority party leadership. The Committee has alternately acceded to this view and fought to retain some autonomous influence in the making of House decisions.

Over the past twenty years factional splits in the Democratic party have made the Democratic leadership's relation to the Rules Committee an unstable one. In 1949 the leadership sought and gained by House vote a 21-day rule, which proved a procedure by which the chairman of a committee might gain recognition by the Speaker and bring a bill to the floor if the Rules Committee refused to act favorably upon it within 21 days of its referral. While it was in force, eight rather important bills were moved to the floor via this route. After a two-year trial and aided by gains in the 1950 elections, however, the southern Democrats and Republicans in the House repealed the 21-day rule and restored the coalition to its position of dominance inside the committee.

In some respects the 21-day rule increased the influence of the Speaker; but it also increased the influence of committee chairmen. Speaker Rayburn regarded it as a very mixed blessing. In any case, during most of the 1940s and 1950s, when it was not in effect, Rayburn frequently had to rely on Republican leader Joseph Martin to provide him with the margin of victory on the committee.

In 1961, in the wake of a number of defeats in the Rules Committee, in the presence of a new and less cooperative Republican leader, and faced with the prospect of implementing the new Democratic President's program, Speaker Rayburn decided to challenge Chairman Howard Smith for control of the Rules Committee. It was a contest that neither man wanted; and it could only have come about, as did the revolt against Speaker Cannon in 1910, under conditions of serious and irreconcilable differences over policy. The Speaker employed the full range of his authority and skills in this contest and pushed his influence to its outermost limits. He succeeded in enlarging the membership of the committee from twelve to fifteen—from eight to ten for the majority-party Democrats and from four to five for the minority. Then he added two personal choices to the Democratic side. With eight dependable Democratic votes, the task of majority-building has subsequently been much easier. Still, it should be noted that the Speaker could not have won his 217-to-212 victory without the votes of 22 Republicans, most of whom were sympathetic to his policy goals. And it should also be noted that a single defection among the "dependable" eight can still thwart majority building by the majority party—as it did on federal aid to education and on the urban affairs bill in 1961.

In the wake of the Democratic landslide of 1964, the party leaders —prodded by the Democratic Study Group—reinstituted a 21-day rule. Under the new version, the Speaker could recognize a committee member "at his discretion." Eight bills that were refused hearings by the Rules Committee came to the House floor under the procedure. And the threat of the 21-day rule doubtless speeded others on their way. In a replay of the earlier sequence, however, a strengthened conservative coalition repealed the rule following the election of 1966. By this time, however, the Speaker's acknowledged control over appointments to the enlarged committee had considerably strengthened and stabilized leadership influence over agenda-making.

Clashes between the majority-party leadership and the Rules Committee go to the heart of the structural separation between House and party. Proposed changes in that larger relationship thus almost inescapably center on Rules Committee activity.

The relations between the Democratic party leadership and the

Rules Committee illustrate something about the social interests served by the majority party leadership. When the same party "controls" both the Presidency and Congress, the majority party leadership is more likely than the committee chairmen to be a vehicle through which interests in society opposed to the *status quo* can assert themselves. Given the fact that presidential programs are likely to be pointed more toward change than many committee chairmen desire, the majority party leadership will most often operate against the influence of the committees. From the perspective of conservatively and liberally oriented groups outside Congress, the 21-day rule and the Rayburn-Smith contests involved the distribution of real advantages and disadvantages.

This identification of the majority party leadership and liberal interests is only approximate, however. Majority leaders are by no means obedient to every presidential desire. Since majority party leaders are chosen for their ability to communicate across party factions, they may work hand in glove with a conservatively oriented committee to preserve the *status quo*. By blocking legislation the Rules Committee, for example, can and often does serve the interests of the leadership. (In some cases it keeps off the floor legislation on which members do not want to have to vote and then provides a whipping boy for them to blame for the resultant inaction.) Neither conservative nor liberal social interests bear a one-to-one relationship to particular elements of the House structure.

Maintenance

Decentralized and yet distributing influence unequally among the 435 members, the decision-making structure of the House is essentially a broad oligarchy. This oligarchical structure has been in existence since shortly after the revolution of 1910. In order to fully understand that structure it is necessary finally to understand those internal processes by which it has maintained itself. Structural stability is the result, in brief, of internal processes which have served to keep the institution from tearing itself apart while engaged in the business of decision-making.

The disruption of the influence structure of the House is prevented through the existence of certain general norms of conduct which are widely held and widely observed by House members and which function to minimize internal conflicts. Foremost among these is the norm that members be devoted to the House as an institution, that they do not pursue internal conflicts to the point where the effectiveness of the House is impaired. Immediately after he is elected and sworn in, the Speaker customarily voices this norm and his total allegiance to it. Similarly, the minority party leader graciously accepts the results of the election, thereby symbolizing the minority commitment to the House as an institution. From this over-arching rule of conduct follows the norm that all formal rules and informal traditions of the House should be observed.

Two distinguishable clusters of such rules and traditions are of special importance to the preservation of the existing structure. One cluster functions to maintain harmony between those who hold leadership positions in the House and those who do not. It is the seniority-protégé-apprentice system of norms. A second cluster functions to maintain harmony among those members who hold leadership positions. This is the negotiation and bargaining system of norms. Together the two systems maintain the degree of centralization-decentralization which gives to the House its oligarchical characteristics.

These clusters of norms represent what most members regard as proper behavior. By word and by example they are taught to the newcomers of the House in the earliest years of their tenure. Members who learn them well and whose behavior demonstrates an attachment to them are rewarded with increased influence. Conversely, members who seriously and persistently deviate from them are punished by diminution of their influence. Members may be denied or given the potential for leadership that goes with such formal positions as subcommittee leader or party leader. Or, if they are committee chairmen, rewards and punishments may affect their capacity to maximize the potential for influence. But for these socializing and sanctioning mechanisms, the structure of influence would be quite different from the one just described.

THE SENIORITY-PROTÉGÉ-APPRENTICE SYSTEM

The seniority rules which govern the selection of committee chairmen draw a great deal of attention in commentaries on Congress. What does not draw attention is the fact these rules are only the most visible ones out of a large and complex body of norms which superintend the House career of every member. Seniority governs ultimate leadership selection; but for all those who do not hold leadership positions, the rules which count represent the other side of the coin. Seniority rules rest on the basic assumption that a man must first spend time learning to be a representative, just as he learns any other occupation. Seniority signifies experience, and experience brings that combination of subject-matter knowledge and political wisdom which alone is held to qualify a man for leadership in the House. Before a member can be certified as an experienced senior member, he must first be an apprentice and a protégé. In recent years, the length of the apprenticeship has been shortened and its prescriptions diluted. But the essence of the apprenticeship—that the freshman is not expected to be as influential as the non-freshman—remains.

The prescriptions of the apprenticeship are very general. A new member is expected to work hard, tend to his constituency, learn his committee work, specialize in an area of public policy, and cooperate with the leaders of his committee and of his party. Within each committee, the interpretation varies. For Education and Labor members, the apprenticeship is virtually nonexistent; for Appropriations members, it is palpably constraining. Naturally, this is the time in their careers when House members are most critical of the system which denies them influence. The proportion of newcomers to nonnewcomers is, therefore, a key index of potential conflict in the House influence structure. It was, for example, the extraordinarily large number of new Republicans that made possible the overthrow of Charles Halleck, the Republican floor leader, in 1965. Normally, however, the number of newcomers is sufficiently small so that they have difficulty in organizing to combat the existing leadership structure.

House members believe there is no better judge of a man's worth than the institutional judgment of the House. The assessment and reassessment of one's colleagues—the calculation of each member's "Dow Jones average"—goes on without end. Indeed, this searching scrutiny of one another is an occupational necessity for men whose business is majority-building. After a couple of years or so of apprenticeship, men on whom the judgment of the formal leaders is favorable will be rewarded—with an assignment to one of the most prestigeful committees or with an assignment to one of the committees or working units of his party. The more promising among the newcomers will become the protégés of committee and party leaders. Protégés of a committee chairman may turn up as special confidants, as subcommittee chairmen, or at the chairman's side during floor debate. Protégés of the Speaker turn up as chairmen of the Committee of the Whole, as participants in strategy meetings, or as "a leadership man" on various committees. No mark of preferment, however slight, escapes the notice of the membership. These protégés, with three, four, or five years of service, have reached an intermediate stage in their House careers. They will have demonstrated their talent, their devotion to the House and their willingness to cooperate with its leaders. They will be expected to assume the grinding responsibilities of House decision-making and to exercise an independent influence in the chamber. As other members see them, they have gained in stature and are marked as the future leaders in the chamber. As the protégés see it, they have been rewarded for their apprenticeship with a gratifying measure of influence. They have been given, too, time in which to ponder and prepare for the eventualities of formal leadership.

The seniority-protégé-apprentice system emphasizes a gradual and well-modulated ascent to positions of formal leadership. In its early stages this process of leadership selection is affected by the behavior of the individual member and by the reaction of the leaders to him. The idea of a ladder is basic; but members are sorted out and placed on different career ladders. By their third term most members will be embarked on a House and party career that will follow a fairly predictable path. And in its climactic stage, the process is totally predictable, automatic, and quick. Custom has made this nearly as true for the succession from majority leader to Speaker as it has for the succession to committee chairmanships. The seniority-protégé-apprentice system is basically a system for minimizing conflict among members over who shall exercise influence and who shall not. Its apprentice norms damp down a potential conflict over leadership between newcomers and the more experienced members. Its rules for rewarding the newcomer with a predictable degree of influence keep most of those in mid-career reasonably satisfied with their prospects. Finally, at the point where conflict would be greatest, namely, where formal leadership positions are at stake, the system proscribes conflict almost entirely.

The seniority-protégé-apprenticeship system is a regulator of many relationships in the chamber—not merely a way of picking committee chairmen. The system must be considered in its entirety as it functions to stabilize the internal structure of influence. It must be considered, too, as a system which touches almost every activity of the House. Consequently, proposed changes in the seniority-protégé-apprentice system cannot be considered as minor. They would produce a new distribution of influence in the House.

THE NEGOTIATION AND BARGAINING SYSTEM

An organization like the House, in which influence is distributed among 70 or 80 different leaders, risks the danger of irreconcilable conflict among them. And it is to prevent such internecine struggle from destroying the institution that a system of norms has developed to govern the business of majority-building.

The negotiation and bargaining system of norms defines for the members how majority-building should proceed. The over-arching norm of this system is that compromise through negotiation be accepted as the proper way of making decisions in the chamber. No individual or group ought to expect to get exactly what it wants from the process. Each must "give a little and take a little" if majorities are to be built and the institution is to survive. A corollary of this norm is that all conflicts should be as depersonalized as possible and that policy disagreements should not produce personal animosities. Members should "disagree without being disagreeable." Only thus will it be possible to negotiate and bargain with one's colleagues on a continuing basis and to construct new alliances with former opponents. From these basic norms of conduct flow other rules to govern those interactions between specific leaders or specific groups where conflict might be expected to arise.

Working back through the structure as we have described it, one obvious point of conflict is that between committees or between a committee and the rest of the House. One source of such conflict was reduced considerably by the elaboration of committee jurisdictions in the Reorganization Act of 1946. Committees which authorize programs still conflict, however, with the Appropriations Committee, which must act on the money for those programs. Between the two, however, there normally exists a mutual recognition that the Appropriations Committee should not define programs, i.e., legislate, in an appropriation bill and that the authorizing committee must accept the dollar figure set by the appropriating committee. To keep this conflict to a minimum, informal consultation between the two committees frequently occurs so as to exchange information and to negotiate outstanding differences of opinion. In general, it is the acceptance of the norm of specialization that minimizes intercommittee conflict. On this basis, committees negotiate treaties of reciprocity ranging from "I will stay out of your specialty if you will stay out of mine" to "I'll support your bill if you will support mine." Committee leaders share the desire to preserve their autonomy within the House and will often come to each other's aid when they perceive a threat to the committee system in general. The survival of them all demands, and produces, a norm of mutual respect one for another.

Inside the various committees, conflict is frequently held down by similar norms of negotiation. Where influential subcommittees exist, as on the Appropriations Committee, the rules of specialization and reciprocity underpin a system of mutual subcommittee support. To the degree that the committee leaders share their influence and bargain with other members of the committee in working over a piece of legislation, internal conflict may be averted by obedience to norms which stress a minimum of partisanship—as they do on the Armed Services Committee—and which produce a close working relationship between chairman and ranking minority member and their respective party groups.

One especially delicate relationship involves that between the majority party leadership and the committee chairmen—the sore point of House and party structure. The disruptive potentialities of this kind of conflict are well illustrated by the struggle between Speaker Rayburn and Chairman Smith of the Rules Committee, causing damage that took Speaker McCormack much of his first year to repair. But this case is an extraordinary one precisely because actions taken in accordance with the usual norms of negotiation and bargaining failed. Most of the time the two kinds of leaders cooperate—sometimes on the basis of a policy agreement, but always on the basis of a mutual need. The party leaders need the support of the committee leaders if they want any bill at all to get to the floor; the committee leaders need the support of the party leaders if they want procedural assistance and sufficient supporting votes on the floor. So committee leaders remain amenable to the wishes of the party leaders; but the party leaders by and large defer to and support the specialized committees. Sanctions and the threat of sanctions are, of course, available on both sides and may be used. But knock-down, drag-out battles within the majority party are events to be avoided at nearly any cost. The committee leaders risk a loss of influence inside and outside their committees; and the party leaders risk the permanent loss of sources of support which they may need on later issues.

Given the fact that partisanship runs deep in the structure of influence, the norms which keep interparty conflict at a minimum are perhaps the most important of all. Without them the House could not survive as we know it. The existence and the observance of such rules were symbolized in the trust, the friendship, the consultation, the exchange of information, and the mutual assistance between Sam Rayburn and Joseph Martin and, similarly, between Nicholas Longworth and John Garner before them.

Most basic to interparty relations are the continuous consultations between the respective leaders on the legislative program. The rule that the majority should schedule the business of the House is accompanied by the rule that the minority should be apprised of that schedule in advance and that minority objections or suggestions should be entertained where possible. Here again, there is mutual need. For the majority, speed and order may be of the essence. The minority cannot obstruct indefinitely, but it can surely disrupt the smooth flow of House business. On the other hand, for the minority, predictability is critically important. They do not want to live under constant threat of parliamentary tricks, snap roll call votes, or unscheduled sessions. Informal working agreements and trust between majority and minority lubricate House decision-making. Similar agreements as to the size and party ratio of each committee, together with the agreement not to interfere in each other's committee assignment processes, undergird the committee system.

The fact that all-out conflict between the parties is subject to certain limiting norms at every stage in decision-making means that when a majority is built, its decision is more likely to be accepted as legitimate and supported as such by the minority. This is doubly essential in a system where much of today's majority may be found in tomorrow's minority.

Since the divisions within each party make intraparty conflict likely, some note should be made of those norms which help to keep such conflict from disrupting the party altogether. Foremost, perhaps, is the rule that no man is required to show complete party loyalty. A great many reasons are acceptable as excuses for going "off the reservation" and against "the leadership." Constituency and conscience are recognized as taking precedence over party, and a vote cast on these grounds will not be held against a member. On the other hand, in return for this degree of freedom, party leaders do expect that when a man is importuned specifically and directly on a vote, he will do everything he can to "go along." Party members who seek immunity even from this degree of give and take will receive no rewards at the hands of the leadership. But, as we have seen, the leaders must take the party coalition as they find it. Thus they preside over negotiations which take place among the elements of the coalition and preserve its loose unity. Such negotiations dominate internal party organs. Committee assignments are negotiated among party blocs in accordance with formulas that give proportionate representation to party factions. Similarly, all factions will be represented on party policy organs. And party leaders, as we have noted, will be chosen from those most able to communicate on a basis of trust and respect with all factions.

Conflict is the very life blood of a decision-making body in a free society. Yet it is amazing how much of the time and energy of House members is devoted to the business of avoiding conflict. The reason for this is simple. Excessive conflict will disrupt and disable the entire internal structure. In the interests of stability, therefore, a cluster of norms calling for negotiation and bargaining is operative at every point where conflict might destroy the institution. In view of the criticisms frequently pointed at bargaining techniques—"back scratching," "log rolling," "pork barrelling," "vote trading"—it should be noted that these techniques are designed to make majority-building possible. Negotiations in which exchanges of trust or exchanges of tangible benefits minimize conflict pervade every attempt to exercise influence in the chamber. If they were replaced with new rules of conduct, a wholly new structure for decision-making would have to be inaugurated in the House.

Conclusion

This essay has attempted to describe the existing structure of influence inside the House of Representatives. And it has used the problems of decision-making and maintenance as the vehicles for that description. The reader has been invited to view influence relationships in the House as they function to solve these two basic organizational problems. Present relations within and between committees and party units have been treated as one solution to the problem of decision-making. Seniority and bargaining norms have been considered in terms of their contribution to maintenance. Obviously, many other structural arrangements can be devised to deal with these same problems. The pre-1910 Speaker-centered structure comes most readily to mind. This essay, however, offers neither blueprints nor prescriptions. To those who may be concerned with alternative arrangements, the suggestion here is simply that they focus their attention on the twin problems of decision-making and maintenance.

In choosing to highlight decision-making and maintenance as crucial *internal* problems, the essay declares a bias in favor of an influential House of Representatives. If one believes that the House should be dominated either by a powerful president or by a national party organization, then neither decision-making nor maintenance are significant internal problems. They will have to be solved—but the solution will come from outside the chamber. And the internal structure of influence will be a mere shadow of the external structure of influence. To those, therefore, who would prefer a weaker House of Representatives, this essay will miss the mark and, hence, have little to offer. To those who wish to preserve or strengthen the influence of the House of Representatives within the American political system, this analysis of one kind of internal structure may help in assessing the likely consequences of another.

Ralph K. Huitt

4

The Internal Distribution
of Influence: The Senate

The Senate of the United States is a small and special world. The chamber is quiet. It must be, because there is no public address system and business is conducted in conversational tones. It is dignified: somber-suited men, a few quite old, move in the perpetual twilight of its high ceiling lights. There is a feeling of continuity; in the bottom drawer of the Victorian desks the men who sat there have signed their names and some, at least, must stir the least imaginative newcomer.

It is the place of the states, as the Founding Fathers meant it to be. No teeming state may override the constitutional guarantee of perfect numerical equality, and no man is bigger simply because he comes from a big state. Indeed, men from small states have walked this floor with a heavy tread: Borah of Idaho, Norris of Nebraska, LaFollette of Wisconsin, Mansfield of Montana. It is the place of the individual; most business is done by unanimous consent, and one man with ruffled feelings must be pacified, if he knows the rules.

It is a small world, ingrown and not wholly immune from narcissism, yet its nerve ends are in the great world outside, and its reaction to events can be instantaneous. It does not forget, nor does it let the executive forget, that it has unique powers over and responsibilities for the conduct of foreign policy.

RALPH K. HUITT *is executive director of the National Association of State Universities and Land-Grant Colleges. He was assistant secretary for legislation in the Department of Health, Education and Welfare, and his direct experience of the United States Senate has included service on the staffs of Lyndon B. Johnson and William Proxmire. He is director of a study of Congress sponsored by the American Political Science Association.*

Its members are accustomed to deference; their elevators carry them where *they* want to go while the public waits. Nevertheless all of them must return, sooner or later, to account to the people who sent them, and not one may be absolutely sure he will come back.

The small and special world of the Senate is not easy for the outsider—nor all the insiders—to understand. Prestige outside and inside the body are not necessarily equated, and prestige both outside and inside does not necessarily mean influence inside. Formal powers are less important than the brains and self-confidence to assume a large role, tempered by the sensitivity to internal controls necessary not to overplay it. The tranquil outer surface is deceptively simple; the complex and largely unstated rules of its inner life may be missed or misunderstood even by men who live with them a long time.

Sober and sophisticated men have fallen in love with the Senate, and some of them have betrayed their infatuation in print. Others, including some members of the body, have excoriated it in harsh despair.

All this seems worth saying, or trying to say, at the beginning of what is intended as a dispassionate analysis of some of the elements of power in the Senate. It is a way of saying that the Senate is not easy to write about with confidence. Some familiarity with senators and their world brings with it a hesitancy to say very much with certainty. Nevertheless the Senate *does* have a public life, and some insights may be gained from it.

Formal Party Leadership

In the House of Representatives the chair is more than a symbol of authority; it is the seat of the most powerful man in the body, the Speaker. He is there when great business is afoot and many other times besides. Not so in the Senate. The Constitution says the Vice-President (a man of prestige if not much power) should preside and sometimes he does—during the opening prayer, perhaps, or when a tie vote (which he can break) seems likely. His surrogate technically is the President *pro tempore,* a venerable majority member who may spend more time in the chauffeured limousine the office provides than in the chair itself. Presiding is the special burden of the freshman senators of the majority party, who among them do it most of the time. Their staff people like to send constituents over to the gallery (with a pardonably deceitful hint of pride in his quick success) "to see our senator preside." It is a good joke but a small one—poor pay indeed for hours spent at the most tedious and least influential job in the Senate. Nevertheless their chore underlines a basic truth about the Senate, that power is not where rules say or appearances suggest it should be, but where it is found.

The men who sit in the front seat on either side of the aisle, the floor leaders of the respective parties, have much influence, as have the chairmen of the standing committees in varying degrees. Besides these incumbents of formal positions there are senators who exercise influence in informal groups which set the tone and shape the norms of the body. The relative effectiveness of these extra-constitutional power-wielders depends upon a combination of personal aggressiveness and sensitivity to the climate of the Senate, of time and circumstances and external influences, which makes generalization hazardous indeed. Generalizations must be tried just the same. Political power of the magnitude of that exercised by and within the Senate demands that repeated attempts at analysis be made.

THE FLOOR LEADERS: SOME STABLE ELEMENTS

There are elements of the floor leader's power in the Senate which are relatively stable and permanent, others which are variable; among the variable elements there are some about which he personally can do much and others about which he can do little.

The most important stable element by far is the character of the American political system. Governmental power is divided between the national government and the 50 states, and at the national level it is shared in a shifting balance by the executive, Congress, and the courts. These are basic constitutional arrangements about which the leader can do almost literally nothing. He can do little more to change the kind of political parties these arrangements have helped to produce. The leader is the principal officer in the Senate of a national political party. What does this mean? If his party has captured the White House, he can expect some policy guidance from the President; but if that is not the case, he would be hard put to it to find anyone with a claim to national party leadership superior to his own. "National" party in America is an ambiguous concept: ideologically, it is a cluster of ideas, symbols, and associations which its "members" share more or less; operationally, it is an agglomeration of state and local parties, interest groups, and temporary associations which want for one reason or another to elect a President. Its quadrennial platform, compounded of principle and expediency, may be ignored or even denounced by the presidential candidate himself. The most astonishing thing about this remarkable organization, the party, is that it *does* command considerable loyalty from its members, inside and outside public office.

But it is not a loyalty which binds a congressman to a party line, no matter who enunciates it, when it goes contrary to his own convictions or strongly held wishes his constituents appear to hold. Party identification may be the strongest influence on voters without meaning the same thing to all voters; so a high score on party votes will not necessarily get a campaigning senator in free. Survival in office rests ultimately on his relations with his own constituency. The leadership cannot help him or hurt him very much, and he knows it. Great careers have been built on party dissidence, and he has seen party giants go down. The leader understands this, too, because his party office gives him no immunity. What leader did more than John Worth Kern, who put Woodrow Wilson's massive legislative program through the Senate virtually intact? And what was his reward but to be retired by Indiana voters in 1916? What else happened to Scott Lucas in Illinois and Ernest McFarland in Arizona, both Democratic leaders, in successive elections? For each man defeat closed his senatorial career; there is no device in American life by which a party may restore a defeated leader to office. Moreover, congressmen know that a trip to the party woodshed may smart but is seldom fatal; not even Franklin Roosevelt could purge intransigent Democrats. No member of Congress can escape the lonely awareness that he is essentially on his own. This explains a basic fact of life in the Senate: no one finally can make anyone else do anything.

A second element affecting the leader's situation which changes little is the relative paucity of formal powers attached to this position. He is not a national officer in the government. He is not a national officer in his party. He is not even an officer in his house, as the Speaker is in the House of Representatives. He must put together "fragments of power," as David Truman has said, combining them with great personal skill and tenacity, if he is to succeed.[1] The majority leader has, for instance, the right to be recognized first when he pleases, which gives him substantial parliamentary advantage. Through the Policy Committee he may control the scheduling of floor consideration of bills; through the Committee on Committees (or the Democrats' Steering Committee) he may influence his party's committee assignments. If he is a Democrat both are made easier, because he is also chairman of the two committees. Because he is the center of the senatorial party's communications network and has access to the President if they are of the same party, the leader knows more than other senators and can share what he knows as he chooses. He may use these advantages, with some small favors he can bestow, to help other senators get what they want and expect them, in return, to help him. Democratic leader Mike Mansfield certainly was too modest when he said he had no more power than any other senator. On the other hand, there is no reading of these formal powers which will support the notion that they amount to much.

The converse of the leader's powers is the very considerable freedom of action reserved to the members themselves. This freedom is tenable only because it is exercised in the main with moderation and good

[1] David B. Truman, *The Congressional Party: A Case Study* (New York: Wiley, 1959), p. 115.

sense. The Senate transacts most of its business through unanimous consent; debate is limited, schedules agreed to, rules set aside without objection because leaders respect the rights and interests of individual senators, who in turn go along with reasonable arrangements proposed by their leaders. But nothing is surrendered. One man may object and slow business to a halt. The ultimate expression of a latent institutionalized anarchy in the Senate is, as everyone knows, the filibuster—the privilege of unlimited talk—which permits a determined minority, and under certain circumstances a single member, to impose a negative on the entire body.

The Senate has never been entirely easy with its rule of "unlimited debate." Henry Clay tried unsuccessfully in 1841 to get adoption of a one-hour rule to limit debate. Nearly a century later the Senate accepted a cloture rule after a "little group of willful men" had, in Woodrow Wilson's opinion, "rendered the great government of the United States helpless and contemptible" by successfully filibustering his proposal to arm merchant ships. Cloture has gone through several variations since then, but it has always been hard to invoke and slow to take effect. Sixteen senators must sign a petition for limitation of debate, which brings the question to a vote two days later. At times the votes of two-thirds of the whole membership have been required to adopt cloture, but in 1959 this was reduced to two-thirds of those present and voting. After adoption of cloture each senator still may talk an hour on the measure.

Cloture undoubtedly is difficult to achieve. It has been employed successfully only eight times between 1917 and the close of the Ninety-first Congress, and four of these came in the first ten years of the rule's existence. Perhaps it will be easier in the future; the last four times have come close together. In 1962 a cloture motion was adopted 63–27 to overcome a liberal filibuster against the creation of a private corporation to develop and manage communications satellites such as Telstar. In 1964 every member of the Senate was present to adopt cloture 71–29 on a civil rights bill, as they were in 1965 to close debate on the voting rights act, 70–30. In 1968 cloture was adopted 65–32 on an open housing bill. But this is a relative matter; there is no prospect that the present rule ever will make it simple to terminate debate on a fiercely controverted matter, and the filibuster (or the threat of it) will remain a potent weapon. It is especially effective toward the close of a session or when much legislation is awaiting action.[2]

Should cloture be made substantially easier to attain? The question seems to be one of the relative importance of majority will and minority rights. The argument for a more liberal rule is that the majority always should be able, finally, to prevail. After extended

[2] See *Congressional Quarterly's Guide to the Congress of the United States*, pp. 26–27.

debate—long enough to correct imperfections, effect all possible compromises, and provide catharsis for the losers—the majority should
work its will. The defenders of the conservative rule point out that
the majority can in fact have its way; what is required is the mustering of more than a simple majority. They argue that a special majority
should be required to override a determined minority which is not
open to being converted by debate. Otherwise resistance and nullifica-
tion are encouraged and enforcement is made more difficult. The rule
of the special majority is a familiar one in the Constitution; it is
required for approval of treaties, impeachments, constitutional amendments, expulsion of members, and overriding presidential vetoes.

What is more important than the leader's powers—and more will
be said about this later—the leader cannot control the vast delegations
of power parceled out by the Senate to those feudal chieftains, the
chairmen of the standing committees. Nor is there any prospect that
the delegations can be recalled; the Constitution has seen to that. The
separation of powers means that to the executive and the legislature
the other must always be "they." The British House of Commons
may rely upon the bureaucracy for assessments as well as fact; the
departments are controlled by ministers who also sit as leaders of
Parliament. If they do not like what they get, the Honourable Members have sanctions which ministers heed. Not so Congress; vigilance
in the committees is the alternative to the forfeit of that equal status
to which Congress is entitled and may, in the rough fashion in which
such sums must be calculated, actually have.

The leader is a man of great influence nevertheless. The basic
reason is that the Senate must be led, and the need will grow more
compelling, not less. It is significant that when the senatorial party
chooses a man to bring a measure of coordination to this body of
specialists, it often abandons the strict seniority principle. Election
by his peers is a mark of confidence in him which is bound to
strengthen his hand.

THE FLOOR LEADERS: IMPORTANT VARIABLES

Some elements of the leader's power potential are variable; of these
the situational probably is the more crucial. Perhaps some illustrations
will support the point.

The three most productive bursts of congressional energy in this
century came in the early years of the administrations of Woodrow
Wilson, Franklin Roosevelt, and Lyndon Johnson.

Congress worked continuously the first 567 days of Wilson's first
term (April 7, 1913, to October 24, 1914) and was *not* in session only
eleven months in four years. Working through Washington summers
without air conditioning, Congress passed the most impressive array of
constructive legislation perhaps in its history. The New Deal's be-

ginning, with its fabulous "hundred days," needs no retelling; why labor a legend? The two periods, in many ways dissimilar, had this in common: Congress felt the hot breath of the country. Wilson's Democrats had been long out of power; his progressivism had brought them back. They bent willingly to his imperious leadership—so much so that Senate Democrats allowed themselves to be dominated by twenty progressives with no more than two years' seniority (including their leader, Kern), eleven of whom were newly elected! Kern, serving his only term, failed to muster his majority on only one bill Wilson really wanted.[3]

Twenty years later, Roosevelt's legions were as eager to go along. Joseph T. Robinson put the emergency banking bill through the Senate in seven hours—including committee and floor consideration— using the only copy of the bill in existence. (The House of Representatives had passed a folded newspaper, accepting the fiction that it was the bill.)[4]

Pressures for liberal legislation had built up once again when Johnson's overwhelming victory over Goldwater brought with it a huge Democratic majority in both houses. Such a margin can be uneconomical; the majority may fall apart in warring factions (as it did in 1937–38 at the beginning of Roosevelt's second term). But most of the newly elected Democrats wanted to pass liberal laws—the happy, if brief, situation enjoyed by Wilson and Roosevelt. Johnson was the man to exploit opportunity; he invested Congress with a sense of urgency, presented a massive program, and drove for its adoption. The Eighty-ninth Congress was the most prolific producer of new legislation in this century.

Randall Ripley has summed up the conditions for successful presidential–congressional collaboration:

> The most successful majority party is likely to be a presidential majority with a large majority, newly come to power, with a President actively involved in legislative tactics, and with innovative leaders. The least successful is likely to be a congressional majority with a small majority, concluding a long tenure in the majority, with a hostile President, and with complacent and unimaginative leaders.[5]

---

[3] Claude G. Bowers, *The Life of John Worth Kern* (Indianapolis: Hollenbeck, 1918). See chapters 14, 17 for Kern's record as leader.

[4] Joseph Alsop, Jr., and Turner Catledge, "Joe Robinson, the New Deal's Old Reliable," *Saturday Evening Post* (Sept. 26, 1936).

[5] *Majority Party Leadership in Congress* (Boston: Little, Brown, 1969), p. 187. Ripley studies ten congresses chosen to illustrate four different combinations of relationships between majorities in Congress and the President. The first congresses of Wilson and Roosevelt are analyzed in chapter 3. For problems and strategies of presidential relations with Congress, see Lyndon B. Johnson, *The Vantage Point* (New York: Holt, Rinehart & Winston, 1971), pp. 440–44, 447–78.

It is not necessary to define "normal" times to say that these were not normal, nor that Kennedy's years, for example, were more nearly so. When a news magazine asked majority leader Mike Mansfield in 1962 "why Kennedy's program is in trouble with Congress," Mansfield replied that Congress responds to sentiment in the country; he believed the country would support the President but there was no sense of urgency yet.[6]

Lucas and McFarland had a Democratic President with a program; they shattered the senatorial party trying to enact the Fair Deal. Johnson had two precious years in the minority to put it together again; he literally sought issues on which the Democrats could be got to vote together. Taft and Knowland, his opposite numbers, could do little with their bare majority and small help from the White House. Johnson's six years as majority leader with Eisenhower raise the question: what difference would a Democratic President have made? Mansfield faced a reaction to Johnson's demanding leadership; a respite of some duration was in order.

The list could go on, but the point is clear: a leader is not free to be any kind of leader he pleases. His alternatives are framed for him by the situation in which he must operate.

At the same time he is not the creature of his situation. The second variable is his own perception of the role of leader. The sharp contrast between Johnson and his successor, Mansfield, is in point. Because he did not drive the Senate as Johnson did, Mansfield was accused (even publicly by a colleague) of being a weak leader. The charge missed the mark: Mansfield had not failed to be like Johnson, he did not *want* to be like Johnson. He was not a weak leader but a deliberately different kind of leader. This is made obvious by interviews held by *U.S. News* with Johnson, in 1960, and with Mansfield in 1962.[7] The men agreed that the majority leader has few real powers, but that is superficial. Johnson made it plain that he meant to use his "only real power," persuasion (by which he meant the employment of every resource he had), to the utmost. Mansfield called Johnson "the best majority leader the Senate ever had," but Johnson would not recognize Mansfield's description of the job. Mansfield did not want the leadership; he was drafted. He was "one among my peers." He had no instruments of authority. He would not use legislative scheduling for leverage nor influence a committee assignment. He would not "think" of telling a senator how to vote. Implicit in his commitments was his basic philosophy that all senators are equal, that there is none, not even the leader, who is "more equal" than the others.

---

[6] "Why Kennedy's Program Is in Trouble with Congress," *U.S. News and World Report* (Sept. 17, 1962).

[7] "Leadership: An Interview with Senate Leader Lyndon Johnson," *U.S. News and World Report* (June 27, 1960). The Mansfield interview is cited in note 5.

How does the leader perceive his relationship with the President? This is bound to affect his performance. There is the President's man; Robinson is an example. Unquestioning fidelity to Roosevelt came easy. He had been successively an ardent Wilsonian, a conservative vice-presidential candidate with Al Smith, an "Old Guardsman" in Congress, a gubernatorial candidate in Arkansas on a strict economy platform. He took the New Deal in stride; party loyalty bridged all ideological chasms. Then there is the man who represents each—the Senate and the president—to the other, but places high value on loyalty to the President. This is the Mansfield view; he said it was easy to follow Kennedy's leadership because they saw eye-to-eye, but he would resign if there was a serious difference. Kern, Barkley, and Lucas felt much the same way. Other leaders have regarded themselves primarily as the Senate's agent to the White House. This was McFarland's view. Taft seemed to regard his relationship with the President as something like a partnership; and Knowland drew a sharp distinction between the leadership and senatorial roles, stepping back several rows to speak in support of the Bricker amendment, which Eisenhower opposed. Again, it is tempting to speculate how Johnson would have worked with a Democratic President. No man ever had more pride in the Senate, but he venerated the Presidency and correctly assessed its unique importance to the successful working of the American system. Despite criticism from the liberal wing of his party, he would not oppose Eisenhower just to make issues nor encourage his Democratic majority to attack the President.[8]

Still another aspect of the leader's perception of his role involves the relations between majority and minority leaders. Ideally, there should be two points of view at a time, which complement each other. Sometimes a leader thinks he must fight all the time; this seems to have been the general notion of Kenneth Wherry, who apparently behaved more as a senator from Nebraska than as the minority spokesman, even siding consistently with a minority bloc in his own party. Other opposing leaders have seen their respective roles much as might contending trial lawyers whose professional obligation is to expedite the business of the court. More than that, some pairs of leaders have been able to make clear distinctions between their partisan roles and their partnership in promoting the general welfare, and these relationships make attractive chapters in the history of the Senate. Johnson with Taft, with Knowland, and with Dirksen, as well as Mansfield with Dirksen, fit this pattern.

[8] Ralph K. Huitt, "Democratic Party Leadership in the Senate," *American Political Science Review*, 55 (June 1961), pp. 333–44; William S. White, *The Professional: Lyndon B. Johnson* (Boston: Houghton Mifflin, 1964), pp. 171–77; Rowland Evans and Robert Novak, *Lyndon B. Johnson: The Exercise of Power* (New York: New American Library, 1966), chapter 6.

Perhaps the variable in the leader role which is easiest to identify and hardest to assess is leadership style. The range of behavior has been broad indeed. The contrast between the highly successful leaders of the New Freedom and the New Deal, whom we mentioned earlier, is relevant. Kern was modest, conciliatory, a man of "infinite patience and never-failing tact." A colleague said of him: "He was a strong partisan, but there was a kindliness about him that turned aside all feelings of ill will or animosity." [9] Of his New Deal counterpart, contemporary observers said "President Roosevelt uses him to push and pull, butt and bludgeon his ideas into legal existence. . . ." Robinson was a man who

> . . . loves a fight, and when it is necessary to make enemies, he never exhibits the usual politician's soft unwillingness to offend. He cheerfully steps on toes that require to be stepped on, and sometimes on some that don't, and he can read the riot act with complete authority.[10]

Mansfield seems to be more like Kern in style than Robinson or Johnson. His leadership has been described as passive and not all his colleagues appreciate it. But he has his own means for advancing legislation.[11] He employs unanimous consent agreements, giving himself flexibility in calling up bills under advantageous circumstances. He is considerate of the minority's rights, which encourages reciprocity, and works well with the minority leader. He has scheduled legislation carefully and kept pressure on committees through the Democratic Policy Committee. The unceasing floor activities of Robert Byrd of West Virginia, the whip, who performs a multiplicity of nearly indispensable services for Democratic senators, has added strength, as did the legislative liaison of administration lobbyists during the Johnson years. Mansfield's tenure is a good example of the interplay of situation and style: he was the majority leader when the Senate passed the avalanche of Johnson legislation, and also during the relatively unproductive years of Kennedy and Nixon.

If these are extremes, Johnson might occupy a middle ground. His determination to "persuade" included everyone who might be got to go Johnson's way. The tactics ranged from the casual but pointed remark in his restless roaming of floor and cloakroom to the saturation bombardment known as "Treatment A," in which the whole gamut of emotions—patriotism, loyalty, selfishness, fear, pride—might be

---

[9] Bowers, op. cit., p. 374.

[10] Alsop and Catledge, *op. cit.,* p. 7.

[11] This brief description is based primarily on Randall B. Ripley, *Power in the Senate* (New York: St. Martins, 1969). Ripley makes use of the transcript of a series of dinner meetings with Democratic and Republican senators and staff members, respectively, sponsored by the Brookings Institution in 1965.

played upon. Johnson's persuasive talents were universally respected but not invariably loved.

Wise leaders have used other men for jobs not quite in their own line. Robinson was not a man for a sensitive situation; when persuasion was needed he called on "fixers" like James Byrnes and Pat Harrison; or at the second level, Vice-President Garner; or as a court of last resort, Jim Farley. One of Johnson's prime skills was his manipulation of the versatile Democratic "bench," fitting men to precise jobs he wanted them to do.

Much has been said here about the leader, particularly the majority leader, because he is the most influential and promising figure in the strongest centralizing agency in the Senate, the party. In his study of party operations in the Eighty-first Congress, Truman found the majority leader in both houses to be a middleman ideologically who sought positions on which a majority could be put together. He worked with the committee chairmen and tended to support committee bills, but when he and the chairman were in opposition on a committee bill the leader tended to carry with him a majority of the committee and the party as well.[12]

There is a limit to what party in the Senate can carry, but it is not a negligible force. Truman has said that the congressional party is "mediate and supplementary rather than immediate and inclusive in function," meaning by "mediate" that "its members' fortunes are not identical with those of the legislative party, but at the same time they are not completely independent of it."[13] The party emerges as the most often-heeded cue-giver in the Senate. A senator may vote with it because there are no competing cues; that is, on an issue he may hear no clear voice from home and may have no strong sentiments of his own. But it goes farther than that: on administration measures in the Eighty-first Congress even the dissident southern wing voted with the Democratic majority more than the Republicans most likely to vote with the administration. This unifying tendency is more evident in the majority party. Lacking the recognized leadership furnished the majority by the President, the minority may lack the capacity to organize a stable majority of its members around a program of opposition.[14]

"Majority" leader in this context usually means "Democratic" leader. Only twice since 1932 have the Democrats been a minority in Congress. What has happened to the Republican congressional party, forced into a position of a virtually permanent minority? Charles O. Jones, in a companion study to Ripley's book on majority party leadership, has demonstrated that "a minority party mentality" has taken hold, pro-

[12] Truman, *op. cit.*, pp. 140, 242.
[13] *Ibid.*, p. 95.
[14] *Ibid.*, p. 192.

ducing negative reactions to majority party initiatives.[15] Beginning in 1959, young junior Republicans in the House of Representatives waged a vigorous fight to build an opposition of constructive alternatives, replacing two floor leaders in six years and breathing some life into party organs. No such effort has been made in the Senate. Minority leader style has been a variable of personality, ranging from the dominating Taft, with a personal position on every issue, to the bargaining Dirksen, a master broker. Jones suggests several reasons why there was no minority rebellion in the Senate. The insurgents in the House were young, new to Congress. Republican senators were on the average more than a decade older than their House counterparts. They had the advantage of long tenure and the independence and visibility of senators. They did not need party alternatives to the majority positions to give them scope for action. *"A minority senator,"* Jones sums up, *"may well be able to satisfy his personal goals as easily as a majority senator."* [16]

OTHER PARTY AGENCIES

Some students and practitioners of American politics have had a dream—an oft-recurring dream—about how the American political system might work. The dream is called responsible party government. There are variations in its details, but the basic notion is always the same, that the parties will perfect machinery through which they will keep the promises they make. The solemn pledges would be made in frequent conventions. The President and his congressional majorities would work together closely. The elected leaders in the two houses would formulate programs through policy committees made up of the chairmen of the standing committees and ratify them in conferences of all the members of the party in the respective houses. Members would be bound, formally or in honor, to support the party position. The chairmen of the standing committees would push through their groups the bills they agreed to in the policy committee. The minority in turn would provide a constructive and loyal opposition through similar party machinery. The majority would bear responsibility for its program, the minority would offer a genuine alternative, and the voter would have a chance to make an intelligent choice.

This is not an idle dream. All the parts of it exist in real life. Some of them are old and some relatively new. All of them work, more or less, but not quite the way the dream would have it.

The conference (or caucus, as it was called) is as old as the republic.

---

[15] *The Minority Party Leadership in Congress* (Boston: Little, Brown, 1970). Not much else has been done on the important problem of constructing a creative minority in this system in which a minority may go for a generation with no opportunity to exercise power. The brief summary here, based on chapter 8, cannot do justice to Jones' insightful analysis.

[16] *Ibid.*, p. 172. Emphasis in the original.

Congressional caucuses nominated presidential candidates before there were conventions. The conference can indeed be an effective party instrument; Kern used it regularly in the enactment of Wilson's legislation. Members were bound and loyalty was expected. It is significant, however, that a substantial bloc of Kern's Democrats were themselves progressives, deeply committed to Wilsonian pledges which they also made. But ideological dedication is not the norm in Congress. Most members chafe at efforts to bind them. They seek that blend of policy positions which they individually can comfortably defend at home. Johnson was bitterly criticized for not holding more conferences, but his critics made clear they did not mean to be bound by conference decisions; they wanted only to advise and be informed. Johnson responded with some conferences, and Mansfield has held them occasionally. Both parties would have found them useful in recent times primarily as means to pass the word.

Policy committees by that designation are relatively new. The Joint Committee on the Organization of Congress recommended in 1946 that policy committees be created to formulate legislative policy of the parties, but the House struck them from the Reorganization Act passed that year. The next year the Senate independently established its own policy committees. The two committees have proved useful without having much effect on policy. They have developed differently in each party.

The Republican committee began with nine members but grew until, in 1955, all Republican senators up for reelection were made members. The practice of inviting other Republican senators interested in issues under discussion was expanded in the late years of the Eisenhower administration to an open invitation to a weekly luncheon meeting where all members could be informed of the President's views. The practice persisted, although attendance dropped off with the loss of the White House.

The real utility of the Policy Committee to the Republicans has been the research staff it has made available to them. The staff has numbered generally from fifteen to twenty. Their importance has been magnified by the fact that the rich professional resources of standing committee staffs were largely the possession of the majority, while the parties divided equally the policy committees' appropriation. The staff resources of the Policy Committee were available to individual Republicans as well as the leaders, and most took advantage of them. Sometimes work done for a single member later was distributed to all along with a series of position papers of general usefulness.[17]

---

[17] Jones found, in interviews with Republican senatorial staff aides, that opinions on the usefulness of the staff, and thus reliance on their assistance, varied widely. *Ibid.*, pp. 163–66.

The Democratic Policy Committee has been what the successive leaders have chosen to make it. The number of members varies, but it has always been small. Barkley chose the members himself and this mode of selection persisted, though *ex officio* members have been added. Some effort has been made to keep an ideological and geographical balance on the committee. Johnson made regular use of the committee to counsel with him. He liked to put friends on it who were men of power in their own right. No announcement of decisions was ever made except for tactical reasons. Mansfield apparently made small use of the committee except for legislative scheduling, which seems reasonable in light of his perception of the leader's role. The staff has also done useful research, but this is less crucial to the Democrats, who have controlled the committee staffs.

The other party agencies of importance are the committees on committees and the campaign committees. The Republican committee takes its committee selections to the conference, where consideration may be heated and prolonged. The Democratic leader may have critical influence over committee assignments if he wants it; he chairs the committee and the conference usually goes along. Johnson used his power deliberately and frankly. One of his first acts as leader was to give all Democrats at least one good committee, a revolution which won the support of freshmen members. He arranged shifts which would put members facing reelection on committees advantageous to them. Mansfield said that he let the Steering Committee freely decide committee assignments. Needless to say, the matter of committee appointments is crucial. The work of the Senate is done in committees; the careers of senators turn on committee assignments. The ability to control committee appointments is power indeed.

The senatorial campaign committees are designed to help senators of their party who are in close races with a chance to win. The committees are in continuous existence, with staff help and substantial assistance to give. They are mentioned here only because of occasional charges that the money and other help at their disposal are dispensed unfairly to penalize partisan colleagues with whom the committee majority are not sympathetic. Whether the charges are true or are merely attempts to get leverage with the committee, an outsider cannot decide.

The Little Governments of the Standing Committees

The ultimate check on party government in the United States is the system of standing committees in Congress. This is another way to say that the ultimate check is the coordinate status of the legislative and the executive branches, so long as Congress is able roughly to hold its own. Because a coordinate legislature must have some way to gather and assess information on its own, if it is not to be a ward of the bureaucracy, the most efficient, practical way is to divide up in committees which specialize and develop a measure of expertise. Committees which specialize and have exclusive jurisdiction over certain kinds of legislation become little legislatures themselves, with power largely independent of the elected leadership of the parent body. Centralized power and dispersed power are contradictions; to the degree that the latter exists the former is limited.

It is necessary, therefore, to see the committees both as organs of investigation and deliberation, indispensable to Congress, and as subsystems of power, crucial both to the interests which seek access to government and to the work satisfactions and career aspirations of their members.

INTERNAL LIFE OF THE COMMITTEES

The chairman of a major standing committee in the Senate is an influential and important man indeed. He usually is in virtual control of his committee. He calls committee meetings, decides what bills will be considered, appoints subcommittee chairmen, controls the selection of witnesses, and, excepting bills of overriding importance, determines which bills favorably reported by his committee really will be pressed for floor consideration. He probably will lead the floor fight for such a bill or designate the man who will. In practice, he chooses committee members who will go to conference with the House on a committee bill and may choose to lead the group himself. The chairman decides whether the staff will be as large and expert as money will buy or funds will be returned to the Treasury; whether the staff will be encouraged to be aggressive or passive; and whether a real fight will be made to carry a bill through floor and conference as the committee wrote it or the effort will be half-hearted.

That is why the mode of selection of the chairman is so important. Certainly the seniority system, which moves the ranking member of the majority on the committee automatically to the chairmanship, provokes hot debate. The principal points are clear. Seniority is good because it settles out-of-hand the most disruptive organizational problem Congress ever faced, which sometimes took months to settle. Seniority is bad because it gives a margin of influence to those states and sections which regularly return the same men—if one happens not to like their point of view. These obvious aspects of seniority obscure others as important, on which not much is known. What is the effect on committee operations and policy when a new chairman drastically different in style or ideology takes over—such as happened to the Senate Judiciary Committee when liberals Kilgore and Langer served as chairmen between conservatives McCarran and Eastland? Are there institutional devices for cushioning the change? What can committees do when the chairman becomes incompetent, perhaps from senility or especially if he has enough wit and obstinacy to hold on to the committee reins? Occasionally the leadership is forced to intervene, as the Democrats had to do with the Foreign Relations Committee chairmanship in Johnson's tenure as a leader, but there must be cases which have not been pushed that far. When a seniority chairman is out of step with a majority of his committee, what happens? Can he tyrannize over them and does he, or are reasonable accommodations made? These are questions to be answered if an intelligent assessment of the seniority system is to be made.

These questions lead to more basic ones. What are the patterns of relationships between chairmen and their committees? Or put somewhat differently, how do individual incumbents perceive the chairman's role? It should be obvious that elements discussed earlier which affect the floor leader's performance should be equally pertinent here. A chairman assumes a job that is fairly narrowly defined by the institutional history of his house. He confronts certain situational aspects: the size of his majority and its temper, the urgency at the moment of his committee's business, the attitudes and demeanor of his party's congressional and executive leaders. But within the limits of this institutional and situational frame he surely is as free as the floor leader to try to behave as he pleases.

Unfortunately, the behavior of chairmen has not been subjected to much scholarly or even journalistic scrutiny.[18] It is not safe or fair, therefore, to try to offer examples. Even so, some "ideal types" of chairmen can be suggested. There is the chairman who successfully dominates his committee. He may use his dominion to make an empire, grasping all the legislative business he can claim title to, or he may suppress committee activity because he is out of sympathy with the majority; either way, he is the boss. A different kind of chairman may not be especially interested in his committee's subject matter, but may see his job as a facilitator of whatever its members want to do. He is a genuine chairman, the servant of the group's goals. Still another may be unsympathetic with what the majority wants but conscientiously helps them; he is a "service" chairman, reinforcing the majority sentiment with assistance only a chairman can give. Still another may regard his committee as a stage for his own performance, an extension of his own personality. He is not so much concerned with what it does as he is with the setting it provides for him. Undoubtedly the list could be extended. What matters, of course, is to discover through comparative studies the *range* of behavior open to chairmen, the patterns it commonly falls into.

The chairman's notion of his own role will probably determine

[18] An outstanding example of what can be done is John F. Manley, *The Politics of Finance* (Boston: Little, Brown, 1970). See especially chapter 4, on Wilbur Mills.

how he reacts to that grievous problem, the need for subcommittees. The Legislative Reorganization Act of 1946 reduced the number of Senate committees from 33 to 15. What it did not and could not do was reduce the volume of committee business. The result was a steady proliferation of subcommittees, each of which tends to carve out for itself some specialized part of the full committee's jurisdiction. The subcommittee chairmen thus parcel out to a degree the chairman's power, as he and his colleagues have parceled out the power of the leadership. Some chairmen we have described do not care; at least one has given a subcommittee to every majority member of his committee (although he *did* later abolish one because he did not like what its chairman did with it). But to the man who hoards the power he has waited so long to get there must be other alternatives. He may eschew subcommittees entirely, putting the whole burden on the full committee. He may try to prevent specialization by the subcommittees, numbering instead of naming them and referring bills of all kinds to each of them. Needless to say, the subcommittee chairmen understand the game; they trade bills around until they have established *de facto* jurisdictions.

A problem faced by every member is what to do about transferring from one committee to another. Not many senators can at once get the committee they most want, and there definitely is a status system among committees. Donald Matthews studied gains and losses of membership on Senate committees over a period of a decade (1947–57) and found a discernible pecking order, with committees tending to lose members to committees above them and to gain from those below.[19] Foreign Relations, Appropriations, Finance, and Armed Services headed the list; the District of Columbia Committee was a predictable last. A transfer, regardless of his *Senate* seniority, is last in *committee* seniority; the agonizing question then is: better junior on a good committee or senior on a less prestigious one? The problem is complicated by the impossibility of calculating the rate at which senior members will die or retire.

Like other institutionalized human groups, committees tend to become small social systems in their own right, reflecting the norms of the larger system but developing nevertheless a group life of their own. Richard Fenno's study of the House Committee on Appropriations is a brilliant pioneering effort to explore the life of one such small system.[20] He found the principal norms to be a dedication to work and a passion for protecting the Treasury. Junior members were socialized to respect these norms, and those who conformed best gained committee status earliest. It is probable that committees with

[19] Donald R. Matthews, *U.S. Senators and Their World* (Chapel Hill: Univ. of N.C. Press, 1960), pp. 148–52.

[20] Richard F. Fenno, Jr., *The Power of the Purse* (Boston: Little, Brown, 1966).

great turnover do not develop a highly integrated group life, but the stable groups with great prestige surely must. If so, the character of that internal life, the norms that shape it, should be of great concern to bureaucrats, interest groups, and party leaders whose success may turn on their ability to placate and influence the committee.

But the balance must be kept: a committee is an institution of Congress; it exists to serve the purposes of congressmen. These are individual purposes as often as they are institutional or partisan. No one who has ever looked seriously at the committees' public activity, the hearing, can doubt that. David Truman has said that there are three functions or purposes of public hearings.[21] The first is to provide "a means of transmitting information, both technical and political, from various actual and potential interest groups to the committee." The second function "is as a propaganda channel through which a public may be extended and its segments partially consolidated or reinforced." The third is "to provide a quasi-ritualistic means of adjusting group conflicts and relieving disturbances through a safety valve." These purposes or functions relate to the performance of the committee as a working unit of the legislature, carrying its share of the work load, representing groups and reconciling their conflicts, reinforcing the authority of the political system. But the committee also affords the member a chance to get *his* job done. He may wish to make himself a national leader, build a reputation as a subject-matter expert, advertise himself to the constituency, do a favor for a supporter, discharge some of his own aggressions—the list could be a long one.[22] What is important is to see that in every aspect of congressional life it is necessary to satisfy both the system needs and the largely personal needs of the member who must keep himself solvent in a free-enterprise politics.

The principal handicap to good committee performance in the Senate surely is the small number of senators. Each senator ordinarily serves on two major committees, perhaps a minor committee, and two or more select or joint committees. More to the point, a senator may be appointed to (a better term than "serve"; subcommittees do the work and no human can "serve" on many subcommittees) literally a *score* of subcommittees. So it is a common occurrence for only the chairman of a subcommittee to sit through a hearing, with two or three others rushing in briefly to ask a few (perhaps the same) questions. The job still would be too big if all the senators were in attendance all the time. But they are not. Senators are much in demand and may be anywhere. Furthermore, the impact of the political shift which makes the Senate the staging area for Presidents is in-

---

[21] David B. Truman, *The Governmental Process* (New York: Knopf, 1953), p. 372.
[22] Ralph K. Huitt, "The Congressional Committee: A Case Study," *American Political Science Review*, 48 (June 1954), pp. 340–65.

calculable. In 1972, aides to four senators reported the absence of their principals during the primaries. The count was: McGovern, 90 days; Humphrey, 85; Muskie, 69; and Jackson, 65 days.[23] These four were by no means the only senatorial hopefuls.

EXTERNAL RELATIONS OF COMMITTEES

Like every other human group, the Senate committee lives in an environment which affects and is affected by it, with which it must somehow get along. Its environment is both congressional and noncongressional—and the latter may extend around the globe. In the congressional environment there are the other committees. The relationship seems to be largely live and let live, which the party leadership, overlapping memberships, frequent transfers, the smallness of the body, and the frequent testimony of members before committees not their own, all make easier. Some tension between the legislative committees and the Appropriations Committee seems to exist beneath the surface, because what the former authorizes the latter may reduce or even deny, but this seems less sharp in the Senate than in the House. Undoubtedly friction is lessened by the Senate committee's practice of inviting senior members of the legislative committee to participate when appropriations for their programs are discussed. Apparently little attempt is made generally for committees with the same jurisdictions in the two houses to work together; sometimes their staffs collaborate a bit, but the committees seem to work independently and meet in conference. The two taxing committees are an exception. Their senior members belong to the Joint Committee on Internal Revenue Taxation, through which they share an expert staff and collaborate effectively.[24] The separateness of the parallel committees reflects the separateness of the two houses, whose majority leaders probably meet only at the White House unless they are personal friends, as Johnson and Rayburn were. It is indeed true that "two houses do not make a home."

In the noncongressional environment, the most frequent and immediate relations of senatorial committees are with the administrative agencies. This usually is called "legislative oversight of administration," a term which is more misleading than not because it suggests a clear legislative mandate to the agency which the committee is determined to see carried out. Undoubtedly there is some of this in the relationship, and committees are directed in the Legislative Reorganization Act of 1946 to supervise the work of the agencies which fall within their jurisdiction. But unfortunately the mandate often is left unclear, sometimes deliberately so, and problems come up not dreamed

[23] Jack Anderson, "The Washington Merry-Go-Round," *The Washington Post,* July 15, 1972.
[24] Manley, *op. cit.,* pp. 307–19.

of when the legislation was passed. Again, the relationship between committee and agency sometimes more nearly resembles a partnership than master and servant.

If oversight is the relationship the committee *does* want, there are traditional tools available to it. The appropriations committees in either house can guide and direct, under the threat of reduced funds. The committee may investigate the stewardship of the agency. The principal agency officers have to come before the committee before confirmation by the Senate. Congress can legislate in detail, telling the agency precisely what is desired. These formidable-seeming tools should be enough, but in practice they raise questions. Can the spending committees actually get to the heart of the matter in the enormous budgets they report, or are they limited to granting an increment, more or less, over last year? After the committee has terrorized the agency, does anything change or do the bureaucrats go back to business as usual? Is confirmation before assumption of office much of a check? How much effect on actual agency operations does the political officer have anyway? How can Congress effectively legislate in detail when the last century of administrative history has been that of increasingly large delegations of legislative power because of the legislature's inability to cope with the bewildering details of modern industrial life?

Moreover, despite a dearth of analysis of the oversight exercised by individual committees, there is enough to show that it varies widely from committee to committee. One may interfere with administrative detail outrageously, another may simply try to keep informed through its professional staff, and a third may decline to supervise at all. A single committee may bear down hard on one agency and be indifferent to another, and its militancy may wax and wane over time. Some variables might be suggested. The first, obviously, is the chairman: one aggressively suspicious of bureaucrats may be succeeded by another who thinks they should be let alone. A second is the character of the agency: a senator who would be horrified at the thought of congressional interference with the Federal Reserve Board may attempt to retry a National Labor Relations Board case in committee. Still another is the character of the program: one with wide interest and visibility will get more attention than another requiring expertise and secrecy. Again there is the closeness to the constituency: the State Department obviously does not affect as many people directly as the Department of Agriculture does. Finally, there is the quality and size of the professional staff: this may in fact be an *index* to the intentions of the chairman. What matters once again are *patterns* of recurring relationships, the *range* of behavior open to committee and staff.

These considerations are not unrelated to the question of power structure within the Senate; far from it. When committee and agency can work out something resembling a partnership, there is advantage in it for both sides. The committee adopts the agency; it protects the agency from other agencies and from executive control to the limit of its (perhaps considerable) ability. On the other hand, if the agency controls what senators (and their constituents) want, the senator with preferred access to the agency has far less need to get legislation. As a man with access to scarce services, he is in a bargaining position with legislator and bureaucrat alike. He can perform services which may make him unbeatable. These are power relationships—perhaps the most important of all and the least understood by outsiders.

Other Sources of Influence

THE INFORMAL SYSTEM

It is unlikely that there is an absolute correspondence in any institutionalized human organization between the formal structure of authority and the actual distribution of influence. Human groups develop "norms"—cultural "oughts" which prescribe proper behavior for their members on which there is a high degree of consensus. The most influential and effective members usually conform most closely to the norms; in their own behavior they represent, in effect, what the group values. Perhaps the formal leaders are these persons, but they may not be; they may instead be members without official power ascriptions who nevertheless exercise a measure of control over what the group decides and does. This is recognized in many groups by the labels attached to this informal influence structure—the "inner clique," the "old guard," the "king-makers."

It would seem highly probable, therefore, that such an informal structure exists in the Senate—but who are they, what do they control, and how do they exercise their influence? One commentator on the Senate asserted in the mid-fifties that such an influence group did exist and described the indirect but effective way they made their weight felt. He is William S. White, an experienced journalist and sympathetic observer of the Senate. He called his dynasts the "Inner Club."

White asserts that "the inner life of the Senate . . . is controlled by the Inner Club." Its members are the "Senate type" (or the "Senate man"). The Senate type is a prudent man. He serves a long apprenticeship before he begins to talk but even then speaks little. He is courteous and forbearing, never allowing the business of the body to affect personal relations. He is helpful to other senators and expects reciprocity. More than anything else he is devoted to the institution; he "speaks to the Senate," not to the country or the world or anyone outside. It does not matter what his political views are; wealth, popularity, social status, intellectual power, party affiliation, or national reputation are not determinants. "At the core of the Inner Club stand the Southerners . . ." but it is not a matter of geography; others may and do belong. Southerners are in because they "express, consciously or unconsciously, the deepest instincts of the 'Senate type' . . ." who is "a man for whom the institution is a career in itself, a life in itself and an end in itself." He is a man who has "tolerance toward his fellows, intolerance toward any who would in any real way change the Senate, its customs or its way of life." How do they operate? Certainly not in conventional ways: ". . . one day the perceptive on-looker will discover a kind of aura from the Inner Club that informs him of what the Senate is later going to do about such and such." In 1956 a proposal to establish a joint committee to oversee the work of the Central Intelligence Agency failed. "Under their bleak and languid frowns the whole project simply died; a wind had blown upon it from the Inner Club and its erstwhile sponsors simply left it." But White admits that the Inner Club members may not have nearly so much influence on what the Senate does that affects the outside world as men who are not truly Senate types at all; they are guardians of the "inner life." [25]

For the student of influence in the Senate these formulations are not much help. White's empathy for the Senate is uniquely his; how does one learn how to discover an aura, to interpret a frown? How does one translate the influence of the inner life of the Senate on the public discharge of its constitutional responsibilities? The informal structure of power in the Senate remains a legitimate problem of research, but it seems reasonable to agree with Truman and Matthews "that the 'real' leaders of the Senate are, for the most part, those in positions of formal authority." [26]

SENATE STAFF

One dimension of power in the Senate which is subtle and complex but largely unexplored is the influence on their principals of members of professional staffs. There can be no doubt that this provision of the Legislative Reorganization Act of 1946 has profoundly changed and vastly improved the performance of the Senate. Like the President of the United States on an appropriately smaller scale, a senator is an institution. He is what he is plus what he can add to himself by the considerable array of brains and skills the law allows him to buy. The work load now carried by the typical Senate office would be unthinkable without the division of labor among roughly a score of

---

[25] *Citadel: The Story of the U.S. Senate* (New York, 1956). All the quotations used here are taken from chapter 7.

[26] The quotation is from Matthews, *U.S. Senators and Their World*, p. 253. Also see Truman, *The Congressional Party*, p. 285ff.

people. Similarly, committees would lose their cutting edge if they lost their staffs. But first-rate professionals do more than carry out assignments. In the offices of individual senators they learn to think like the boss; they determine to some degree who sees him and what importunities reach him. In the committee rooms they identify the problems and provide the facts and questions. The product of the Senate is to some unmeasured and perhaps immeasurable degree their product. Their influence probably would be very easy to overstate, but it does exist. But it is unlikely that staff power has a structure apart from the relationships among senators themselves. Staff actions are little more than extensions of the actions of senators.

The most important staff positions in the senatorial office are administrative assistant (the top job) and legislative assistant. Other professionals may be called legal counsel, press secretary, or other titles. These jobs attract some very bright and able people, who sometimes remain with a senator for years, serving him with sacrificial devotion. They are men and women capable in most cases of achieving successful, perhaps distinguished, individual careers in their own names if they chose to do so. Yet they will submerge their own ambitions and identities in those of a senator, seeing another take credit for their best work, coming in time to think and even talk like him, to exult and suffer with him. Why do they do it?

No one can say with confidence. There is no systematic research into the motivations and satisfactions of these senators' men and women. Surely the possibility of sharing the power and glory of the supreme office must sustain some of them. Kennedy, Johnson, Nixon, Lodge, and Goldwater all were or had been senators when their parties chose them, and Kennedy and Johnson took their senatorial staffs into the White House with them. But some of the most faithful staff people toil for men who never will be notable beyond state boundaries, and there may be a veritable parade of professionals through the offices of some senators with great expectations.

Whatever is revealed by systematic research, one hypothesis may be ventured: the principal staff people share significantly in the exercise of their senators' power or they would not stay. A bankrupt in a millionaire's club is no more contemptible than a man without power in a political system. It is the power over men's lives and fortunes exercised by the national government that attracts ambitious men to the hazards of elective politics, and the prospect of sharing it which enlists and holds the gifted auxiliaries.

How big should senatorial staffs be? Perhaps much larger than they are, in the case of a few populous states. Perhaps not so large as they are, in the case of the smaller ones. But the indispensability of professional staff should not lead to the easy assumption that there is no limit to the number of staff persons who can be properly employed.

Few senators are competent (and some not at all, in fact) to operate a small bureaucracy of their own, and that is not their job anyway. Furthermore, the cushion staff provides between the senator and those who want to see him can become impenetrable, thus destroying the sensitivity to group demands which makes him useful to the system. Finally, any increase in staff beyond what is imperative to keep the work moving probably would be used to court the constituency, making the burden of the nonincumbent opponent—who already must run against the Post Office and the Government Printing Office—quite unbearable.

Are Reforms Needed?

More than any other governmental institution in American life, Congress is under continuous criticism and demand for reform. The Senate shares in the general criticism of Congress and comes in for some directed especially at it. It is not easy to summarize what is said and what has been proposed. *Congressional Quarterly* devoted 62 double-columned pages to such a summary in the summer of 1963, with hardly a wasted word. The literature of reform is overwhelming if repetitive. It is possible, however, to suggest some categories of criticism and reform which are relevant to a discussion of power in the Senate.

One is concerned with leadership. Changes are included which would strengthen the hand of elected leaders and encourage them to work more closely with the national leadership, especially the President, and which would weaken the feudal baronies of the committee chairmen. The seniority system is a special target; if it cannot be destroyed, at least chairmen might be required to relinquish their authority at a certain age or the committee majority might be given some choice among the ranking members.

A second category which is more modest includes proposals to bring some coordination to the spending and taxing programs of Congress. The Legislative Reorganization Act of 1946 required a joint budget committee composed of the four revenue and appropriations committees of the two houses to meet and set a legislative budget by February 15 of each year, but the provision was unrealistic; it still is law but it has never worked. The two taxing committees have proved that coordination is possible just the same. Their senior members, working through a joint committee and a joint staff, have eliminated duplication and conflict between the committees. Once the House Appropriations Committee successfully produced and passed an omnibus appropriation bill and the redoubtable chairman of the committee, Clarence Cannon, never ceased to think it was an improvement over a dozen different bills. The critics argue that a government which spends billions a year of its citizens' money should attempt, at least, to relate income and outgo and bring a measure of planning to the process.

A third category relates to the effectiveness of individual members. Congressional business characteristically lags through the early months of a session and begins to pick up when other people are taking their families on vacation. The hardest work months come in the summer. Congress adjourns, if it ever does, when children are back in school. Scheduling has improved but is still a source of irritation. Only twelve trips back home each year are paid for by the government; many members go nearly every week. In the case of a senator from the state of Washington, say, this is a major drain which may require steady "moonlighting" if he is not rich. Salaries are raised infrequently because members dread the catcalls from home. Allowances for office help and materials are wholly inadequate for senators from populous states. These are nagging nuisances which reduce a senator's efficiency.

A fourth category of reforms is aimed at the conduct of individual members which bring discredit on the whole body. This is not so much unlawful conduct—senators are punished for that like other citizens —but behavior which falls in a kind of twilight zone where the ethics of the individual must be the regulator. A senator belongs to a law firm, makes well-compensated speeches to interest-group audiences, owns securities in businesses dealing with the government. He makes trips abroad at government expense with no public audit of his accounts. He intercedes with government regulatory agencies on behalf of constituents. No one of these activities is necessarily wrong; indeed many are essential to the discharge of his duty. Most members carry them out with scrupulous regard for what is proper. But some members do not, and there is the rub.

The prognosis for reform varies sharply with the categories. The first two involve a restructuring of power arrangements, a matter of taking power from those who have it and assigning it to those who do not. Several observations might be made. One is that there does not exist a model of a legislature as it ought to be. Political institutions grow in the soil of national experience. It is unlikely that one can be proven to be abstractly better than another, but even if it could that would not make it a practical alternative; people simply do not choose their institutions that way. Second, altering the power structure is no cure for inability to muster a majority, because more political force is needed to make the alteration than to win on any single issue. A successful reform is a demonstration of effective massing and use of political power not a prelude to it. National party leadership may dominate Congress one day—when the concern of people with national problems overrides their parochial interests. Third, there may be unanticipated consequences to any change. Reducing the number of committees and clarifying their jurisdictions was regarded generally as one of the unqualified successes of the Legislative Reorganization Act. But the party leader no longer has his choice of several committees for referral of a particular bill; if a chairman is hostile, the leader must try the dubious business of bypassing the committee. Again, when the tyranny of the Speaker was overcome in the session of 1910 and 1911, a strengthened Rules Committee was the chosen instrument. But who was hero; who were villains, in the 1960s? The successful joint operations of the taxing committees provide another illustration: they have resulted in effective domination of federal taxation by the conservative senior members. The liberal members of those committees are not eager to see power over both spending and taxing put in the hands of a single joint committee. They have learned that a coordinating device works for those who control it.

Measures designed to make the congressman's life easier and his work day more efficient ought to be matters better left to the members themselves. This would seem to be true also of standards of ethical conduct, but unfortunately it is not. It is all very well to say Congress should police its own members, but self-regulation is a shibboleth which practically is not within the competence of most groups. What group in American society really disciplines its own members? Doctors? Lawyers? Professors? The public may think so, but the members know better. Perhaps criminal groups do, but adequate documentation is not available. Outside controls are better, and Congress really has none. The electorate obviously should provide them, but just as obviously it does not.

The Senate did pass in 1968 a code of conduct proposed by its Select Committee on Standards and Conduct. The code regulated the outside employment of Senate employees, required a full accounting of campaign contributions and limited the ways they could be used, and required senators and principal staff members to file financial reports each year. But these reports are not published by the Select Committee; public accounting is required only for gifts of $50 or more and honoraria of $300 or more. A proposal for full public disclosure was rejected.

The problem remains and it is a serious one. The effectiveness of a political institution turns in part on the respect in which it is held. Whatever subjects it to ridicule reduces its capacity for winning the unquestioning compliance which is at the heart of civil authority. The Senate should not cease to seek ways to curb excesses, of its committees or individual members, which tarnish the corporate dignity of the body.

Perhaps this has relevance for those two oft-denounced institutions of the Senate, the filibuster and the seniority system. There is weight to the argument that the filibuster has never killed a measure a determined majority really wanted and that the time consumed in a debate of a civil rights measure in 1964 was not disproportionate to that required by the executive and the courts in their efforts to advance civil rights. Nevertheless epithets like "obscene spectacle" were applied to it without challenge, and it would have been hard to find a defense of the filibuster outside the South. What is almost universally regarded as wrong can be maintained by government only at great cost. Perhaps time will prove that a filibuster like that in 1964 was exactly what was needed to make a more effective limitation possible. Cloture has been successfully invoked twice since then.

The seniority rule seems under a like burden of public disapprobation. Most Americans are required by law or private usage to retire by age 70 at the latest; social security and many private pensions are available earlier than that. Common experience suggests to most people that this is about right. They have observed the diminution of powers which ordinarily occurs at that age. Perhaps congressmen are different; certainly exceptional individuals are. But who is to say who is exceptional? That is why a rule is required. At the minimum, a committee might be permitted to decide for itself in the case of its chairman.[27]

These changes and many others will be suggested, and some will be made. No human institution is above criticism or beyond reform. Nevertheless the history of the republic and the prestige of the modern Senate attest to its basic vitality and to its deep-rooted representativeness, and by inference to the judicious use of power by the men who run it.

[27] For a balanced and reasonable analysis of the impact of the seniority system on Congress, which shows that it is more bugaboo than catastrophe, see Barbara Hinckley, *The Seniority System in Congress* (Bloomington, Ind.: Indiana Univ. Press, 1971).

Richard E. Neustadt

5

Politicians and Bureaucrats

In the decade of the 1940s an extraordinary element was added to the government of the United States: an executive establishment, a body of officials, which for size, scale, and corporate survival was a new creation, unlike anything our governmental system knew before. This was the institutional deposit of a series of events: New Deal, World War, the Bomb, Cold War, Fair Deal, Korea. The events are irreversible, the deposit is permanent. For decades our system has been struggling to assimilate it. This chapter deals with aspects of that struggle.

A few figures help to indicate what happened in the forties and thereafter. By 1939, before the Nazis marched on Poland, federal civilian personnel, professional and clerical (excluding postal and industrial workers), numbered a half-million, which then appeared a staggering total. Since 1942 their number never has been less than twice that size, not even at the low point of retrenchment between V-J Day and the Korean War. Before World War II our military forces had an active officer corps of some thirty-five thousand. Since 1945 the number never has been less than ten times that size, save briefly just before Korea when it fell to a mere two hundred thousand. The change has been both lasting and profound.

Congress and the New Executive Establishment

According to the literary theory of the Constitution, Congress as the "legislative branch" makes policy and a President as head of the

RICHARD E. NEUSTADT *is professor of government at Harvard University and has been an advisor on the staffs of Presidents Truman and Kennedy, as well as a consultant to President Johnson. He is the author of numerous topical and scholarly publications including* Presidential Power *and* Alliance Politics.

"executive branch" administers it. If this theory squared with constitutional practice, or even with the Constitution's plain prescription, our new officialdom would be a corporate entity, collectively accountable to Congress through the President and otherwise subordinate to him. But theory is deficient (as it always has been), and bureaucratic structure is a very different thing, the product of a much more complicated context.

Congress, constitutionally, has at least as much to do with executive administration as does an incumbent of the White House. "The executive power" may be vested in his office, but four tangible, indispensable administrative powers rest with Congress: organization, authorization, financing, and investigation. Departments and agencies—the operating arms of the "executive branch"—are created by acts of Congress. They gain operational authority, programmatic jurisdiction, from laws passed by Congress. They gain funds to pay for personnel and programs from congressional appropriations. And their use of both authority and money is subject to "oversight," to inquiry in Congress.

EXECUTIVE REFLECTION OF CONGRESS

Had Congress been a unit tightly organized and centrally directed, its employment of these powers might have brought us something comparable at the other end of Pennsylvania Avenue: a unified executive establishment. But actually, and naturally, what was produced "downtown" reflects congressional *dis*unity. As preceding chapters show, Congress is not one entity but many, mainly the committees and the subcommittees of each House. "Congress," as Clem Miller once wrote, "is a collection of committees that come together in a Chamber periodically to approve one another's actions." [1] In the administrative sphere, as elsewhere, congressional prerogatives adhere most of the time—and most concretely all the time—to these committees and are exercised by them, piecemeal, on the executive establishment downtown. Its character is shaped accordingly.

Our national bureaucracy expanded in a range of separate agencies, corresponding roughly to traditional departments, each dependent on particular congressional committees for its life-blood: laws and funds. These agencies owed little more to Congress as an entity than chairmen of committees owe, which is not much. And they owed almost nothing to each other. Operational authority ran to the heads of agencies, or to subordinates, not to a collectivity. Personnel systems were built up inside agencies, not among them. Even the general career system, "the" civil service—to say nothing of uniformed or diplomatic services—is "general" in name only. For most intents and purposes it functions as

[1] Clem Miller, *Member of the House* (New York: Scribners, 1962), p. 110.

a set of departmental services. Most careerists everywhere live out their lives inside a single agency; their loyalties and perspectives are centered there.

Both organizationally and in terms of personnel the new bureaucracy is a projection of congressional committee jurisdictions—or, more precisely, since 1946, of standing subcommittee jurisdictions. And most committees guard, with jealousy and pride, the separations among agencies downtown. Why, for example, is the Small Business Administration independent of the Department of Commerce? The answer lies in the committee structure of the House. Of course, committee jurisdictions have been influenced, in turn, by organizational developments downtown. Unification of the armed services was matched by unification on the Hill of the committees which had dealt with War and the Navy. Still, the pattern remains one in which particular committees deal with given agencies, and thereby keep the agencies distinct from one another.

EXECUTIVE COMPETITION WITH CONGRESS

Yet in their operations day by day, agencies are much more than "projections" of Congress. They also are competitors with congressmen. Their work defines and embodies public policy, enlisting clients and arousing opposition. They weigh and balance interests while they work. Their regulations have the force of law. Their decisions make news. Their jobs interest partisans. Their expertise helps to get legislation drafted (and committee reports written, speeches prepared, tactics devised). Also, their actions matter at the "grass roots." They carry government into the lives of voters; their "field" officials are in touch with voters. Thirty years ago, aside from postmen and tax collectors (for the well-to-do), the federal presence rested lightly on most citizens. Congressmen could claim to be—and often were—*the* local representatives of "Washington." That time is gone.

Defense contracts and installations underpin the economic growth of many regions. Federal grants-in-aid support the major undertakings of state governments. Federal funds are crucial in the redevelopment of cities. Federal subsidies, direct or indirect, support whole sectors of our industry and commerce—not least commercial agriculture—and become the hope of higher education, private as well as public. And day-to-day decision-making in such spheres as these—on the details of programming and execution which affect constituents concretely— this is done downtown, not on the Hill, and by agency officials, not by congressmen.

This goes hard with the elective politicians who are charged in theory to direct the government and who have won their places through the tests of nomination and election, tests officials do not take. Particularly for new members of the House—among the lowest of the low in Washington's real power structure—it is frustrating to find that their effectiveness in such decision-making matches neither their own expectations nor the expectations of constituents at home. Oftener than not, the pressures of constituents run to the things that only agencies can do, and congressmen perforce become petitioners downtown, a role which often adds humiliation to frustration.

Frustration is compounded by the fact that members of Congress have not only their entitlement to a great voice in government, legitimated by their popular election, they also have wills of their own, views of their own, ideas of their own. Quite naturally these seem to them at least as worthy of attention in detailed administration as are those of any agency official. There is something to be said for this position; congressional ideas are often apt. But as a practical matter, the officials with immediate authority to act, and the necessity, are bound to make decisions day-by-day which reflect their conceptions and their reading of the issues—and which violate the values of some congressmen. This is understood in Congress but it grates. Repetitive experience of offering advice without material result is likelier to make advisers scornful than humble, especially if they are certain of their right to offer. So it seems to be for many congressmen.

CONGRESSIONAL DEVICES FOR CONTROL

Frustration with an overture of scorn has brought a strong reaction from both houses of Congress, a reaction which amounts to vigorous assertion of administrative powers held by Congress. For years entrenchment of the new bureaucracy has given rise to efforts aimed at tightening congressional control over the details of administrative operations. These efforts have been cumulative for a generation, growing in intensity and ingenuity from year to year. New techniques, almost unknown in prior practice, have been devised to meet the new condition of a vast machine downtown. Congress has not been passive in the face of competition from officialdom. It actively attempts to control its competitors.

The reach for control has taken many forms, but there are three in particular. First is a quite traditional device, the patronage, with special reference nowadays to top appointive posts and to those sensitive subordinate positions—so-called Schedule C positions—which are in the civil service but not subject to its tenure rules. Congressional pressure on the President and on department heads is nothing new, but where postmasterships were once the aim, assistants to assistant secretaries and the like are now a natural target, with good reason. And where "senatorial courtesy" was once the means of putting teeth into congressional desires, hints of trouble in the legislative and appropriation processes now take their place alongside that time-honored technique.

A second device is untraditional, a novelty, a postwar innovation, rapidly expanding in the fifties and the early sixties, leveling off since. This is the device of annual authorization for agencies themselves and for their programs. About $50 billion of the federal budget now is subject every year not only to appropriations but to prior legislation authorizing a continuation of existing agencies and programs. Among these are the Agency for International Development with foreign aid, the National Aeronautics and Space Administration with space exploration, and the Office of Economic Opportunity with its poverty programs.

A third device for control also is a postwar innovation: the "committee clearance." In recent years we find numerous statutory provisions— some enacted, some rejected, some enforced without enactment—which require that an agency report particular administrative actions in advance to a committee, or, stronger still, which require that an agency "come into agreement" with committee personnel before action is taken or, strongest of all, which require that an agency respect committee veto in a fixed time-period after the fact. These clearances, whatever their strength, have been asserted in the main by Agriculture, Armed Services, Interior, and Public Works Committees, and by the Joint Committee on Atomic Energy, which has a special statutory right of supervision over the Atomic Energy Commission. Taken together, these assertions seem to aim at giving legislative committees (and their members) a hold on bread-and-butter for home districts: site locations, purchase contracts, surplus sales. The impulse is entirely understandable.

Such devices for congressional control have often made an impact on the details of particular administrative operations, and also on the detailed distribution of administrative powers in Congress. Indeed the latter impact may, in sum, be greater than the former. Annual authorization and committee clearance are, among other things, devices whereby legislative committees gain a share in the surveillance always open to appropriations committees. This frequently redounds to the advantage of the agencies concerned, and probably has often been encouraged by them. For legislative committees often champion "their" agencies against economizers in appropriations committees.

From the standpoint of good management as understood in private corporations or as preached by the apostles of administrative rationality, devices of this sort create a host of troubles for an agency official and for his executive superiors. Annual authorization causes turmoil every year, especially in personnel administration. "Agreement" and "veto" mean delay, uncertainty. (Moreover these requirements are constitutionally dubious.) And "reporting" is a nuisance at the very least. Yet in administrative practice it is far from clear that agency officials are net losers.

On balance, these assertions of control have compensations for officialdom. They sometimes produce good ideas and sensible improvements: congressmen are capable of being very helpful. They may produce a measure of political protection, which is never to be slighted by an agency official. Moreover, they permit an able operator to play his committee "masters" off against each other. Control by two committees of each House can mean control by none, while serving at the same time to dilute direction from above, from the administration.

LIMITATIONS ON CONGRESSIONAL CONTROL

It is significant that the most heartfelt arguments against these new devices have come from central, presidential agencies, such as the Office of Management and Budget and its predecessor, the Bureau of the Budget, especially in Lyndon Johnson's time. Congressional assertions of control are bound to complicate attempts at central management in presidential terms. It does not follow that they have made Congress an effective manager. "Congress" is not involved. Nor are most congressmen.

The competition agency officials offer congressmen is not dispelled by control through congressional committee. Net gainers from this sort of enterprise are likely to be limited in number and are never found exclusively on Capitol Hill. The gainers, ordinarily, are of two sorts: on the one hand, effective agency careerists; on the other hand, well-placed committee members, especially seniority leaders (or their staffs). Control devices can produce a merger, in effect, between particular committees and "their" agencies. Some segments of officialdom are held under the thumb of a strong chairman; others suffer close surveillance by committee staff. Conversely, some staffs are accustomed to take cues from key officials; some chairmen have been known to act as agents of "their" agencies. Either way, there may result a tight relationship between affected agencies and congressmen, restraining competition in the interest of stability for policy and personnel alike. If clients and constituents are brought into the combine to the satisfaction of all sides, so much the better. The outcome then is a monopoly, a true "subgovernment," to adapt Douglass Cater's term, as in the sphere of sugar. Cater writes:

> . . . consider the tight little subgovernment which rules the nation's sugar economy. Since the early 1930s, this agricultural commodity has been subjected to a cartel arrangement sponsored by the government. By specific prescription, the sugar market is divided into the last spoonful. . . .
> Political power within the sugar subgovernment is largely vested in the chairman of the House Agricultural Committee who works out the schedule of quotas. It is shared by a veteran civil servant, the Director of the Sugar Division in the U.S. Department of Agriculture, who provides the necessary

"expert" advice for such a complex marketing arrangement. Further advice
is provided by Washington representatives of the . . . producers.[2]

But congressmen in general gain no measurable benefit from mergers
on these terms, no special hold of policy or personnel, no special claims
with clientele. The benefits accrue to members of particular committees and their friends (both on and off the Hill). For all the rest, officialdom becomes more powerfully competitive than ever, buttressed
by its links to "Congress" *in committee.*

Moreover, the executive establishment is only ripe for "merger" at
the margins of its policy concerns. In central spheres of policy, committees rarely serve the needs of agencies sufficiently to nurture true
subgovernments. Bureaucratic organizations may be molded in the
image of committee jurisdictions. But agency operations are not. For
the very causal factors which brought forth the new officialdom, the
same events both foreign and domestic, mix and mingle operations
among agencies. Neither in military spheres, nor in diplomacy, nor in
domestic welfare, nor in economic management can one agency pursue
its statutory mandates independently of aid or acquiescence from
others, usually many others. Programmatic purposes and operating
problems spill across dividing lines on organization charts, entangling
jurisdictions in the process. This always was the case to a degree; it
now is markedly more so. Thirty years ago the Departments of State
and Agriculture worked in separate worlds. So did the Department of
Justice and the Office of Education. Now even these cross wires often,
while the operations of the Departments of Defense and State are
always intertwined, to say nothing of such Lyndon Johnson legacies
as "poverty" and "model cities" programs. These continuously en-
tangle half the government. Indeed continuous entanglement is characteristic of the hundreds of new ventures in education, health care,
housing, transportation, welfare passed by Congress during the triumphant part of Johnson's term.

Committee "domination" of an agency is constantly imperiled by
these jurisdictional entanglements. "Mergers" do not flourish in the
midst of mingled programs. Overlapping operations force entangled
agencies to deal with one another day by day, and to appeal over each
other's heads when bargaining breaks down. The need for bargaining
arenas is endemic; so is the need for arbitrators. But in central spheres
of policy, the spheres of greatest overlap, congressional committees
rarely offer either adequate arenas or authoritative arbitrators. Committee jurisdictions usually are too confined for that. And bargaining
between committees rarely meets the needs of daily work downtown.
As a forum for administrative bargaining, our legislative process has

[2] Douglass Cater, *Power in Washington* (New York: Random House, 1964), pp.
17–18.

its uses in securing and defending fixed positions, not in reaching or applying operational accommodations suited to a job in hand. Thus even for the privileged few, controls exerted through committee may break down just when and where their use becomes most interesting. For operators with a job to do will sidle out from under the committees and will deal with one another or appeal against each other in executive arenas at the other end of Pennsylvania Avenue—the White House end—where congressional seniors, however potent in their own committee bailiwicks, have limited access and a (relatively) weak voice.

In general then, the politicians on the Hill reach for control of their competitors downtown without securing a surcease from competition. On the contrary, these efforts at control have rather helped than hindered agency officials—and indeed have spurred them on—to play committees off against each other. For most intents and purposes, much of the time, detailed decision-making with direct impact on voters still eludes the politicians, while their agency competitors still flourish as before. Who controls whom is a nice question. Perhaps officials are as often the manipulators of committees as congressional seniors are the managers of agencies.

Congressmen continue to have reason for frustration. When they compare their nominal administrative powers with the actualities of who-does-what in Washington, the fact that their committees can assert control of relatively marginal affairs is little comfort. When they look down the Avenue toward the White House and perceive the Presidency, with its own officialdom, asserting the prerogatives of central management—as any President has done since Franklin Roosevelt's time—their comfort grows the less. And when they add what they are bound to see, and so to feel, that policy initiatives are centered in the White House too, the pain in their position grows severe. Constituents rub salt into the wound. So does a proper pride in the traditions of a parliamentary body.

When the elective politicians on the Hill voice their frustration they are likelier than not to pass over its source, competitive officialdom, in favor of a target more traditional and easier to watch: their constitutional competitor, that Man in the White House. Yet he, an elective politician in his own right, struggles with officialdom no less than they. He too is in a competition with their new competitor.

The President and the Executive Agencies

The Presidency's character shapes what there is of unity in the executive establishment. Every agency is headed by a presidential appointee (Senate consenting). These appointees are not immune to the old charge of Charles G. Dawes that "members of the Cabinet are a

President's natural enemies." But they and their immediate associates do have some things in common with each other and the President which their career subordinates do not: temporary tenure and a stake in his success. Our terminology acknowledges their semblance of community; we speak of them collectively as "the administration," something wider than "the White House," looser than "the Presidency," but different from "officialdom," an intermediate layer neither truly presidential nor wholly bureaucratic.

Within limits, these distinctions have reality behind them: presidential appointees are men-in-the-middle, owing loyalty at once to the man who put them there, to the laws they administer, and to the body of careerists, backed by clientele, whose purposes they both direct and serve. They also owe some loyalty to their own careers, which may make for dependence on each other. And being similarly placed they may have fellow-feeling for each other. All these are two-edged swords. In many circumstances these induce a "scatteration" rather than community-of-interest. But insofar as this exists, the Presidency lies back of it.

The Presidency is a binding force in other ways as well. In many spheres of action the executive establishment can scarcely move except as it invokes the President. One such sphere is a traditional "royal prerogative" where Presidents are heirs to English kings: command of the armed forces and the conduct of foreign relations. A second sphere is of more recent origin, a modern prerogative: the initiative in legislation, authority and funds alike. A third sphere, rooted in our politics, has been transformed by our technology: the appeal to the people, the defense of new departures. In each sphere presidential acts, or delegations, or approvals (as a matter of form at least) are vital for official action, legitimating it as nothing else can. Thus each sphere weaves a bond around all those concerned in action—the bond of common need.

DEFENSE AND DIPLOMACY

The President's place in defense and diplomacy turns on his role as commander-in-chief, a role created by the Constitution, deepened by history, confirmed by modern practice. The Vietnam War, part of that practice, has made this role more controversial lately than at any time since 1940, but like FDR before him Richard Nixon is constrained only by prudence. The excuse is that no one else can make him use the nation's troops—or its nuclear weapons for that matter—and no one else can stop him except (in theory) Congress if it cares to intervene after the fact by changing force-levels or cutting funds; hard to do. A President's place in foreign policy has other sources also, but they pale by comparison with this. The same thing can be said of his authority, long since acknowledged by the Supreme Court, to guard the "peace of the United States" *internally*. Again, the fact that *he* commands the troops is paramount. So, when the use or threat or possibility of force comes into play, officials of all sorts in every agency concerned will keep the President in mind because they must, and each will seek his sanction for the course of action each prefers. The twenty years *since* the Korean War are marked by Dien Bien Phu, Suez, Quemoy, Lebanon, Berlin, Congo, Cuba, Santo Domingo, Laos, Vietnam, Thailand, Cambodia, where troops were either sent or quite deliberately withheld—to say nothing of Little Rock, Arkansas, or Oxford, Mississippi, or Detroit, Michigan. From the standpoint of government agencies there is no need to labor the point.

LEGISLATIVE INITIATIVE

The President's initiative in legislation is a rather different matter, more a product of convenience, of pragmatic adaptation, than a constitutional imperative. Presidents have always had a role in legislation: the veto power and the right to recommend stem from the Constitution. But the process of enlarging these foundations to support initiative across-the-board began only with the Budget and Accounting Act of 1921. Congress then imposed upon the White House—having nowhere else to put it—the duty to propose an executive budget, a statement of financial need for every agency, in the President's judgment, not theirs. This was conceived by its sponsors as a way to cut expenditures. It also proved a way to make the White House matter more to agencies than it had done before. No other single innovation has so markedly enlarged the practical importance of the Presidency to the whole executive establishment; those sponsors got more than they bargained for. Nevertheless, once done the thing was irreversible. Congressional committees remained ultimately "in control": witness the successes of an Otto Passman, terror of the foreign aid program. But the Presidency held an intermediate control; oftener than not this proved conclusive for the agencies, always, at the least, a problem to them: the starting line for Congress was the *President's* proposal. So it has remained.

In the years of FDR and Harry S. Truman, the initial years of our contemporary "big government," White House initiative spread from the sphere of money to the sphere of substance.[3] Ultimately it encompassed the full range of measures coming before Congress. By 1939 the central clearance of all agency proposals and reports on pending measures—whether money bills or not—had been established in the Bureau of the Budget. By 1949 the legislative "program of the President" had come to be a fixed, defined, and comprehensive entity, laid down by annual messages and spelled out in a set of special messages

[3] For details on this development see my "Presidency and Legislation," *American Political Science Review* (Sept. 1954 and Dec. 1955).

in each session. Continuation of both practices through subsequent administrations has accorded to both the sanction of long usage, "ancient custom." There are not many civil servants left who can recall when things were different. In the forties some agencies habitually evaded central clearance. This is rare today. In the fifties the White House still stopped short of sending bill-drafts with its messages; these went instead from a department head to a committee chairman for introduction "by request"; the fiction was preserved that Presidents themselves did not send bills to Congress. By 1961, however, "John Kennedy" became the signature on draft bills sent with messages directly to the Speaker and the President of the Senate, very much as though the White House were Whitehall. While this has not been the invariable practice since, the fiction disappeared—and no one noticed.

The fact that "no one noticed" is suggestive of the character of this entire half-century development. It has been among the quietest pragmatic innovations in our constitutional history. The reason for the quiet is that it has proved at every stage to have advantages for all concerned, not least for Congress. What Congress gains is a prestigeful "laundry-list," a starting order-of-priority to guide the work of each committee in both houses in every session. Since it comes from downtown, committee and house leaders—and all members—can respond to or react against it at *their* option. But coming from downtown it does for them what they, in their disunity, cannot do for themselves: it gives them an agenda to get on with, or depart from.

The President's initiative in legislation is accepted on the Hill because it serves a purpose there. And since it serves a purpose there it is respected by officialdom downtown. Inclusion of their own aims in "the program of the President" matters to most agencies—and to their clientele—for reasons both of prestige and of practical advantage. Exclusion is distasteful, at the least, sometimes disastrous. In consequence, both budgeting and program-making are among the binding forces fostered by the Presidency.

So in recent years is "legislative liaison," a matter not of setting the congressional agenda but of keeping up relations between houses and with agencies in the pursuit of presidential programs on the Hill. The White House has become, long since, a place—almost the only place— where Senate and House party leaders meet with one another on the tactics and prospects of congressional action. The White House telephone has been for many years a major weapon in the hunt for votes, especially when it conveys the President's own voice. But more than this, since Eisenhower's time a special staff for legislative liaison has been established in the White House to monitor the progress of all presidential bills and to assist in rounding up the votes. This staff makes claims on congressmen, and they in turn assert their claims on operating programs in the agencies. The staff attempts to harness agency resources, and the agencies respond by claiming White House help for *their* congressional concerns. Agencies will often have the better of that bargain: a President's connections with the leadership will often serve their purposes more nearly than their help serves his. Because they stand to gain from White House liaison—and liaisoners —this is still another binding tie.

APPEAL TO THE PEOPLE

A President's preeminence as spokesman *for* the government and *to* the country is again a different matter, a compound of many things: Madison's Constitution, Washington's propriety, Jackson's politics, Lincoln's martyrdom, TR's energy, Wilson's earnestness, FDR's voice—all mingled with the human need to personalize "government," a need which grows the greater as the government enlarges and its work becomes arcane. Since the thirties, first radio then television fed that need by offering the *President* at work and play for everyone to hear or see directly, through a form of personal encounter which by now becomes a settled expectation, a matter of course.

After FDR, all Presidents have felt impelled to go before the country, into people's homes (and bars), at every time of gravity in national affairs and at each major turn in governmental policy, to soothe, explain, defend, or urge, as circumstances required. The public expectation is so clear—or seems so—that a Kennedy, who had no native taste for "fireside chatting," nevertheless put himself through these encounters gamely, while elaborating televised press conferences as a congenial form (for him) of partial substitute. A Nixon shuns the Kennedy-style press conference while reaching for new forms of media exposure. But he too follows the "fireside" format, with radio and television talks at appropriate moments. So did LBJ (who reportedly liked such set pieces no better than Kennedy). Almost certainly their successors will feel bound by the tradition.

For agency officials who have new departures to espouse, or risky courses to pursue, or clients in deep trouble, it seems natural and proper, often indispensable, to make the President their television spokesman. Presidents may demur, and often do, but their presumed utility is none the less for that. Accordingly, officials never cease to urge. The net effect is still another force for unity originating in the White House—again a force of need.

The President and the "Institutionalized Presidency"

These spheres of presidential primacy give every part of the executive establishment the shared experience, the mutuality of interest (such as it may be), which stems from common claims upon the President. The claims have grown the stronger as officialdom has grown.

The same events fed both. But if, while this was happening, the White House had proved institutionally incapable of dealing with these claims, then shared experience would have been sheer frustration, and those spheres would have become bone-yards for agency contention, dog-eat-dog. Actually, White House capabilities have kept pace just enough to counter separations of that aggravated sort.

It is the "Institutionalized Presidency," another constitutional innovation of our time, which gives concreteness to the elements of unity in our "Executive." The Presidency began to change from man to institution while our bureaucratic apparatus still was relatively small and still in flux, during the New Deal years. The change was guided by a President whose grasp of office and whose continuity in office were extraordinary: FDR. Both timing and guidance appear providential in the light of what came after: stabilized, entrenched officialdom. The Brownlow Report of 1937 and its sequel "The Executive Office of the President" established not alone an organization, but a doctrine: the rightness of a "President's Department," the need for staff resources of his own. These were established in the nick of time. The organization changes, but the doctrine remains. Otherwise, the Presidency as we know it scarcely could have weathered the subsequent years. By now it would have been a hollow shell.

CONFLICTING DEMANDS

Yet having said this much, it remains to be said that the institutionalized Presidency has not proved an unmixed blessing for the President. In its evolution since the second Roosevelt's years, this institution vividly suggests a basic conflict, probably irreconcilable, between bureaucratic claims upon the White House and a President's own claims upon officialdom. Agencies need decisions, delegations, and support, along with bargaining arenas and a court of last resort, so organized as to assure that their advice is always heard and often taken. A President needs timely information, early warning, close surveillance, organized to yield him the controlling judgment, with his options open, his intent enforced. In practice these two sets of needs have proved quite incompatible; presidential organizations rarely serve one well without disservice to the other.

The National Security Council is a case in point. This Cabinet committee got its statutory start in 1947, as a product of reaction against FDR's secretiveness and "sloppiness" and "meddling" with the conduct of the war and its diplomacy. Yet barring some extraordinary lapses—the German zonal agreements above all—he had managed by his methods to maintain a high degree of personal control during the war, which is what *he* was after. That heightened the reaction. Its ultimate results were seen in Eisenhower's NSC, which came to have a formalized and "paperized" procedure, buttressed by an elaborate interagency substructure. This produced a counterreaction. In 1961 Kennedy abolished both procedure and substructure to escape bureaucratization of his business. He replaced them, in effect, with a handful of personal aides enjoined to do no business but his own. In the main they gave him what he wanted, and the Cuban missile crisis served to vindicate his whole approach, at least in White House eyes. But outside White House precincts in the great departments, especially at levels twice removed from Cabinet rank, memories of those Eisenhower regularities—and of the access they provided—grow fonder every year. By 1966 senior officials had succeeded in persuading Lyndon Johnson to restore the forms of regularized procedure: the SIG-IRG system, so-called, with the State Department nominally at the center. This never worked to anybody's satisfaction, partly because Johnson's operating style was incompatible with it. In 1969 Richard Nixon replaced it by a still more formal system manned by a larger staff, avowedly intended to eliminate Johnsonian "disorder." Ostensibly this was a move back toward the Eisenhower regularities. Officialdom, however, found in it cold comfort. For the Nixon system's center was removed from State to White House more decisively than ever in the past. The NSC became a peg on which to hang not Kennedy's few staffers but a massive White House agency headed by a single, presidential confidant, Henry Kissinger. At second levels of Defense and State, officials now yearn to dismantle Nixon's system.[4]

PRESIDENTIAL VS. AGENCY JUDGMENT

What this instance suggests has pertinence beyond the realm of staffing: not only is officialdom competitive with Congress; it also is in competition with the President. Granted that officials need his sanction, he needs their resources; the dependence being mutual is no bar to competition.

Agency officials, seized by a given problem, rarely seem unequal to the task of making judgments for the government. Nor do they seem inclined to seek a presidential judgment, their's aside, for any other reason than because they cannot help it. The White House would be treated to a novelty if bureaucrats began to ask the President's opinion out of nothing but respect for his good sense. Most careerists see authority as hierarchical—such is the world they live in—and consider that the President is nominally at the top. Because he is on top they can accept his *right* to judge, at least when he asserts it with a show of real authority or when they find it a useful thing to assert against

---

[4] For a further statement of the issues in the national security sphere see my *Afterword* (written jointly with Graham T. Allison) to Robert F. Kennedy's classic *Thirteen Days* (New York: Norton, 1971), esp. pp. 130–6.

their colleagues. But this is not because they think his judgment better than their own. That thought seems a stranger in officialdom. The usual official view of Presidents is rather like the academic view of businessmen: respect for power, a degree of resignation, a tinge of contempt. Given any chance to work the government without the President, officials will proceed to do so in good conscience, except as they may want his voice or acquiescence for their purposes.

If this does not seem quite the disciplined official style respectful of authority à la Max Weber, ours is not a European civil service. In certain other well-established governments, relationships are rigged to minimize, as far as possible, the personal and institutional insecurities of everyone in public life. This seems to be the situation in Great Britain, for example. Not so with us. With us it is almost the opposite: we maximize the insecurities of men and agencies alike. Careerists jostle in-and-outers (from the law firms, business, academic life) for the positions of effective influence; their agencies contend with the committees on the Hill, the Office of Management and Budget, other agencies for the prerequisites of institutional survival, *year by year*. Pursuit of programs authorized in law can be a constant struggle to maintain and hold support of influential clients, or the press. And seeking new authority to innovate a program can be very much like coalition warfare. Accordingly, most agencies have need for men of passion and conviction—or at least enormous powers of resistance—near the top. American officialdom may generate no more of these than other systems do, but it rewards them well: they rise toward the top. And there they tend to set the tone of bureaucratic views about all comers from "outside," not least the President.

Yet any modern President will see things very differently. It is routine for White House aides to seethe with irritation at the unresponsiveness of "them," the almost-enemy, officialdom. And aides are but more royalist than the King. Their principals tend to become resigned, but not less irritated. For a President combines in his own person a unique perspective with unique responsibility. Naturally he will consider that the one is relevant to the other, that his own outlook has bearing on the issues which invoke his own official obligations. Moreover, he is not himself an "office" but a human being, eager to make marks upon events, conscious of *his* place in the republic's history, and mindful—now that ICBM's are held in Moscow too—of a shared capability to terminate that history. Besides, the human being sees himself in office as the outcome of his own career, topped off by national nomination and election. Ordinarily this is the hardest course to run in our political system. He has run it; in his first term he faces it again; in his second term he faces it at one remove, for a successor (he will hope) of his own choosing. So at least have our Presidents seen things up to now.

To an observer from outside, this seems a reasonable vision of the President's own place. Indeed, our governmental system sanctions it, what we have called "democracy" requires it, the system is legitimated by it, and our history confirms its practical utility—which is with us no small consideration. Despite the present failures-in-particular recorded by our history, not least recent history, too many of our Presidents have done too well in exercising judgment for observers to dismiss their claims upon the role. Historically, the averages still seem to support them.

In exercising judgment, Presidents quite often have contributed themselves what none of their executive associates could offer with an equal skill: a first-hand feel for feasibilities across the board of politics, from publics, interests, partisans, to Congress, and officialdom, and governments abroad—a feel for current prospects of support, indifference, toleration, opposition, with respect to lines of action wherever they lead.

This contribution is the province of elective politicians, those who bear the burdens, take the heat, and face the risks of sudden death by ballot box, especially when they share in administrative power and have learned the risks peculiar to that line of work as well. But in the whole executive establishment there are no such risk-takers, short of the White House. Aside from the Vice-President, whose role is bound to be ambiguous at best, the President stands quite alone. Officials cannot make his contribution for him. Few can help him very much to make it. For no one stands on a spot like his, with comparable duties, facing comparable risks. A Lincoln in the months before emancipation, a Franklin Roosevelt in the years after his "quarantine" address, a Kennedy in the weeks after Birmingham, or in the days of his climactic confrontation with Khrushchev, a Johnson in the early months of 1968—all these men were engaged in calculating feasibilities, and it is not of record that associates could have been counted on to come up with their answers for them. In this trade there is no reliable apprentice system.

A President does have some fellow journeymen, of course, but they are far away, a long mile down the Avenue on Capitol Hill.

The Common Stakes of Elective Politicians

The separations between President and congressmen are partly constitutional, partly political, partly attitudinal, and in no small degree a matter of semantics. The Constitution's barriers look higher than they are. The barriers of politics may soon start to decline. But differences in attitude may still be on the rise, fed by the connotations of our words.

EXECUTIVE VS. LEGISLATIVE

Constitutionally the President and Congress share each other's powers, from the veto, to appointments, to administrative "oversight," and
so down the list. Practically this is a sharing between one man at the
White House and a scattering of others who hold key positions in the
two congressional "bodies"; they share powers with each other even
as they share with him. Politically, these sharers are kept separate by
their differing dependence upon different electorates. These differences
are sharpest at the stage of nomination: senators and congressmen will
owe their seats to separate sets of nominators; chairmen owe their
powers to seniority acquired by repeated nomination. The President,
by contrast, owes his place and powers to a nominating contest of another order, as far removed from theirs, in timing and geography and
personnel alike, as theirs are separated from each other. The fact that
nominators everywhere would like to win elections has not served to
produce like-minded party candidates—far from it. Terms of party
competition and conditions of survival and electoral arithmetic have
differed far too much. Realignment of congressional districts, reapportionment of legislatures, and Republican gains in the once "solid
South" *may* now combine to change this situation, to reduce those
differences, to force more uniformity on nominators, and hence on
candidates. If so, then there will be a narrowing of separations among
senators and congressmen and Presidents—a narrowing, at least, of
gaps induced by politics. But that time is not yet.

Even if it comes, there will remain the gaps induced by attitudes of
mind, by habit, custom, way of life, and ways of doing work. In some
respects our Constitution and our politics tell less about what separates
the Presidency from Congress than our architecture does. For the
White House and the Capitol as structures almost perfectly express
these underlying differences of attitude: the former has an exterior
which at first glance looks simpler than it is, and inside all seems
orderly: rectangular rooms mostly, connected by straight corridors, as
neat-appearing as an organization chart. The latter is almost rococo in
externals, appearing more complex at first than on long knowledge,
and within it seems all twists and turns: passages which lead in circles,
little-known connections, sudden detours, hidden treasures, obscure
sanctuaries, walls in curves. The men who work inside these buildings
literally work in different worlds. Their attitudes are shaped accordingly.

The Senate and the House, of course, are not identical workplaces.
For most of its inhabitants the Senate is a pleasant place, possessed of
quite enough prestige and power (or its semblance), and amenities of
staff and space, and time to enjoy them (six years at a crack), so that it
alone remains what much of government once was, a refuge for the

spirit of political free-enterprise, unfettered either by undue responsibility or the restraints of size. The House, however, offers comparable enjoyments only to a few, the men of great seniority or great good luck. The rest either content themselves with marginal existences or scramble for political and personal identity amidst the ruck and ruckus of large numbers, rigid rules, demanding lobbyists, disdainful agencies, unheeding press, importunate constituents, and pitifully short tenure. No wonder that the House is seen by many of its members as a stepping stone, a place to be endured on the way up and out. It may well be the most frustrating place to work in Washington. It certainly ranks high among such places.

Even so, the contrasts between houses pale compared to those between the work of either and of men downtown. Tiber Creek is gone, but there remains a great dividing line across the Avenue.

This is the product not alone of work-ways but of substance, not merely who-works-how but who-does-what. So much of the decision-making critical for all of us is centered nowadays in the executive establishment that congressmen and senators feel cheated of a birthright. They are, for the most part, men of seriousness, intelligence, and patriotism, to say nothing of experience. They also are men of elections, voted into office by a portion of the citizens and sharing with the President the risk of death by ballot box. Yet others have a greater voice than they in numbers of decisions, day by day, which touch the lives of citizens. They may accept this, but they cannot like it.

For instance, the most critical of government decisions, the war-or-peace decisions, have been snatched away from Congress by technology, at least where nuclear war is risked, despite the plain words of the Constitution. As for limited war, Congress may now vote itself authority to do what it always could have done anyway, namely stop hostilities once started. But while the threat of legislative veto might deter a President, the evidence of history makes it appear remote that Congress actually would call a halt once troops had been engaged. No congressman disputes the fact that Congress has lost hold of war-making. Few have any eagerness to take upon themselves the heat of presidential choices. But many, perhaps most, dislike to draw the corollary, that they have no choice at all and not even a voice, except by presidential courtesy, in presidential prudence. When it comes to lesser instances, where courtesy and prudence are prerogatives of a mere appointee or even of a careerist, then their sense of deprivation will be stronger still, and for good reason.

Hurts like these are rendered the more painful by the press, which centers its attention on the President. Publicity is far too great a prize for politicians to make this a happy outcome for most members of Congress. Only elders can remember when the Hill was the best-covered part of town. Franklin Roosevelt's Presidency put an end to

that. But even juniors are impelled by sheer professional concern to
nurse their disadvantage as a grievance.

Such feelings are returned with interest from downtown. In executive eyes, Congress is at best a necessary nuisance and at worst a great
conspiracy against efficient government. All Presidents will wish they
could make Congress serve them as a rubber-stamp, converting their
agendas into prompt enactments, and most Presidents will try to bring
that miracle about, whenever and as best they can. Most presidential
appointees will grow despairing about drains upon their time, skill,
energy, and ingenuity—to say nothing of reputation—occasioned by
the legislative (and investigative) process with its "endless" repetitions
in committee hearings, correspondence, phone calls. Most careerists,
even if their agencies show profit, will grow sick, or cynical, at seeing
"rational" solutions twisted out of recognition by committee compromise. And most of them, reacting in anticipation, become do-it-yourself types, compromisers-in-advance, despite the risks of amateurish
outcomes. (Amateur careerists, in turn, sicken the politicians; some,
however, do acquire near-professional standing.) Underlying all of
this is a persistent puzzle: why should "they" be so blind to imperatives
of good administration? It is the obverse of a question constantly oc-
curring on the Hill: what makes "them" so obtuse about the necessities
of the legislative process and of political survival?

"They" and "them" are optical illusions, but these make the sense
of separation all the sharper. Administrators may know well, from
personal experience and frequent exploitation, how disjointed is the
power structure on the Hill. Yet most of them would say and feel with
Kennedy:

> . . . the Congress looks more powerful sitting here than it did when I
> was there in Congress. But that is because when you are in Congress you
> are one of a hundred in the Senate or 435 in the House, so that power is
> so divided. But from here I look at a Congress, and I look at the collective
> power of the Congress, particularly the bloc action, and it is a substantial
> power.[5]

And most members of Congress may be quite aware that any one of
them, with influence enough, can penetrate or even dominate the programs of some agency or other. Yet looking down the Avenue at the
array of agencies—the rows of office buildings, the outpouring of
officials, the interminable corridors, the bustle of department heads
departing for the White House from their grandiose office-suites—
these legislators see an entity of monolithic aspect, the executive
branch, apparently commanded by one man, the President: that other

[5] Television and radio interview, December 17, 1962, *Public Papers of the President: John F. Kennedy* (1962), p. 893.

and more grandly placed elective politician whose hold upon the agencies seems mighty in comparison with theirs.

These visual impressions are confirmed by our semantics, reinforced by words in common use: *the* Congress, *the* Executive, "legislation," "administration." Decades ago the coming of the "Institutionalized Presidency" was justified by experts outside government (and by officials near the White House) as essential to the role of "Chief Administrator," a presidential role read into constitutional provisions by analogy with private corporations. The analogy has stuck, and with it the suspicion that all efforts to enlarge a President's resources threaten the prerogatives of *Congress*, striking at committee rights to authorize, finance, investigate, and "oversee." Presidents in fact are merely fighting for their rights as independent operators, threatened with engulfment by official claims upon them. This is a fight which should enlist the sympathy of fellow politicians on the Hill. But phrases twist the fact into a contest between President and Congress.

POLITICIANS VS. BUREAUCRATS

This is symptomatic of a great confusion about who is fighting whom and who is winning in our government. Bureaucracy has brought a new contestant into play: the great prospective struggle is between entrenched officialdom and politicians everywhere, White House and Hill alike. Officialdom already is competitive with both. Its strength is sapped by institutional disunity, the gift of Congress. Temporarily, at least, this shields the politicians from the consequences of their own disunity. But it seems far from certain that the bureaucrats will not learn how to close their ranks in better order, faster, than their showing up to now. What then would happen to the politicians separated as they are by all the factors just described?

The first edition of this essay written during LBJ's first year as President took that last question as a peg on which to hang three final paragraphs. These follow:

We now are entering our second generation of experience with an executive establishment in modern dress. Even now, experienced officials tend to work across their lines of jurisdiction with an ease and understanding little known some twenty years ago. Relations between the Departments of Defense and State exemplify the trend. Their disputation still remains incessant, as before, but temperature and tempo are decidedly below the levels of, say, 1949. If this trend should continue and accelerate, encompassing domestic agencies as well, a President and congressmen might confront competition too intense for them to meet in isolation from each other. If so, they either must array their own ranks or our government will risk losing what they uniquely bring to public

policy: the feel for feasibility of men who take the heat from an electorate. It is a risk not only to their power but also to our polity.

Fortunately for the politicians, there is little likelihood that bureaucrats
will soon be tightly united. The separations among agencies, induced by
separations on the Hill, run far too deep. The risk lies not in an official
unity but simply and more subtly in a heightened sense of official community. And nowadays not only are there signs of fellow-feeling among
"second-generation" bureaucrats, there also are great efforts being made
by private sources to induce community spirit through enhanced professionalization. Our schools, foundations, and study groups make no such
efforts for our politicians.

The moral is plain. To paraphrase Karl Marx: Politicians at the two
ends of the Avenue unite! You have nothing to lose but your pieces of
power—and even now these may be slipping out of reach. To call for
unity in form would be absurd. To call for sheer subservience of Congress to the President, or *vice versa,* would be futile. But to urge some
change of attitudes at both ends of the Avenue, to urge awareness of
joint stakes and common risks is not perhaps to ask too much of our
established system. This might induce a unity sufficient for the purpose.
Moreover, politicians might enjoy it when they thought about it. Opportunities to think, however, will come hard unless outside observers
—academic and other—set about repairing our semantics. We might
begin now.

RECENT DEVELOPMENTS

So much for commentary circa 1964. Like all else dating from that
year those words convey an atmosphere often curiously remote. "Pre-
war" we probably will start to call it soon. A lot has happened since.

Three developments especially affect the near-term prospects for
relations among Congress, Presidency, and officialdom.

One of these developments is the spread of congressional mistrust,
of grievance nurtured by deprivation, into the realms of defense and
diplomacy. These are realms where presidential leadership was relatively uncontested for the generation from Truman to Johnson. On
Capitol Hill, as well as outside Washington, a legacy of Vietnam's
long-drawn course becomes frustration tinged with fear. Such feelings
are not universal, but are widespread and in some minds deep. The
sense of separation between President and congressmen deepens accordingly. Snarls at "they" and "them" are heard on every hand. In
Nixon's time, of course, these are abetted by the lack of party ties between the White House and congressional majorities.

A second development is what appears to be progressive diminution
in the relative positions of most Cabinet officers, a weakening of the
traditional "Administration." These men and their immediate as-

sociates are caught between a burgeoning White House staff—enlarged four-fold in Nixon's time alone—and ever more entangled departmental jurisdictions consequent upon the outpouring of laws in Johnson's time.

Departmental heads now seem distinctly more subordinate to Presidents than twenty years ago, or even ten. Presidents do not seem to have profited thereby, not anyway in their own estimations. Johnson seriously considered and Nixon has proposed a sweeping scheme of departmental reorganization, meant to produce fewer but more potent Cabinet members tied to one another and the White House in such fashion as to strengthen central management of Federal agencies.[6] Whether structural reform along these lines is possible congressionally, and if so whether it could actually induce the benefits now claimed for it, are both uncertain quantities. Meanwhile, presidential staff grows at a frantic rate, as does the burden of coordination thrust upon it. Every entanglement means more work up top.

The third development is an appearance, possibly deceptive, of progressive loss of confidence, morale, assurance, perhaps also of quality, in many different parts of the executive establishment. Public and congressional suspiciousness of soldiers—for the first time in a generation—plays some part. So does White House suspiciousness of diplomats. So does Republican suspiciousness of career staffs. So do the suspicions in reverse of some careerists, especially among professionals, for example lawyers. Party separation of the White House from congressional committee chairmanships no doubt feeds such suspicions on all sides. So does the vocal discontent of many publics.

Deeper down, the operational experiences of the sixties have left bafflement, confusion, apprehension, in a lot of minds not only at the Pentagon, not only in response to ineffectual warfare, but also at HUD, OEO, some parts of HEW, and other "home" departments in response to ineffectual administration. The massive task of turning legislative mandates into actual results, implemented in the field, often under budgetary stringency, has proved far harder, more demanding, less assuredly achievable, than was foreseen in the initial years of LBJ when all those laws poured in. Discouragement and disillusionment—and often bafflement—accompany the implementation struggle.

What these developments portend for the long run is hard to say, possibly nothing. In the short-run, however, they assuredly defer the day when bureaucrats cohere sufficiently to confidently reach for governmental leadership. They also reduce reasons for the politicians to

[6] See Executive Office of the President, Office of Management and Budget, *Papers Relating to the President's Departmental Reorganization Program, Revised, February, 1972.*

cohere among themselves. Their electorates, of course, may force them to it. Television, crime, and race, combined with war, may have profound effects upon the separations between President and Congressmen by reducing the separations of their electorates. But consciousness of bureaucratic challenge will not do it, not anyway in the short run.

Harvey C. Mansfield

6

The Congress and Economic Policy

Any observer can assert, and none can prove, that the country is lucky the Congress does what it does; or to the contrary, that we would be better off if it stayed home, or if some other body, somehow differently organized, replaced it. This chapter has a more modest, expository aim: to illuminate the ways in which the Congress and its component parts go about their varied activities in the field of economic policy; to account for some of the whats and hows and whys of their actions; and to identify types of policy and policy-making to that end.

A general theme is the continuing tension between the needs and forces calling for an overall view of national policy—usually a distasteful discipline for congressmen—and the more congenial course of responding to special claims. Not all particular interests, luckily for everyone, are inconsistent with a general interest, however defined. But the notion will not down, vague as it is, that there is a general interest to be advanced; and its identification and fostering require analysis and policies addressed to the aggregate performance of the national economy. These, the institutions of Congress are ill-adapted to supply. For the Congress is itself a part of a larger political system, and so only partly a master of its own destiny. It is internally fragmented, as well. It is seldom the source of major economic initiatives or innovations; its typical outputs are the products of interaction with forces outside, and display patterns characteristic of the ways those

HARVEY C. MANSFIELD, *since 1965 professor of government at Columbia University, was for a decade the managing editor of the* American Political Science Review. *During World War II he served the Office of Price Administration, and has since been consultant to a number of government commissions, federal and state.*

forces combine and collide in the Congressional setting. Some of these patterns can be specified.

Congressional Power in the Premises

In the field of domestic economic policy, Congress deals from constitutional strength. It can have a large say if it wishes to—if it is moved and organized, that is, to exert its full potential. Its enumerated and implied powers (Article I, section 8) are sweeping if not plenary: to tax, borrow and spend; to regulate interstate and foreign commerce, currency and credit (and the lack thereof, bankruptcy); to grant patents and copyrights and establish post roads; and to order the organization and procedures of the judicial and administrative establishments, as well as its own. These powers have been broadly construed in their exercise; and in the realm of economic policy they are not seriously hemmed in by the constitutional powers lodged with the President or with the courts.

The President, to be sure, is vested with the power to make appointments to the offices that Congress creates or authorizes. This is a source of influence over policy; and he has other means of influence. But his overriding constitutional power as commander-in-chief, which bulwarks his position in foreign and military affairs and also enables him ultimately to intervene decisively when domestic federal authority is forcibly defied—as in the school desegregation cases—is of little avail in economic controversies in peacetime. This much, at least, is the teaching of President Truman's experience when he ordered the seizure of the steel mills in 1952—a lesson no successor, however tempted, has tested. The President's "executive power" and his responsibility to "take care that the laws be faithfully executed" have not, for present purposes, proved to be significant sources of independent power either.

The federal courts have done much to vindicate congressional power in economic affairs and little to curb it except by insistence on procedural requirements—at least since 1937 when the Wagner Act and the Social Security Act were sustained. With constitutional controversies since then transferred in the main to the field of civil liberties and the rights of defendants in criminal cases, the function of the courts in economic disputes has been confined chiefly to statutory construction and to enforcement injunctions. Where the statute involved is broad and vague, like the Sherman Act, this still leaves a good deal of scope for judicial discretion. But when the Congress does not like the result—for instance in the *Southeastern Underwriters* case (1944) in which the Supreme Court reversed long-settled doctrine and held insurance to be interstate commerce subject to the Antitrust law—it has been possible to undo the effects of the decision by changing the law, as was done in that case. During a sample five sessions, from 1957 to 1961, at least eight acts or amendments were passed to reverse the results of some thirteen Supreme Court decisions. Most of these were tax cases; the best known of them cushioned the duPont divestiture of General Motors stock, but two dealt with transportation rates and one, the Landrum-Griffin Act, with labor relations. Occasionally the Congress pushes an economic regulation to the limit of its power, approaching absurdity. There is the law, for example (U.S. Code, Title 21, section 347c), which says that every restaurant in the United States must, if it serves oleomargarine to its patrons, serve it in triangular pats—lest they mistake it for the high-priced spread. But ordinarily the politics of legislative processes keep the final exertions of congressional power well within the borders of constitutionality.

As nearly any enactment has some economic aspect, there is no precise answer to the question, what proportion of congressional time and attention is devoted to those regulations of "interfering interests," deriving from the unequal distribution of property, that Madison saw as the "principal task of modern legislation." Some crude notion of the distribution of activity by subject can be gained from an analysis made some years ago and summarized in table I which classifies—but does not weigh—the bills acted on in the 1962 session. There is no reason to suppose that the proportion has lessened over the ensuing decade. Lumping together the items tabulated there under the headings of Agriculture, Appropriations, Welfare, Housing, Public Works and Resources, and Taxes and Economic Policy, it appears that 384, or 44 percent, of the 872 public bills that reached at least the stage of a committee report, and 272, or 45 percent, of the 599 bills that ultimately passed in that session, can be counted in the realm of economic affairs primarily. This only sets the stage for the question, what kinds of policies and interests are at stake in these bills? For Madison the answer to this question was plain: interests are particular, and interfering interests must be moderated by public authority, lest the society fly apart. Today this answer is only a partial truth, because its premise—that economic activity is private—is no longer descriptive. Today public authorities are direct and large-scale sponsors, participants, and managers; and "private" organizations perform public functions.

Macro- and Micro-Economic Policies

Economic thinking about the economy, and in its train political thinking and congressional actions regarding what the government could and should be doing, have undergone a revolutionary transformation since the impact of John Maynard Keynes became felt in

Table I

DISTRIBUTION OF BILLS ACTED ON (COMMITTEE REPORT OR BEYOND), BY
SUBJECT CATEGORY, EIGHTY-SEVENTH CONGRESS, SECOND SESSION (1962)

Subject of bill	Completed	Unfinished
Agriculture	41	9
Appropriations	19	3
Education and welfare		
Education	3	12
Health	3	2
Welfare	17	8
Housing	3	0
Veterans	26	12
Foreign policy		
International affairs	22	7
Immigration	4	1
General government		
Congress	18	5
Constitution and civil liberties	1	5
Government operations	17	6
Post Office and civil service	14	17
District of Columbia	52	30
Indians, territories	37	15
Judiciary	34	17
Commemorative	38	20
National security		
Armed services and defense	48	10
Atomic energy and space	10	2
Public works and resources		
Lands	29	12
Resources and public works	51	28
Taxes and economic policy		
Economic policy and regulations	31	6
Commerce	21	9
Labor	4	5
Transportation	27	16
Taxes	14	11
Tariffs	15	5
Totals	*599*	*273*

Source: *Congressional Quarterly Almanac 1962* (Washington, D.C., 1962), pp. 770–795.
The tabulation includes one Senate Resolution and eleven House Resolutions deemed
substantively significant by the *Congressional Quarterly* compilers; these are neither
"laws" nor "bills."

this country during the 1930s. After a generation of controversy, a
neo-Keynesian doctrine triumphed, and was vindicated in the event,
during a brief period around 1964. But by 1972 the links between
doctrine, diagnosis, and policy were again in doubt, and in contest.
As domestic inflation and unemployment persisted despite the return

of troops from Vietnam, and the dollar cheapened abroad, and monetarists attacked Keynesians, a Republican President confounded critics and supporters alike, from the left and from the right. He appointed a persuasive Democrat to be his secretary of the treasury, and adopted a program of the sort Democrats had talked about: massive budgetary deficits, a devalued and inconvertible dollar, and direct, if mild, wage and price controls. What policy course was left for a Democratic Congress in an election year? What could economists teach congressmen?

DOCTRINAL DEVELOPMENTS

Prior to the Great Depression economists—following in the steps of Alfred Marshall and the classics—concentrated on price analysis, since every transaction has a price, and setting that price seemed to be the key decision for the participants. On the limited range of economic questions the government could decide, economists lined up for or against free trade or protection, the gold standard, and free competition as against the regulation of monopolies or public ownership of utilities. A maverick Veblen scoffed at them from the sidelines without deflecting their concerns. After World War I, specialties with practical and political applications began to develop in agricultural and labor economics and Wesley Mitchell launched his pioneering studies of business cycles. Orthodox public finance economists preached the virtues of an annually balanced budget, on the assumption—not always tacit—that the government should be a neutral factor in the economy, taking out only as much as it had put in—and the less of either, the better. Texts on money and banking taught the need for a system of currency and credit firmly anchored to hard money reserves and regulated in volume automatically by the level of business demands.

Keynes' doctrine, that the national government should use its fiscal and credit powers to play a deliberately compensatory role in the economy—buoying it with deficit spending in times of slack demand and running a budget surplus in inflationary periods—found a cordial reception (where and when it did) partly, no doubt, because it provided a theoretical rationale for what the government was, after a fashion, already doing—and being criticized for doing. The Congress that in the Economy Act of 1933 virtuously piled deflation upon deflation by directing cuts of 15 percent in federal salaries and veterans' pensions, by 1935 was voting a $4.8 billion appropriation outside and beyond the regular budget, for work relief and public works. But the Keynesian impact was more than political. It directed attention away from preoccupation with the behavior of prices to focus instead on aggregate income and savings in relation to consumption and investment, and on output, actual and potential. Looking at aggregates meant taking a national view of the behavior of the economy as a whole—a view that would inevitably influence policy judgments.

In the state of the art at the time such a view was not easy to get. For some sectors of the economy statistical series were highly developed; for many they were inadequate or nonexistent; nowhere were the parts put together regularly and comprehensively. In the late 1930s Simon Kuznets and some co-workers set about developing a statistical basis for expressing the then novel concept of the Gross National Product. This might have occupied a quiet academic generation, but for the advent of World War II. The imperative need of the War Production Board to know the GNP and its components as a prerequisite to refashioning that product to serve the purposes of war mobilization, put the full resources of government into the statistical task. Starting in 1940 the Budget Bureau circulated confidentially to the upper ranks of officialdom in Washington, particularly among those connected with the war agencies, a monthly statistical compilation under the title of *Defense Progress* (August, 1940–December, 1941) and *War Progress* (January, 1942–October, 1945). This was the precursor of *Economic Indicators,* prepared by the Council of Economic Advisers since 1947 and published monthly by the Joint Economic Committee of Congress. All the main federal agencies concerned with financial and economic affairs—Treasury, Federal Reserve, Budget, Commerce, Labor, SEC, and so on—contribute their figures to this compilation. Since the war, analysis of the national income and of the GNP have been the starting points for official as well as private professional studies of economic policy; and the technical terms have entered congressional vocabularies.

STRUCTURAL DEVELOPMENTS

Statistics and computers, of course, are the instruments, not the authors of policy. Complementary developments in the institutions and financial practices of the government have had more weight in bringing about the transformation in economic thinking and in congressional approaches. The passage of the Budget and Accounting Act in 1921, which created the Budget Bureau, was the first long step—since the days of Hamilton and Gallatin—toward focusing on the President a government-wide responsibility for a government-wide view of fiscal policy. The Bureau's practical effectiveness was enhanced after 1935 by the renovation in Treasury accounting procedures and organization—introduced in order to keep current and accurate track of federal relief expenditures—that for the first time provided reliable monthly data on governmental cash outlays. The Bureau's position was strengthened further in 1939 when it was moved from the Treasury to become the key unit in the newly formed Executive Office of the President, following the passage of the Reorganization Act of that year. The Bureau introduced another tool of overall analysis after the war when it began reporting the consolidated cash budget—reflecting Social Security and other trust fund receipts and payments—alongside the traditional administrative budget, which was limited to new obligational authority. After 1967, in pursuance of the report of the President's Commission on Budget Concepts, the Bureau enlarged the coverage and refined the categories of transactions included in the budgetary presentation so as to emphasize their economic implications and thereby doubled the apparent size of the newly "unified budget." Since 1961, and in contrast with prior years, the budget director has invariably been an economist by training. Reorganization Plan 2 of 1970 renamed the Bureau the Office of Management and Budget (OMB), increased its allowance of super-grade positions and directed it to pay more attention to managerial concerns. It remains to be seen how far OMB will transcend the Bureau's traditional preoccupation with appropriation requests.

The passage of the Employment Act of 1946 consequently marked a second long institutional step toward the development of national economic programs. For although it endowed the government with no new powers beyond the vehicle of an annual economic message and report, it announced a set of goals for the economy as a whole—not just the government sector—and committed the government to a new degree of political responsibility for pursuing them. To provide organs of planning and deliberation it created the Council of Economic Advisers in the Executive Office and a congressional Joint Committee on the Economic Report, later renamed the Joint Economic Committee (JEC), both of which have become influences to be reckoned with.

Other institutional developments fit in with the trend. By the Reciprocal Trade Agreements Act of 1934 the Congress gave over its nineteenth century practice of piecemeal enactment of individual tariff rates, in favor of a process of collective bargaining with other nations. The Trade Expansion Act of 1962 reaffirmed and extended this approach; since then a foreign trade policy adviser has had a regular niche in the Executive Office staff. President Nixon's abrupt Executive Order of August 15, 1971, imposing, among other things, a temporary surcharge on imports across the board and setting in train a round of negotiations over import quotas and currency values, underscored the need for central direction in economic foreign policy. In the realm of domestic policy the organs established simultaneously with the surcharge—the Cabinet-level Cost of Living Council, the Price Commission and the Pay Board, together with the *ex officio* Domestic Council already designated in the Reorganization Plan of 1970 noted above—have yet to prove their viability. Meanwhile, without any new statute and with only one apparent lapse (in 1966) in over a decade the Federal Reserve and the Treasury entered in the 1960s a new era of close and informal cooperation—in sharp contrast to the tensions that had often marked their previous relations—in the exercise of their powers over money and credit; this because of their converging concern over the international position of the dollar and its domestic ramifications.

Underlying these institutional changes and furnishing the basic drive toward an overall perspective were a series of developments in federal finances too familiar to need elaboration: the income tax, which established a revenue base sufficient to sustain federal borrowing on an unprecedented scale without bringing the government's credit into question; Supreme Court decisions that quieted any doubts about the constitutionality of federal spending; the power of the Federal Reserve to create money (in the form of bank reserves) and so to sustain a market for government securities in virtually unlimited volume; the technological innovations such as machine checkwriting on IBM punch cards that made it physically and administratively possible to issue checks by the millions, quickly; and federal outlays on a scale that in 1944–45 approached 45 percent of the annual GNP and in fiscal 1972 amounted to an estimated 229 billions. Governmental instrumentalities of such capabilities called for conscious management and direction with an eye to their aggregate impact. They were too potent to be left to the chance play of private influences.

POSTWAR FISCAL POLICY

The deliberate marshalling of economic processes in wartime was one thing; to talk of economic planning after the cessation of hostilities, unless in the most general terms, was something else again, as the debate on the Employment Act showed. An appreciation of Keynesian teachings spread slowly from professional to political quarters. During the Truman and Eisenhower administrations the virtues of balancing the budget—i.e., ignoring the Social Security fund surplus and neutralizing the aggregate effects of government budget spending—and of reducing the public debt, an anti-inflationary move, were still official doctrine. But practical responses in Congress to practical conditions in the country and to soundings in the electorate belied the doctrine on decisive occasions. In 1948, with price inflation waning and the Treasury running a heavy surplus, a Republican Congress preferred tax reduction to debt reduction in an election year—to the extent of overriding a Democratic President's veto. In the 1958–59 recession a Republican administration, with the acquiescence of a Democratic Congress, ran a deficit of unprecedented proportions (over $12 billion) by sustaining expenditures while revenues fell off sharply. Finally, in the early 1960s, bipartisan political judgments and Keynesian doctrine converged overtly. At a time when the balance-of-payments deficit dictated a rise in short-term interest rates, while a lagging growth rate forbade higher long-term rates and an unemployment rate near 6 percent called for an expansion of aggregate demand, the administration in 1963 proposed a major tax reduction even though a budget deficit was already in prospect. The Revenue Act of 1964 was the result, but only after more than a year of congressional debate. In the event the reduced rates produced a sharply higher total yield because the income base had grown; hence talk for a time of a "fiscal dividend" to be distributed. Reviewing the experience, Secretary of the Treasury Douglas Dillon crowed a little:

> . . . the past three and one-half years constitute a significant watershed in the development of American economic policy. For they have borne witness to the emergence, first of all, of a new national determination to use fiscal policy as a dynamic and affirmative agent in fostering economic growth. Those years have also demonstrated, not in theory, but in actual practice, how our different instruments of economic policy—expenditure, tax, debt management and monetary policies—can be tuned in concert toward achieving different, even disparate, economic goals. In short, those years have encompassed perhaps our most significant advance in decades in the task of forging flexible economic policy techniques capable of meeting the needs of our rapidly changing economic scene.[1]

The secretary nevertheless included one *caveat* in his otherwise optimistic survey:

> There remain, in my opinion, great obstacles to the use of tax policy for purely counter-cyclical purposes. The chief of these obstacles is the fact that, within our constitutional system, a long lag typically intervenes between a request for a change in tax rates and legislative approval. Unless and until some method is worked out—acceptable to the Congress and consistent with its prerogatives—whereby tax rates can be varied without undue delay, the purely counter-cyclical function of tax policy will remain outside our arsenal of economic tools.[2]

This episode probably marks the high point in the influence of economists and economic teaching on fiscal policy as voted by the Congress, culminating the transformation in thinking that had taken place over a generation. It would be pleasant to report that the lesson controlled policy in succeeding years, but the record is spotty and sometimes perverse. A frontal assault in the Goldwater campaign of 1964 was turned back. After 1965, however, the escalation of the Vietnam War, the enactment of LBJ's Great Society programs, calling for expanded domestic outlays, and the continuing deterioration in the balance of

[1] Speech at the Harvard Business School, June 6, 1964.
[2] *Ibid.*

payments contributed to inflationary conditions that sooner or later dictated restraint and an increase in the proportion of public to private expenditures. The political obstacles to applying the "new economics" in reverse gave fresh evidence for Secretary Dillon's *caveat.*

President Johnson, conscious that asking for higher taxes would help conservative opponents in Congress to defeat his administration's responses to rising expectations for social welfare spending, put off making his request; congressional leaders would not move without it. When he did ask, in 1967, Chairman Wilbur Mills of the House Ways and Means Committee raised the price of action to include matching cuts in already approved appropriations and larger reductions in pending budget requests; action was blocked for months while contending forces tried to get their way. By the time the Revenue and Expenditure Control Act of 1968 (P.L. 90–364) passed, on June 28, and imposed a temporary compromise, the Senate Finance Committee had made an end-run around the House committee, attaching the tax increase to a routine House-passed bill and so throwing the issues into conference, where seniors count for more, and also challenging the historic constitutional priority of the House in tax matters; the Ways and Means Committee had encroached on the territory of the Appropriations Committee in forcing rescissions; and the President had been obliged to accept a statutory duty to impound large sums for non-defense appropriations he had previously secured. But for the general anxiety stirred by the gold crisis that spring, virtually unanimous business lobbying and labor acquiescence, there is no telling when the bill might have passed. A similarly complicated and controverted process attended the passage of the similar act in 1969.

Measures such as these affect the long-run balance of power between the executive and Congress by making delegations of discretionary authority; between the two houses, as to whose will shall prevail; between their committees, over jurisdiction—i.e., constitutional issues—; or else they effect a significant redistribution of income and influence in the population at large, taking from some in order to pay others, in the name of social justice; or they sacrifice environmental quality to current consumption and exploitation, or vice-versa. Such measures arouse ideological issues and appeals to class interests, and array the administration against major pressure groups. The scope of conflict is too broad to be contained within the confines of a committee, and floor fights take time to organize and bring to a conclusion.

So it is that the political commitments of the Employment Act, or, in economists' terms, an adequate and sustainable growth rate, near-full employment, price stability, a tolerable balance of international payments, satisfactory minimum standards of living (health, education, and welfare) for the underprivileged, and more recent environmental concerns, are widely accepted in general terms as the legitimate agenda of the federal government, and yet are perennially in contest. Where they can be forwarded under existing statutes, as by Federal Reserve operations in the money market, little objection is heard. But where they depend on new and timely legislation that runs counter to still-cherished doctrines, a major political battle in Congress ensues. All the resources of the administration become engaged in such a battle and these may not suffice to carry the day, the distribution of power and prejudice in Congress being what it is. Victories in any one year can usually be counted on the fingers of one hand. At any given time a considerable list of such measures on the agenda, long agitated, are indefinitely stalled: tax reforms like ending the exemption of municipal bond interest; revenue sharing and block grants; a negative income tax; universal health insurance, among others.

CONTESTS FOR ADVANTAGE

Meanwhile, and alongside these major grapplings, the Congress continues to be preoccupied with the never-ending and far more numerous contests for advantage among interfering interests that make up the ordinary stuff of politics; who gets what and when. Several categories under this general heading can usefully be distinguished, marking different types of advantages to be had and perhaps suggesting characteristic patterns of conflict and accommodation.

One such category is the disposal of the public domain—literally and figuratively the parcelling out of the tangible and intangible resources and benefits that are inherently within the power of the government to bestow on claimants. Historically, titles and rights to public lands and protective tariffs exemplify this category; it includes also a good many kinds of appropriations, for public works, subsidies and grants-in-aid, for instance. Latterly, access to the virtually unlimited store of government credit (or credit guarantees or insurance) and commodity price supports have become favorite forms: for two decades after World War II at least, more federal money was invested in the stockpiles of strategic materials than in holdings of farm surpluses. Whatever their intrinsic merits, all these function also as types of patronage. Various general principles may be mustered against them, but seldom any major organized interests outside of the government—at least before Ralph Nader, Common Cause, and the Sierra Club began their crusades; for it is a thankless task to argue that the government should keep what it can give away if someone really wants it. So congressional committees listen to the claimants and preside over the process of disposal, in ways that tend, like patronage generally, to fortify the *status quo* in the political system. If the supply is ample the process is painless. If giving to one means denying another, a test of access and power ensues. If the claimants are individually vulnerable, a logrolling omnibus bill is the typical result. If they grow increasingly numerous, the goodies may be subdivided into smaller pieces.

A second category consists of regulations that the Congress may impose, directly or by delegation to administrative agencies. Here the benefits conferred on some come not from a government store but from restraints laid upon others who are regulated. In the long run it may well turn out that the regulations benefit the regulated too, as by increasing the confidence of their customers or by eliminating some troublesome forms of competition; but they do not usually see it that way at first. So a regulatory proposal—for example, the Motor Vehicle Act of 1935 that brought the trucking industry under ICC control, or the Bank Holding Company Act of 1956 and its 1966 amendment, or the Federal Mine Safety Act amendments of 1966 (P.L. 89-376)—typically arrays well organized interests (and stimulates their formation or strengthening pro and con) in a parallelogram of forces operating in a congressional matrix with allies and opponents among federal bureaus that are affected. A common variant of this category occurs when it is proposed to upset the *status quo* by repealing or relaxing an existing regulation around which settled expectations have grown up—for example, by permitting commercial banks to open branches outside their home-office territories, or by letting savings and loan associations into the personal loan business. Parties with a stake in the continuance of the regulation react as though they were themselves about to be regulated.

A third category is made up of exemptions and dispensations, partial or complete, from burdens otherwise generally applied. Any broad regulation brings applications for exceptions or special treatment, on grounds of hardship or inequity, fancied or real. Much of the language of the revenue code is devoted to spelling out congressional responses to such applications. In considering a plea of this sort a congressional committee confronts a highly concentrated and sharply focused pressure from a limited source, working often through a single, friendly, well-placed congressman. The Treasury or another government agency may take a stand in opposition, on behalf of a more general interest, but countervailing pressures from other organized interests are ordinarily not in evidence unless the exemption sought will confer a marked competitive advantage. If that proves to be the case, the easiest course is to broaden the exemption, to cover the competitors as well. On the other hand, if the exemption has no merit but the influence of the member sponsoring it, the committee may write the exemption so narrowly that only a single person or firm will qualify under its terms. Such was the "Louis B. Mayer Amendment" of 1951, shepherded, it is said, by Senator Taft, that was estimated to have saved the movie executive $2 million in taxes on the settlement of his contract with MGM after his retirement. Another case involved a Wisconsin mortgage guaranty company, MGIC, and gained some temporary notoriety from its connection with the Senate's Bobby Baker investigation and with the ranking minority member of the Ways and Means Committee. A knowledgeable reporter observed:

> No one denies that there are a dozen or so cases in an average year in which one-company legislation is passed by Congress because of the intense interest of a single member who is accommodated by his fellow legislators. These cases are not secret, however. It is just that no one other than those concerned generally pays any attention.[3]

A third example, the "Christmas Tree" bill of 1966 (P.L. 89-809), passed at the end of the session, helped American Motors, Harvey Aluminum, and buyers of hearses, among others, and attracted attention only because Chairman Long of the Senate Finance Committee chose to include also a later-aborted amendment allowing any income-tax payer to check off a dollar of his tax to be given by the Treasury to party campaign funds.

The same forces and methods that secure legislative dispensations commonly operate also in reverse, by logrolling, to defeat most efforts to close tax loopholes—a lesson that caused President Kennedy at an early stage to abandon his attempt to combine tax reform with tax reduction in 1963. The one major loophole-closing salvaged in the 1964 tax act, the repeal of the 4-percent dividend credit, is reported to have cost the administration a federal judgeship in Kentucky.[4] And this repeal illustrates a further lesson: in the absence of a consensus on where the burdens of taxation—or of any economic regulation, for that matter—should be laid, one man's justice is another man's loophole. The dividend credit was advocated by the Eisenhower administration as a measure of equity; it was repealed by the Kennedy administration in the name of reform. The Tax Reform Act of 1969, the only broad-scale attack on loopholes to be carried to the statute book since World War II, was a redistributive measure of the sort

---

[3] Eileen Shanahan in *The New York Times*, Nov. 11 and 18, 1963. Private laws are common in other fields; the judiciary committees, for instance, handle a great many that give relief from the stringent provisions of the immigration and naturalization laws. When they are passed as individual acts they are subject to a presidential veto; special tax relief measures, however, are usually incorporated as amendments to major tax bills that are veto-proof.

Congressman Patman on Feb. 29, 1972, headed a group of liberal Democrats who blocked, at least temporarily, House passage of a score of "members' bills" from the Ways and Means Committee, called up on the Consent Calendar. The tax reformers demanded hearings on such potential giveaways. Chairman Mills said hearings were impractical. He concluded that another procedure for handling the bills, not vulnerable to individual objections, would have to be found. *The New York Times*, March 1, 1972, p. 1.

[4] *The New York Times*, Feb. 27, 1964, p. 19.

noted above, the culmination of years of agitation, and in the end a pale version of the bill it started out to be.

The fate of particular measures in any of these categories is affected by a great many factors, of course, including chance. Nevertheless, some tentative generalizations can be pulled together at this point. Professor Lowi, in a highly original analysis based on the premise that policy types make for corresponding types of politics—more than the other way around—has argued that distributive policies entail patronage politics and logrolling tactics in a process in which the congressional committee's role is determinative. Regulatory policies are worked out by pressure group politics and bargaining tactics; again the committee's role is creative if not always decisive. For both these types the committee is characteristically stronger than the executive if a contest develops. Redistributive policies, on the other hand, stir class politics and ideological issues; they cannot be contained within the committee's control, and succeed or fail in floor outcomes that depend largely on the effectiveness of the administration's intervention. So a President, when several different types of policy are being contested, may simultaneously appear to be the voice of the people, a power broker, and a passive observer.[5]

Within this general framework the disposition of particular proposals depends a great deal on the structure of the organized economic interests involved, and on the nature of the relevant congressional committees.

Sources and Channels of Influence

Economic interests seeking to influence congressional action may follow any of several paths, all leading sooner or later to the various committees having jurisdiction in the two houses. Giant firms, major labor unions, and farm co-ops can take up their specific legislative concerns directly or by way of top officials in whatever departments or agencies are also involved. General Motors, Kodak, Chase Manhattan, International Telephone and Telegraph, the railroad brotherhoods, the teamsters and mine workers, the Farmers Union, and the like have permanent offices and informal contacts in the capital; they know their way around and do not need intermediaries; they have connections with both parties. New firms and small firms without permanent Washington representation can start with their congressmen, or possibly go to the select small business committees in either house if they can interest a member in their problems, or they can employ *ad hoc* brokers or lobbyists, usually attorneys. But for problems that are generic rather than specific, associations are the main

---

[5] Theodore Lowi, *Four Systems of Policy, Politics and Choice* (Syracuse, N.Y.: Inter-University Case Program, 1972, mimeo).

channels for aggregating and applying pressures, direct and indirect. And because the attitudes of the administration and the agencies affected by a particular proposal are apt to be critically important— especially if these are negative—the associations cultivate executive as well as legislative ties.

We can put aside here the ideological pressure groups like Common Cause that seek a better world for no mercenary reason and the status groups—veterans, AMA, NAACP—that seek a better standing for their own order, though their demands may have economic overtones. We can put aside too the advisory committees set up by departments for expert consultation. Our present concern is the organization of frankly economic interests.

Characteristically, in each of the broad areas of business, agriculture, and labor there is room for one or two nationwide, all-embracing, general-purpose organizations—the United States Chamber of Commerce, the American Farm Bureau Federation, the AFL-CIO. These speak with a mighty voice before Congress on issues that command a fair degree of consensus among their members—taxes, price supports, labor relations. But like the Republican and Democratic parties, their members are divided or indifferent on most specific matters; the corn grower's price is the poultrymen's cost; sectional producers compete in metropolitan markets; fruit growers do not care what wheat growers get, and so on. So except on a handful of major issues the voices of the peak organizations are muted or ambivalent, their wills paralyzed by internal divisions. This leaves room for a host of more specialized associations, organized around a commodity, a product or service, a craft, a distinctive method of doing business, a limited geographical area, or some combination of these. Specialization is carried as far as is needed to express an undiluted interest with a stake sufficient to warrant the costs of maintaining an organization. Most legislative proposals start as specific fragments and most of the arguments over them are urged before Congress by these specialized and inherently parochial associations. If no one else is paying attention they may get their individual desires piecemeal. More commonly they jostle each other and must work out their cross-purposes by the tactics of coalition. The proliferation of committee staffs and congressional office space since the Legislative Reorganization Act of 1946 has greatly facilitated and regularized the maintenance of lobbyists' contacts.

Policy Sectors and Committee Controls

Congressional action depends so much on committee action and the committees differ so in their attitudes and modes of operation, that economic policy-making tends to be a function of committee jurisdiction—or, conversely, it might be argued, committee modes of operation are a function of the types of policy-making categorized earlier in this chapter. Two pairs of committees—Appropriations and Government Operations—as well as the House Rules Committee and the Joint Economic Committee, all have in varying ways, nearly universal jurisdictions. The Small Business Committees likewise can roam at large wherever their clients' interests reach, though their targets are generally inconsequential. By contrast the taxing and other legislative committees—Banking and Currency, Commerce, and so on—have sectors defined by rule and precedent, designed to effect a division of labor and responsibility. As between the two houses, committee names and jurisdictions correspond roughly but not exactly. Assignment to the House Appropriations Committee excludes a member from service on any legislative committee, though not from a joint or select committee. In the Senate, by contrast, Appropriations Committee members on the majority side usually have two other major committee assignments—in 1971 including half a dozen committee chairmanships, not to speak of subcommittees—and minority members one. Moreover, a Senate rule dating back to 1922— the price of consolidation then—gives *ex officio* membership, sometimes limited, sometimes plenary, on its Appropriations Committee to three ranking members from each of seven legislative committees and to six members from Public Works. Left to themselves, committees tend to go their separate ways, but inevitably they impinge on each other. Jurisdictional rivalries are consequently endemic, reflecting contests for power and its policy stakes.

The Spending Power

By rules of the two houses adopted in conjunction with the passage of the Budget and Accounting Act of 1921, jurisdiction over all appropriations was vested in a single committee in each house; and corollary rules, imperfectly observed, forbade legislation in appropriation bills. In this way the Congress braced itself to deal with the unified budget it directed the President to submit. Since very little moves without money, it might be supposed that the appropriations committees, thus endowed, if they were so inclined and adequately informed, might control the fiscal policy of the government—allowing a discretion to the taxing committees in raising the sums appropriated. In fact, the appropriations committees wield formidable concentrations of power, but not to that extent and not in ways designed to effectuate a general economic program. They have to reckon with some practical limitations, and they also have objects in immediate view that are inconsistent with an overall concern for fiscal policy.

The limits are of several sorts. One is the sheer labor of reviewing the details of budget estimates, totaling in the neighborhood of a quarter of a trillion dollars in the unified budget for fiscal 1973—lending authority and new obligational authority (NOA) included as well as direct appropriations. So burdensome a labor forces reliance on subcommittees which ratify each other's work when the full committee assembles. For 99 percent of the items, subcommittee action is committee action and House action as well. No subcommittee can get its own work done and also take an overall view. Another limit is the independence of the taxing committees and the variable yields of the tax laws, depending on the state of the economy. The appropriations committees must take the revenue estimates as given.

A third limit consists of legislation handled by other committees that makes certain appropriations mandatory. Some of this is ground previously abandoned; some of it is territory conquered by rival committees. The appropriations committees may themselves mitigate the rigors of an annual review by making permanent indefinite appropriations (as for the interest on the public debt) or lump-sum appropriations (as for military pay) or "no-year" appropriations (as for major construction and military hardware development projects); but their hands are forced by laws that set salary scales or stipulate payments (benefits to veterans, for instance, or formula grants-in-aid to states, or farm price supports) at specified rates to all applicants who qualify. Their discretion is altogether foreclosed by laws that earmark the proceeds of specified taxes as trust funds or automatic appropriations for designated uses, such as the Highway Trust Fund, social security taxes, and the 30 percent of customs receipts allocated to the enlargement of outlets for farm products. And not only discretion but also jurisdiction is foreclosed by laws that authorize various agencies to operate with funds borrowed from the Treasury (e.g., the REA) or from the public (the TVA, Farm Credit and Home Loan Bank Board agencies), or generated by their own operations (Federal Reserve Banks, Export-Import Bank), or assessed against their clienteles (Board of Governors of the Federal Reserve System, Farm Credit Administration, FDIC). The Government Corporation Control Act requires some, but not all of these agencies to get appropriations for their administrative expenses and approval of their planned scale of operations.

APPROPRIATIONS COMMITTEES' PROCEDURES

Within these limits the appropriations committees go about their work, toward goals largely of their own devising over the half century since 1921—goals that differ somewhat for the two committees and, in the case of the House group at least, have become embodied in a set of settled doctrines for committee behavior.

The House committee and each of its dozen or so subcommittees for the bills assigned to them, aim first of all to reduce the President's total budget figure, whatever that may be ("I've never seen a budget that couldn't be cut"); and in this they succeed, with occasional exceptions, at least until the conference stage is reached. They aim next to revise the judgments expressed, and reduce the amounts allowed below the authorizations established, by the legislative committees for programs the appropriations group is not enthusiastic about. The legislative committees are thought to be "soft" on the agencies, and in need of disinterested discipline. But this is a delicate operation, involving the confidence of the whole House in the committee: the committee must listen to the importunities of other members and distribute or withhold its cuts in ways that consolidate support—it cannot rely altogether on moral exhortation and rhetoric. Next, the committee has its own sparing enthusiasms and must make room for additions to the budget estimates under these headings without pushing the total back up to the President's figure. Further, the committee aims to make it unmistakably clear to agency spokesmen that, in any conflict of purposes, they are to take their marching orders from the committee. A variety of sanctions, mild and harsh, are available to enforce this intent. Finally the committee, extrapolating the revenue-originating prerogatives of the House, aims to oblige the Senate to accept its judgments; in this it is only partly successful.

In aid of these objectives the committee and subcommittees have traditionally met only in executive session and heard only agency spokesmen and, infrequently, other members of Congress; the printed testimony is released when a bill is reported and floor action scheduled—too late and too voluminous (and unindexed) for general use in debate. In what may be a harbinger of change the House committee in 1971 commenced its budget hearings with a few open sessions. The committee maintains a small permanent staff, supplemented by investigators detailed for limited periods by the FBI and GAO for field studies to go behind the justification sheets that accompany the budget. Its prime concerns are the requests for appropriations and new obligational authority, not the "cash budget" or the national income accounts also presented in the unified budget.

The Senate Appropriations Committee, unlike its House counterpart, makes no effort to canvass all the items in the estimates. Instead, it waits until the House has acted, listens to appeals from cuts the House has made—granting some, denying others—and then makes some additions of its own. When it listens, it hears the same general kind of evidence the House had heard. In 1972 it, too, experimented with a broadened record by hearing some "public witnesses" from "diverse elements of society," as Senator Ellender put it. Its members are fewer (24 as against 55 in 1971), also senior, and frequently ex-members of the House; they choose their subcommittee assignments, according to seniority and interest, instead of being appointed by the chairman or ranking minority member; and the subcommittee compartments are not so impermeable as in the House. Because of the freedom of floor debate, legislative riders inserted in the House, and protected there by the Rules Committee from points of order or separate votes, can be more easily removed in the Senate; and conversely, riders not sponsored by the committee are more easily attached on the Senate floor. And because appropriations usually reach that floor late in the session, the floor leader's help in scheduling means a good deal to the subcommittee chairman managing a bill. So late, indeed, that a good many of them in recent years have not reached that stage until well into the fiscal year to which they apply, necessitating interim continuing resolutions to enable the administration to carry on. The foreign aid appropriations for fiscal 1972, an extreme case, did not clear the Congress until March 1972, scarcely three months before the year's end.

The final shape of appropriations is fixed in conference, where the senior subcommittee members from both houses meet and bargain. Occasionally the managers on one side or the other are adamant on some particular item, prolonging a deadlock, but the pressures for agreement are very strong. Concessions come from both sides, especially at the expense of insertions sponsored by junior members or added by floor action; some items are taken to conference only for trading purposes. The Senate managers usually succeed in making most of their changes stick, wholly or in part. As likely as not, the final bill is higher than the President's budget, unless in election years. Since the Senate considers only a few of the items, however, and is more apt to raise than reduce what it looks at, the House subcommittees have the more pervasive influence. This fact, coupled with the stability of membership on the House committee, makes it, or some of its subcommittee chairmen, in the eyes of many bureaucrats, the nearest thing to tyranny in our legislative institutions. Nevertheless, there are reasons for believing that in recent years, relatively speaking, the House Appropriations Committee has lost ground to the erosive influences that surround it.

The final shape of appropriations, of course, is not the final shape of expenditures. Alterations in the range of $2 billion or more annually are made within military appropriation accounts alone, in addition to transfers between accounts there and elsewhere that are authorized by statute. The relevant subcommittees attempt to monitor reprogramming by requiring advance notification and committee approval—given by letter—of changes from the detailed budget justifications in excess of stipulated threshold amounts.

COUNTERFORCES

One device for frustrating the appropriations committees, as already noted, is the "back-door financing" method of authorizing the spending of funds borrowed from the Treasury—public debt transactions instead of appropriations—for designated agencies or programs. This device came into wide use during the depression and again during World War II when the Reconstruction Finance Corporation, itself a borrower from the Treasury, was an alternate source of funds for emergency purposes. The Government Corporation Control Act of 1945 was a compromise attempt, reinforced by the demise of the RFC, to curb the practice, but it has survived for at least a score of agencies. The lure of a government loan is potent. It was the Penn-Central's last hope before bankruptcy in 1970; a $250 million loan guarantee enabled Lockheed to avoid that fate the next year. The Securities Investor Protection Act of 1971 gave the insurance corporation it chartered a billion-dollar line of credit to the Treasury in case of need. For a decade or more during the 1950s and 1960s senior members of the House and other "economizers" attacked "back-door financing" as an evasion of constitutional controls, but several legislative committees —notably Banking and Currency, Veterans, Foreign Relations, and Agriculture—and powerful agencies enjoying their protection, as well as many senators and "spenders" generally, had too much of a stake in preserving it. *Ad hoc* balances of power rather than constitutional principle have settled the outcome as particular cases have arisen.

Another and more unwieldy device, introduced in the 1950s and progressively extended, is the requirement of an annual authorization act, emanating from the legislative committee, prior to consideration of an appropriation bill. First employed in connection with foreign aid, it has been applied also to atomic energy, space, military construction, and procurement and research, among others—in fiscal 1968 to nearly a third of the administrative budget. Against it are the delays and duplications of testimony involved; in its behalf, Foreign Affairs Committee members argue that since appropriation bills are considered only in executive session, the open hearings of the legislative committees give the foreign-aid agency its only chance to get its case before the public. Plainly, annual authorizations increase the leverage of the legislative committees.

A third counterforce is the growing practice of presidential impoundment and transfer of appropriations previously made. Impoundment began modestly with Budget Bureau gleanings and set-asides for contingency reserves, in the name of economy. During World War II it embraced domestic road and construction projects laid aside in aid of industrial mobilization. In postwar years it was an occasional means of presidential intervention in interservice rivalries over strategic weapons. But the Revenue and Expenditure Control Acts of 1968 and 1969 directed the President to impound sums sufficient to keep total outlays within prescribed ceiling formulas; and in 1969 and 1970 President Nixon ordered impoundments of funds for social programs so as to make room for the supersonic transport, for NASA, for an enlarged merchant marine, for Safeguard ABM installations, and so on—a reordering of his predecessor's priorities. Again in January 1972 press reports disclosed that without public announcement he had impounded $200 million added by Congress the previous summer to his budget request for food stamp payments—a decision that was reconsidered after it became known.[6] Clearly, a President equipped with discretionary authority that can be used in substance much like an item veto can second-guess the Appropriations Committee, whose influence and credibility depend so heavily upon its ability to have the last word.

For present purposes, two related conclusions can be drawn from this sketch of familiar matters. First, the appropriations process has only an inadvertent bearing on the fiscal policy of the government. And second, the appropriations committees are mainly concerned with the oversight and control of executive agencies and their programs, as against other contenders for that prerogative. They are not oblivious of the economic effects of individual appropriations on particular industries and areas—far from it—but they do not employ their powers as instruments for achieving a calculated impact, in the public sector, on the national economy.

Investigating Committees

The two Government Operations Committees (successors since 1946 to the old and ineffective Committees on Expenditures in the Executive Departments) typify but by no means monopolize investigative activities in Congress. Like the appropriations committees, they have government-wide jurisdictions and the authority as standing committees to report bills. Conceivably, their investigations might sometimes take them into the realm of economic policy and lead them to make broad analyses and recommendations. In practice, however, this function has been assumed by the Joint Economic Committee, as will be noted later. The Government Operations Committees deploy their energies almost entirely through subcommittees that enable their members to ride individual hobbies—which may be broad themes or particular cases. The jurisdictional base once exploited by Senator Joseph McCarthy later served Senator McClellan in his crusade against racketeering and, on the House side, Congressman Moss in his campaign against secrecy in government. During the Nixon administration it enabled Senator Ribicoff to expose black markets in Vietnam.

The subcommittees touch economic questions sporadically, and when they do, members encounter the fact that one or another of the other legislative committees also has jurisdiction and may be jealous

---

[6] *The New York Times*, Jan. 12, 1972.

of intruders. If congressmen with prime interests in economic affairs, like Henry Reuss of Wisconsin, are placed on the Government Operations Committee, it is an accident of the processes of committee assignment that gave him an alternate base when he found himself lacking support in the Banking and Currency Committee. Government Operations does not rank high on the ladder of prestige. For both reasons the investigating committees are unlikely locations for sustained attention to broad economic policy or influence upon it.

Taxation

Congressional control over the revenue and borrowing side of fiscal policy is centralized in the Ways and Means Committee of the House and the Finance Committee of the Senate; and in practice, largely concentrated in the hands of the ten senior members—five from each body, three from the majority and two from the minority—who comprise the Joint Committee on Internal Revenue Taxation. The Joint Committee's grip in the early 1970s was neither so centralized nor so conservative as it was in the 1940s and 1950s when Harry Byrd, Sr., Walter George, and Robert Kerr dominated the Senate side; Russell Long, successor to the chairmanship there, was less predictable and sometimes given to populist moves. And on the House side, Chairman Wilbur Mills had perceptibly broadened his constituency from the days of his reluctant conversion to tax cuts in 1963 and to Medicare in 1965, on to his 1972 position as an avowed presidential aspirant, promoting a block-grant bill. Nonetheless, the House committee has retained its jurisdiction intact.

COMMITTEE CONTRAST

The full committees have an older tradition and a higher rank than the appropriations committees in prestige. The leverage of Appropriations members is matched by the opportunities of taxing committee members to be helpful to others. In the House the Democratic members of Ways and Means, each with a geographical cluster of several states as his province, also constitute the party's committee on committees. By cooptation (in consultation with the leadership), Ways and Means itself, on the Democratic side, is a self-perpetuating body. Other House Democrats who wish to improve their committee assignments are well aware of the bargaining situation this entails. This explains why, at a critical stage in floor consideration of the 1963 tax-cut bill, Chairman Mills preferred to use his Democratic committee colleagues for a canvass of the close prospective vote on the recommittal motion coming up, rather than depend on the parallel organization of the party whips, who also had zone captains assigned to keep track of Democratic voting.

Two differences in the work of the spending and revenue committees are inherent. Most appropriations are annual, so that the round of bills must be done over each year. Tax legislation, except for some excises with expiration dates needing periodic renewal, is "permanent" —i.e., fixed until changed. So the Appropriations Committee always has a dozen balls in the air at once, while Ways and Means concentrates on one major bill at a time. The public debt ceiling is the only measure the revenue committees have kept on an annual—or even shorter—basis. Another difference is that the appropriations committees are acutely sensitive to the geographical distribution of federal outlays, while the revenue committees deal with classes of taxpayers, wherever located. The whole domestic wine industry is regulated by the Alcohol Tax Act; extractive industries have their own depletion allowances; manufacturers have one set of rules for valuing inventories, department stores another; savings banks, commercial banks, and insurance companies have different allowances for tax-free reserves, and so on.

Two other contrasts between Appropriations and Ways and Means are sharply marked. Appropriations gets nearly all its work done through subcommittees; ratification of their decisions is nearly automatic.[7] Ways and Means, on the contrary, has no standing subcommittees, and when *ad hoc* subcommittees are occasionally employed they are not empowered to draft or report bills. Further, the House Appropriations Committee has a tradition of fierce independence, not only of other House committees (except Rules) but more especially of the Senate; it is forever insisting on its prerogatives as against Senate amendments. The senior members of Ways and Means, on the other hand, while they will not delegate power to their junior committee colleagues via subcommittees, cooperate with their Senate counterparts—this despite the fact that their prerogative of originating revenue bills is clearly spelled out in the Constitution, while the corresponding assertion by the Appropriations Committee is plain usurpation.

THE JOINT COMMITTEE

The mark of these differences is the Joint Committee, established in 1926 to monitor large tax refunds after an investigation of dubious cases during the regime of President Harding's commissioner of in-

---

[7] An exception to prove this rule occurred during floor action on the District of Columbia appropriation for fiscal 1972. Two northeastern liberals on the Appropriations Committee, Robert N. Giaimo (Dem., Conn.) and Silvio O. Conte (Rep., Mass.), with President Nixon's help, succeeded in restoring funds for the projected District of Columbia subway, deleted by the District subcommittee—this in defiance of the subcommittee and full committee chairmen and of the leadership on both sides of the aisle. It was a mass transit versus highway fight, with racial and class overtones. *The New York Times*, Dec. 3, 1971, p. 82.

ternal revenue. It still performs that statutory function. But like so many institutions, it has since acquired others, not mentioned in the statute nor anticipated by its founders, that dwarf its formal duty and give its members a generally firm hold on congressional tax policy. Although, as already observed, that hold is neither so concentrated nor so conservative in the 1970s as it was in the 1950s, the Joint Committee nevertheless is limited to seniors; it is bipartisan; its membership is quite stable; it employs the principal staff that works for Congress on tax bills; and its members are usually the conferees who settle differences between the two houses in the concluding stage of tax legislation.

The staff, headed since 1963 by Laurence Neal Woodworth, was the first genuinely professional and nonpartisan staff maintained by a congressional committee, antedating the Legislative Reorganization Act of 1946. Woodworth had already served nearly two decades under the tutelage of Colin Stamm, who was staff director for a quarter-century and before that, reaching back into the 1920s, had spent ten years codifying the tax laws for the committee. The staff is a team—numbering 18 in 1972—of lawyers, economists, and statisticians who work closely with Treasury staff but keep their loyalties exclusively for the senior committee members. Since the accession of Chairman Mills the Ways and Means Committee has also supported a staff, in 1971 comprising half a dozen professionals (all men) and a dozen "staff assistants" (nearly all women); and Russell Long, reversing the practice of his predecessor as Senate Finance Committee chairman, had six professionals on his committee staff, where Harry Byrd had limited himself to one. Even so, junior committee members, not on the Joint Committee, must generally depend on their own resources, or look outside, for technical help. The tax laws are too complicated, and the consequences of changes too uncertain and potentially far-reaching, for anyone to intervene effectively without skilled help.

TAX REVISIONS

In this general setting, tax revisions—since the abrupt Korean War increase in 1950—have come about slowly, with the attention of nearly all participants preoccupied for the most part with the details of particular provisions. The Joint Committee staff are technicians, not policy analysts or planners. They stay with the process from the beginning stage of months of homework through House, Senate, and conference action. They are concerned with the complexities of drafting and calculations of the revenue consequences of alternative figures and phrasings. The senior committee members utilize their positions and skills to distribute the burdens and benefits of tax provisions as they think best, and to keep others from imposing different views. To do this they must win votes or forestall them from being taken. Much of their time therefore must be occupied in assessing the opposition to particular provisions, finding acceptable alternatives, and assembling and mustering the shifting coalitions that produce majorities at the successive stages when votes are needed. This does not leave much time, if they had the inclination, for escape from the narrow concerns of organized interests in order to entertain questions about the use of the taxing power to attain broad social goals. A case in point, too intricate for recital here, is the handling of the issue of continued exemption for the interest on municipal bonds, particularly so-called industrial development bonds—issued by municipalities to subsidize the location of new plants in their jurisdictions but backed only by the guarantees of the beneficiary firms—during the tax reform drive in 1968. Neither Wilbur Mills nor Russell Long, coming from states where such bond issues were actively used, would touch the issue. Ultimately a watered-down Ribicoff amendment (Dem., Conn., sixth in Finance Committee seniority), limiting the exemption to issues of no more than $1 million, was carried by the joint lobbying efforts of an unlikely combination: Treasury, Investment Bankers Association, National Association of Real Estate Boards, AFL-CIO (fighting southern relocations of northern industries), and the National Association of Counties.[8]

Experience in the era of fiscal conservatism in the 1950s, and again in connection with the Revenue and Expenditure Control Acts of 1968 and 1969, teaches that it is possible to concentrate power in Congress in the tax field when ideological consensus pervades the senior ranks of the revenue committees. This is not, however, the kind of concentration that champions of party responsibility advocate. As Professor Huitt observed a decade ago in an incisive study for the Commission on Money and Credit:

> There is almost no way that the nation's voters could register "no confidence" in the tax policies of a handful of senior congressmen of both parties and absolutely no way they could turn them out so long as Congress continues to work as it has in this century.[9]

It does not follow that a similar concentration could be put together and maintained over other fields, as has often been suggested—say, over all appropriations, let alone over expenditures and revenues combined—or that, if feasible, it would long be politically tolerable, the legendary reputation of Wilbur Mills notwithstanding.

Social Security legislation is a special case. Because taxes are in-

[8] P.L. 90-364, the Revenue and Expenditure Control Act of 1968. See *Congress and the Nation: 1965–1968,* II, pp. 177–78 (Washington, D.C.: Congressional Quarterly, 1969).

[9] Ralph K. Huitt, "Congressional Organization and Operations in the Field of Money and Credit," in *Fiscal and Debt Management Policies* (Englewood Cliffs, N.J.: Prentice-Hall, 1963), p. 456.

volved it lies in the jurisdiction of the revenue committees, not those
that handle other labor and welfare matters. And because the forms
of an autonomous trust fund are observed, that jurisdiction extends
to the scale, scope, and other features of the benefit payments as well.
The Ways and Means Committee, on conservative principles, made a
virtue of keeping the trust fund in surplus—an easy matter during the
first generation, when nearly all covered workers paid in and relatively
few were as yet eligible to draw out. During the 1950s the taxing committees, facing pressures from employers and beneficiaries in direct
opposition, were on the defensive against significant enlargements of
the benefits. Ideological controversies were more prominent and more
clearly polarized than the obscure moralities of income tax amendments
and selective sales taxes. By the 1970s, with the voting strength of the
beneficiaries steadily growing and inflation a special hardship for
them, the committees had settled into the congenial practice of raising
the benefits and lowering the eligibility requirements in even-num-
bered years, while coupling them to subsequent increases in the trust
fund's take, either by turning up another notch in the rate screw or
by raising the wage ceiling below which the tax is applied. The conservative consensus on the Joint Committee was more secure when it
did not need to be explicit.

Management of the Public Debt

The management of the public debt—the timing and terms of
borrowing and refunding, and so on—has been confided to the Treasury by broadly phrased delegations of authority and permanent indefinite appropriations of whatever is needed to pay interest and
principal when due. A statutory limit on the total debt outstanding
at any one time—first fixed in the Liberty Loan Acts of World War I—
however, requires frequent revision as the debt mounts upward. In
form the amendment permits a stipulated "temporary" excess for a
limited period, usually a year or less, over a "permanent" ceiling that
was exceeded some time ago. It has been common practice for the
Ways and Means Committee to make a "cliff-hanger" of this amendment, getting it to the President for signature only on the last day of
the previous extension.

The original rationales for this ritual—that, as in the case of a
private corporation, unlimited and large-scale borrowing might cast
doubt on the public credit; or, that the prospect of exhausting the
debt allowance might somehow put pressure on the Treasury to make
good the failure of the appropriations committees to avoid a deficit
by reducing outlays—have long since lost credibility. Economists and
study groups like the Commission on Money and Credit (1961) have

repeatedly urged the outright repeal of any apparently fixed limit: the debt is the inevitable accumulation of an excess of deficits over surpluses, with some allowance for Treasury cash balances. Yet the limit remains, and not just from inertia. Evidently, the ritual has a latent function. Realistically, it appears that the expiration date gives the taxing committees what the budget gives the appropriations committees, an automatic occasion for summoning high Treasury officials to listen politely to some public badgering and to respond to some informal exertions of leverage. The confrontation with a deadline creates a bargaining situation the taxing committees are unlikely to forego. With annual deficits on the order of $30 billion, however, such as occurred in 1971, calculated in the terminology of the unified budget, the cry of "wolf" seems more mockery than menace.

Legislative Committees

Apart from the taxing, spending and government operations committees, subject-matter jurisdiction is parcelled out among fourteen other standing committees in the Senate and eighteen in the House. All but four or five of these on each side have substantial segments of the economy within their province; none have more than segments. Space precludes any comprehensive review of their work, but some generalizations more or less applicable to all of them are in order, as are some examples.

First, they tend to go their autonomous ways, and to multiply these ways by setting up subcommittees that, once established, tend to develop their own permanence and autonomy. Jurisdictional alternatives and rivalries accordingly are frequent; on balance this is probably wholesome. Significant issues may be agitated under surprising auspices. For instance, Senate hearings in 1971 that called OMB officials (and inferentially President Nixon) on the carpet for impounding appropriated funds, and thereby thwarting supposed congressional intentions, were conducted not by the Appropriations or Government Operations Committees but by a Judiciary Subcommittee on the Separation of Powers. A good many questions of economic policy, that is to say, have as many partial answers as there are committees and subcommittees participating. If it be asked, say, what congressional policy governs the granting and use of patents on inventions developed by federal contractors in the course of fulfilling their contracts, or the determination of the federal share of outlays supported by grants-in-aid, or the terms for lending federal funds, across-the-board canvasses of a great many distinct committee actions would need to be compiled before an answer could be attempted. The House and Senate leadership, moreover, are not program-makers for the committees. They may prod a committee chairman for a bill that can pass, and help to see that it does; the contents of the bill, within some limits, are up to the committee.

Second, as the saying goes, "everything depends on the chairman," and the caliber of staff he assembles. A change in chairmanship is seldom so dramatic as the one that occurred when Adam Clayton Powell (Dem., N.Y.), first Negro to be elected to Congress in the twentieth century, succeeded Graham Barden (Dem., N. Car.) as the head of the House Education and Labor Committee in 1961, but a substantial reorientation of committee activity is to be expected from any change in leadership. To take purely hypothetical illustrations, a change in party control in the Senate after the 1970 elections would have made Senator Tower of Texas chairman of the Banking, Housing and Urban Affairs Committee in place of John J. Sparkman, and Wallace F. Bennett of Utah chairman of Finance in place of Russell Long.

Third, the extent of discretion already conveyed to administrative agencies by past legislation shapes the room left for committee activity. The Federal Reserve Act, for instance, launched an agency that has become self-sufficient in authority and more so in funds; it needs little from Congress but to be let alone; the banking committees are outsiders looking in. The same is true of the Farm Credit Administration's complex of banks, which have repaid their federal grubstakes, *vis-à-vis* the agriculture committees. The Interstate Commerce Commission has a broad statute, a tradition of independence, an unwieldy top structure with eleven commissioners, and an unmanageable case load. It needs annual appropriations for administrative expenses, but the legislative committees leave it alone, too, lest they get caught in a thicket of trucking rivalries. On the other hand, where regulation is combined with subsidies, as with public lands, public works, defense installations and development contracts, education, welfare, housing, merchant marine, air transport and many other fields, the legislative committees are active intervenors.

Fourth, the legislative committees tend to attract members with a special interest—usually promotional, but sometimes antagonistic—in some part of their jurisdiction, though this is not the only consideration in committee assignments. This shows up most vividly on the agriculture committees, where farm constituencies have been the nearly universal rule—Shirley Chisholm, the black congresswoman from Brooklyn, when she drew Agriculture as her first assignment in 1969, took the risk of protesting publicly and demanding a transfer rather than accept what to her was an exile to Siberia. The banking, interior, and merchant marine committees display the same affinity for members with constituency interests closely tied to their committee work. Notwithstanding the codes of ethical conduct adopted by both houses in 1968, most actions by members are matters for their individual consciences as elected legislators—subject to review upon complaint lodged with the standing Committee on Standards of Official Conduct in the House or the Select Committee on Standards and Conduct in the Senate—so a wide range of behavior, from the near scandalous to the austere, may be found in the same committee.

BANKING COMMITTEES

These generalizations can all be illustrated in the two banking committees. Their names and jurisdictions are extensive but not exactly co-extensive. The Senate Committee on Banking, Housing and Urban Affairs controls securities legislation but not the international lending agencies, which are under Foreign Relations; in the House, the former belongs to Interstate and Foreign Commerce, the latter to Banking and Currency. Both have an active housing subcommittee to handle the omnibus housing bill, which has become a popular annual feature, somewhat after the model of public works. The Senate committee had a period of broad activity on many fronts when Fulbright headed it (he took with him the international lending agencies, which Vandenberg had not wanted, when he moved to Foreign Relations), while his successors, Willis Robertson (Dem., Va.) until 1967, and thereafter John J. Sparkman (Dem., Ala.), have pursued inconspicuous courses— the latter was more active earlier, as chairman of the Housing subcommittee. The House committee had an unaggressive era in the regime of Brent Spence (Dem., Tenn.); Wright Patman (Dem., Tex.), an inheritor of the Populist tradition, has made the committee a gadfly of large eastern financial institutions, bank holding companies, supposedly philanthropic foundations, the Penn-Central railroad, and especially during William McChesney Martin's long tenure as chairman, the Federal Reserve System—a case of pursuing an interest in order to reform it, rather than to profit from it. By 1972, after eighteen years' service, fourth-ranking Henry Reuss (Dem., Wis.) had become the outstanding intellectual and moral figure on the committee. By contrast, five years earlier a twenty-year veteran on the committee, Abraham Multer (Dem., N.Y.), chose to retire in retreat to a Brooklyn judgeship after his connections with savings and loan institutions became a campaign issue in his district. Senator Robertson's demise at about the same time was also attributable at least in part to charges of subservience to banking interests.

Little formal collaboration between the two committees is in evidence, beyond the necessities of conferring on legislation pending between the two houses. The sharp divisions, however, are within the committees rather than between them. Staff relations are proper but not close; the House committee staff, except for its minority member, turned over almost completely in 1963; its general counsel left to become legislative counsel to the Federal Reserve.

Staff contacts with downtown agencies in the committees' realms are maintained with some, like the Department of Housing and Urban Development, much more than others, such as the Export-Import Bank. In part, staff assistants are alert to cues from members, especially senior members, as to agencies and topics they want watched, or are indifferent to. In part, some agencies are more in the limelight.

But it does not follow that because a controversial situation develops, the committees will necessarily plunge in to resolve it. In a textbook example in 1963 the comptroller of the currency, reversing previous interpretations of the apparently flat prohibition in the Banking Act of 1935, ruled that national banks could underwrite municipal revenue bond offerings. The Federal Reserve protested publicly. Commercial bankers came to the House committee, pressing a bill that would have confirmed the comptroller's interpretation and extended it to state-chartered banks as well. The investment bankers' association appeared in opposition to this. Facing the unlikely line-up that ranged Chairman Patman alongside Chairman Martin and the investment bankers against the comptroller and state banks, the committee looked for an out. Instead of acting on the bill it suggested that an official opinion of the attorney general be secured, construing the 1935 law—an opinion it was not altogether clear the incumbent comptroller would accept as binding, though the Federal Reserve, in an even more independent position, promised to do so.

Similarly, the committee took no action on several other bills, implementing recommendations made by the Commission on Money and Credit in 1961 or by the President's interdepartmental Committee on Financial Institutions in 1963. These would have realigned bank supervisory jurisdictions and relaxed restrictions on competitive practices among various types of banks. It took no action either on recommendations of the comptroller's Advisory Committee on Banking, a clientele group he sponsored as an offset to the ABA and the IBA, to advance the competitive position of national banks. A decade later the situation was much the same. President Nixon's Commission on Financial Structure and Regulation (the so-called Hunt Commission) reported late in 1971 with scores of detailed recommendations affecting interest rate ceilings, allowable functions of the main types of depository institutions, chartering, branching, reserve requirements, taxation, deposit insurance, pension funds, and so on. Pension funds had already generated a wider concern from other quarters and in 1972 seemed headed for major regulatory legislation, not necessarily through the banking committees. For the rest there was little prospect of significant action. In this regulatory arena, where changes in the competitive *status quo* are regarded all around as a zero-sum game, the normal inclination of disinterested committee members is to listen but not act, while the interested ones thrust and parry to a draw. Ideological splits prevent the kind of cohesion the Appropriations Committee has developed, and the Ways and Means Committee's formula for concentrating power requires more muscle to begin with than the banking committees possess.

The House committee is willing to study what it will not act on. On the fiftieth anniversary of the Federal Reserve Act it commissioned a series of studies and summoned all the Reserve Board members and Reserve Bank presidents in turn to extended hearings and grillings. But it did not back Chairman Patman's bills to alter Federal Reserve structure. More recently it has delved into topics involving the international position of the dollar; but with one or two exceptions committee members are out of their depth in these waters.

FUNCTIONAL REPRESENTATION

Two House committees with jurisdiction over far-reaching questions of economic policy deserve note not so much for what they do as because in different ways, their bases of composition exhibit in an unusual degree the forces of functional representation rather than the more usual geographic dispersion. These are Education and Labor, and Agriculture.

The Education and Labor Committee ever since World War II has been the arena for contesting issues—labor-management relations, public school aid and its corollaries, help for parochial schools, and racial desegregation and busing—animated by many of the most burning emotions in American politics. Consequently, as a student of the subject put it, "this assignment is no place for a neutral when there are so many belligerents around." [10] On this ground George McGovern, a South Dakota Democrat and later a senator, but a history professor and Ph.D. when he was elected to congress in 1957, was given a transfer from Education and Labor to Agriculture after it developed that school aid had become a major campaign issue in his farm district. Any position he took in his previous committee only hurt him at home. For two decades the Democrats put on this committee some anti-union Southerners, all Protestants, and more northern city representatives with strong union support, often Catholics; while the Republicans named members who could safely survive union opposition. The ensuing battles between rival forces resulted usually in a standoff and lengthy periods of stalemate within the committee until the breakthrough on civil rights and school aid in 1964 and 1965, under pressures LBJ mobilized. Since then the pattern has shifted decisively.

[10] Nicholas A. Masters, "House Committee Assignments," *American Political Science Review,* 55 (June 1961), p. 354.

In 1972, of 22 Democrats on the majority side, Chairman Carl D. Perkins and two others were from the border states of Kentucky and Missouri; all the rest were from northern or Pacific coast (including Hawaii) constituencies. The sole committee member from south of the Mason-Dixon line was Earl B. Ruth of North Carolina, a Republican and former athletic coach. But the ideological spectrum spanned the range from John M. Ashbrook (Rep., Ohio) and Louise Day Hicks (Dem., Mass.) on the right, to such union stalwarts as Frank Thompson (Dem., N.J.) and John Brademas (Dem., Ind.) and minority crusaders Shirley Chisholm (Dem., N.Y.) and Herman Badillo (Dem., N.Y.).

The Agriculture Committee is responsible for programs entailing budget expenditures in the range of $8 to $10 billion annually in the years 1970 to 1972, distributed according to the political strength of the claimants as well as to need. Compromising the claims has become increasingly complex and difficult in recent years, both because of divided counsels from farm interests, which tend to paralyze the committees, and because of a rising tide of urban and suburban consumer sentiment in the House membership, in the face of higher food prices, which threatens trouble for the committee when its bills reach the floor. The Agriculture Act of 1970, an omnibus measure, was sixteen months in the works. It was delayed a month at the end when, after the House had passed the conference report, Senator Robert Byrd (Dem., W.Va.), the assistant whip, prevented the House messenger from entering the Senate chamber to deliver it to the presiding officer's desk—in order, so Republicans charged, to save fifteen Democratic senators from having to vote on it before election day.

Agriculture Committee seats, all but one, are a monopoly of members from farm areas and are distributed with attention to commodity coverage as well as geographic dispersion. Six of the committee's ten subcommittees in 1972 had a commodity focus: (1) cotton; (2) dairy and poultry; (3) forests; (4) livestock and grains; (5) oilseeds and rice; and (6) tobacco. Commodities have partisan as well as sectional affiliations: wheat, corn, livestock (except in Texas), and dairy products are mostly Republican; while cotton, rice, and tobacco (and peanuts when they were on the support list) are mostly Democratic. Sugar is a separate and complex story, involving foreign quotas as well as Democrat cane and Republican beets; it has a separate bill, unchanged in principle since 1934 and renewed in 1971 for four more years—a bill handled in the Senate by the Finance Committee.

The committee's traditional procedure, still observable in the tortuous course of the 1970 act, operates on logrolling principles—letting each subcommittee write its own ticket in a succession of titles in an omnibus bill, in order to get something the full committee can report; and modifying or abandoning the more vulnerable of these on the floor, in order to get something the House will pass; and then huddling in conference with the secretary of agriculture, White House aides and farm organization leaders, in order to get something the President will sign. Increasing emphasis on programs for feeding the hungry, such as the food stamp plan, school lunches and Food for Peace—and not just dumping surpluses—has been part of the price for continued commodity price supports from urban and suburban members.

The single non-farm seat on the committee has existed at least since the 1950s; it has had a bizarre history and a rapid succession of occupants—no more than two terms per incumbent. For reasons somewhat obscure—perhaps as a sop to consumer sentiment, perhaps as a form of freshman hazing, perhaps as a deterrent demonstration of the power of the Ways and Means Democrats to reduce a deviant to impotence if they are so minded—the seat has regularly been assigned to a Democrat from New York City or its environs. Early recipients of this honor, a regular organization man from Brooklyn for instance, were docile and pleaded good behavior as a ground for transfer at the first opportunity. Latterly, they have not been so tame. Joseph Y. Resnick, a wealthy manufacturer from Ellenville in the Catskills, used his chairmanship of the Subcommittee on Rural Development in 1967 to hold hearings and denounce the American Farm Bureau Federation as a network of big insurance companies, with half its members not farmers; this resulted in a 27-1 vote by the full committee, "disassociating" themselves from his charges. In 1969 Shirley Chisholm, as already noted, got herself excused in disdain. In 1970 Allard K. Lowenstein, of Nassau, dissented publicly when the committee reported its omnibus bill, objecting that the fifty-thousand-dollars ceiling on farm support payments to any one farmer was too high. The incumbent in 1972 was John G. Dow of Newburgh, a corporation systems analyst in his third term.

Nonlegislative Committees

RULES COMMITTEE

The Rules Committee commands a reviewing position over all legislative business headed for floor action, but not, supposedly, an initiative of its own. Since its enlargement in 1961 and the demise of its legendary chairman Howard Smith in 1967, it has been generally cooperative with the leadership in its scheduling role. But an isolated incident early in 1972 was a reminder of its power of selective intervention in economic policy when its chairman is alert and has the votes.

The occasion was the longshoremen's strike, following the exhaustion of Taft-Hartley remedies, that shut down the docks east, west, and Gulf; and the imminence of the traditional Lincoln's Day recess. President Nixon had submitted and asked for immediate action on an *ad hoc* bill peremptorily requiring an end to the strike, with compulsory arbitration; and Senate approval was assured. But the House Committee on Education and Labor, in a temporizing mood, refused to approve this course, and formulated a milder bill, more acceptable to the spokesmen for organized labor, which it had not yet reported. In these circumstances the Rules Committee brought to the floor a resolution calling for an immediate vote on the administration bill, forbidding the offering of the House committee's bill as a substitute, and making in order another vote to accept instead the Senate bill (similar to the administration's) forthwith, so as to avoid a conference and get that bill directly to the President. Chairman Colmer (Dem., Miss.), of the Rules Committee, aged 81, who had previously announced his own intention to retire at the end of the session, had correctly gauged rank-and-file sentiment in the House as desirous of a vote before the recess. His resolution prevailed, against the opposition of the Speaker and most committee chairmen. It was a coup.

A formal way for Congress to transcend the jurisdictional boundaries it has set for its standing committees, in order to focus concern on a problem that cuts across them, is to establish a study committee. Without authority to report bills, it avoids the jealousy a claim-jumper would arouse. It can study, hold hearings, issue reports, and agitate. Its members also sit on legislative committees; if they are persuasive they may obtain results there.

SMALL BUSINESS COMMITTEES

Two examples of this approach are the Select Committees to Study the Problems of Small Business, one in each house, created in 1940 and made permanent in 1950. They undertake to help small firms get attention from government agencies, get credit when it would otherwise be unobtainable, get government contracts or subcontracts, and so on. They are a convenience to other members, who can refer constituents to them as a complaint bureau. As official lobbyists, so to speak, for a frankly labeled bias and clientele, they give strength and legitimacy to what might otherwise be dismissed impatiently as a nuisance.

The Senate committee has owed much to the energy of Senator Sparkman (Dem., Ala.), its chairman for many years and in 1972 still a member, though he had relinquished the chairmanship to Alan Bible (Dem., Nev.). The House committee also had an outspoken champion in its long-time chairman, Wright Patman, still a member in 1972 though he had handed over the lead to Joe L. Evins (Dem., Tenn.). Working with the other committees, they have sponsored a surprising amount of legislation that has been enacted, including the establishment of the Small Business Administration, chartering of Small Business Investment Corporations, tax concessions, and set-asides of procurement orders. Patman also used the House committee as a base and outlet for voluminous studies of chain banking, and of the operations of tax-exempt foundations, both later the subject of legislative restrictions. It may be no accident that the committees have had their greatest successes with projects in the legislative province of the banking committees since Sparkman moved up the ladder to the chairmanship of that committee on the Senate side, as Patman did likewise in the House.

The small business committees demonstrate an effective method of institutionalizing a bias, a needed reminder and sponsor of a neglected interest. It is their virtue that no one mistakes them for more than that.

THE JOINT ECONOMIC COMMITTEE

A very different sort of study group is the Joint Economic Committee, the nearest thing to a central economic analysis unit that Congress possesses. As seen in the early 1960s:

> In many ways the Joint Economic Committee is the most exciting contemporary invention of Congress. Established originally to react to the annual Economic Report of the President, it roves at will over the economic spectrum, studying broadly or intensively any problem which attracts the interest of Committee or congressional leadership. The Joint Economic Committee is a congressional anomaly. It is a planning and theory group in a culture fiercely devoted to the short run and the practical. It is committed to the panoramic view in a system which stresses jurisdictional lines. It signifies recognition that economic problems are related, by a body which deals with them piecemeal.[11]

This appraisal perhaps required some qualification in the early 1970s as the committee addressed some very practical problems with evident political ramifications, such as the economic justification of the supersonic transport program; but it conveyed the essential distinction between the JEC and other congressional committees.

The JEC in 1972 comprised twenty members who had requested the assignment, divided six and four, majority and minority, from each house. The chairmanship alternates biennially—from 1955 on, between Senator Paul Douglas (Dem., Ill.) and Congressman Patman, until the former's enforced retirement in 1967, when Senator Proxmire (Dem., Wis.) took his place. None of these was in the inner leadership circle of his chamber—on the contrary—but the group has had muscle as well as brains: on the Senate side in 1972, two from Appropriations, three from Finance, four each from Foreign Relations and Government Operations, two each from Banking and from Agriculture, with

[11] Huitt, *op. cit.*, p. 477.

representation also from Armed Services, Labor, Commerce and Public Works; on the House side, the majority leader, two from Ways and Means and one from Rules, and five from Banking and Currency. Noticeably absent from this array, after an early nominal trial, is any representation from House Appropriations.

The JEC publishes an annual report in the spring, commenting on the President's Economic Report. It publishes the monthly *Economic Indicators* prepared by the Council of Economic Advisers, a compendium of current statistical series without commentary. And it makes and publishes studies of its own selection. Senator Douglas inaugurated a style for some of these, resembling an academic seminar, that was novel to Congress and designed not only to enlist first-rate professional advice but also to overcome two of the notorious frustrations of congressional hearings—the tendency of senior members to monopolize the time for questions and the tendency of witnesses with axes to grind to contradict each other without ever meeting on the issues. For such studies the JEC commissioned papers and monographs from outside experts, and sometimes also arranged for panel discussions with the authors, as well as staff analyses. The staff is stable, and on easy terms of professional familiarity with experts in the CEA, Treasury, Federal Reserve, and other agencies. One side effect has been to give economists an official forum and an elevated degree of professional recognition. Many JEC publications have sold in the hundreds of thousands of copies and have found their way into college course reading requirements. The committee's work therefore has a double effect, one direct, as the members go about their other business in Congress, and the other indirect, as the outside impact of their publications is reflected back on other members. Unquestionably, the committee has been a notable educational influence and has contributed to a marked increase in the level of sophistication since 1947 in public debate on economic policy.

If the JEC has helped change the climate of thinking, it would be something else again to argue that it has been specifically responsible for any identifiable policy change. A study group is not an action group, let alone a policy-making group. Before 1955 its annual reports were unanimous, or nearly so; since then, majority and minority reports, strictly along partisan lines, have been the rule. These form probably the least influential part of the committee's output. On the other hand, Senator Proxmire had a leading part in the cancellation of the supersonic transport program in 1971. It is perhaps significant that the committee's work has attracted the greatest attention in periods when Democrats controlled the Congress and Republicans the White House. When the same party controls both, there is less room—and less incentive—for developing, from a congressional committee base, major alternatives in policy to those espoused by the administration in office.

The Quest for Coordination

At this point the problems of Congress and economic policy merge into the larger problems of the place of Congress in the general scheme of things. We confront dilemmas not apparently soluble without larger readjustments.

Congress acts on economic matters nearly always in piecemeal fashion, from limited perspectives. The committee system permits both technical expertise and political appraisals to be brought to bear on these actions, the appraisals reflecting the dominant organization of power at the particular time and place. Most of the time this is perhaps as much as can be asked. It is congenial to regulatory and distributive types of actions, involving pressure groups and patronage principles and moving incrementally. The economy is huge and complex, and most people prefer changes in small doses at a time.

Nevertheless, though the economy is huge and complex, it is not beyond the reach of human purpose in furtherance of macro-policies of a redistributive character that rouse class politics. Economic understanding has advanced sufficiently so that its larger movements, and forces behind them, can be apprehended, if not always with a desirable degree of clarity or precision. Even in the novel conditions of the early 1970s, with simultaneous inflation and unemployment, economic goals were formulated and programs to secure them developed. Potent instruments are available to the government to further such goals, or alternatives to replace them. Once their potentialities begin to be appreciated, it is idle to say that the instruments should be put away, and it is better that they be used consciously than blindly. Even small moves need the guidance of larger perspectives. Yet these perspectives are missing in the ordinary conduct of congressional business.

The experience of the Joint Economic Committee testifies that it is possible to organize a unit in Congress that can open up national perspectives on the economy and avail itself of the most advanced techniques of economic analysis to make prescriptions. But it is not conceivable that the JEC could acquire the power to enact them; it is a teacher, not a governor.

The experience of the Joint Committee on Internal Revenue Taxation, and of the Ways and Means Committee in 1968 and 1969, testifies that it is possible to organize a unit in Congress sufficiently powerful to control the use of the taxing power. But it is not conceivable that the taxing committees, in doing so, will apply more than fragments of JEC prescriptions, or adopt its perspectives unless rhetorically. Except for atomic energy, it is doubtful that any other subject-matter field lends itself to as much concentration of power across the two houses at the committee level as does taxation.

The experience of the leadership in both chambers testifies that power over procedure will bear no corresponding responsibility for the substantive content of a program. And precedents from bygone days when the leadership could control the substance of legislation do not encourage efforts to return to them.

Three general conclusions emerge. First, at any given time those who control the proceedings in any segment of congressional machinery can be expected to use their power to impose their own terms. Power is not neutral.

Second, the basic problem is not in the organization of Congress as it acts on economic policy, important as structure is. A growing organization can confer power, but a growing power can also create organization. It would be unrealistic to expect that creating new committees on economic policy would bring about material changes unless the forces that control present arrangements were somehow realigned. This could come about imperceptibly through education; gradually through shifts in the electoral base such as are brought about by demographic movements, redistricting, and lowering the voting age; and inadvertently in consequence of changed habits of the participants.

Third, experience with the Budget and Accounting Act and the Employment Act suggests that the way to influence the Congress to view the economy in a broader perspective is to impose on the President a duty to do so first, and in a public stand that requires a response. A focal point for a coordinated approach is to be found in the White House, or nowhere. If one is articulated there, in connection with action programs that Congress cannot disregard after he has committed himself, wider influences will be released, as became evident after President Nixon's economic turnaround in August 1971. In a political system as loose of access as ours, Congress is a poor place to assemble sufficient force for a coordinating, i.e., a governing initiative; but it cannot avoid being a reactor, or ignore the perspective in which the initiative is publicly presented.

Holbert N. Carroll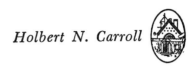

7

The Congress and
National Security Policy

In the spring of 1972, the Senate, by a vote of 68 to 16, sent off the War Powers Bill to an uncertain fate in the politics of House-Senate relations.[1] In essence, for the first time in history, the Senate sought to place comprehensive limits on the President in committing the nation's armed forces to hostilities abroad. While providing him flexibility to meet contingencies, the bill required specific congressional approval for the use of military forces beyond 30 days.

To a sponsor, the bill was "one of the most important pieces of legislation in the national security field that has come before the Senate in this century." [2] To another sponsor, the head of the Armed Services Committee, Senator Stennis—whose credentials in supporting military and presidential leadership in foreign-military affairs were impeccable—the bill was a necessary measure "to try to bring back into focus the responsibilities of Congress." [3] In Senator Ervin's view, the measure undertook "to usurp and exercise, in part or in whole, the power of the President to perform his constitutional duty to defend the nation against invasion." [4] To the secretary of state, the bill was "unconstitutional and unwise," an attempt by legislation "to alter our historic constitutional system." [5] He voiced no objections to a House-

---

HOLBERT N. CARROLL *is professor of political science at the University of Pittsburgh. Among his publications is* The House of Representatives and Foreign Affairs.

[1] S. 2956, 92–1.
[2] Senator Javits, *Congressional Record,* 118 (March 29, 1972, daily ed.), p. S 5153.
[3] *Ibid.,* April 11, 1972, p. S 5897.
[4] *Ibid.*
[5] Secretary Rogers in a letter to Senator Allott, *ibid.,* March 29, 1972, p. S 5186.

approved bill which called for reporting by the President to Congress
on the use of force abroad.[6]

Some perfecting amendments were accepted. A move to send the
bill—which had been incubating for almost two years, with hearings,
reports, and studies covering history, law, and politics over two centuries—to the Judiciary Committee for further study was refused. The
Senate quickly abjured an opportunity to declare war on North Vietnam. All of the major Republican leaders voted for the bill which
their President opposed.

Within a few days, in the midst of a massive step-up of North Viet-
namese military activity in South Vietnam and renewed American
bombing of the North, the Senate Foreign Relations Committee voted
to sponsor an amendment to a bill to cut off all money for military
activities in Vietnam at the year's end, provided the North released
American war prisoners.[7] In a rare move, the House Democratic caucus
voted 144–58 to instruct the Foreign Affairs Committee to report a
bill within 30 days to accomplish the same objectives.[8]

These events may survive only as decorative footnotes in future
scholarly accounts. They illustrate the recent upsurge in Congress for
a more influential voice in foreign-military affairs as well as phenomena reaching back to 1789.

The stirrings in Congress to assert more influence date from the mid-
1960s. The unrest mainly has focused in the Senate. Distress over the
war in Southeast Asia was the principal catalyst, but the sources were
more complex. The unrest coincided with the end of the post-World
War II era and abatement of the Cold War and containment. It coincided with the growing belief that executive-legislative balances had
become distorted, with a search for a redefinition of the nation's vital
interests in a vastly changed world, and with the imperatives of rear-
ranging warped domestic priorities.

Congressional questioning and activity during this recent period
were expressed in diverse ways. Defense budgets were scrutinized more
thoroughly than for decades. Congressional challenges compelled the
President to retreat from proposals for extensive deployment of anti-
ballistic missiles. For the first time in its history, the Congress repealed
an area resolution, the Tonkin Gulf Resolution of 1964. For months,
the Senate was bogged down on challenges to the draft, questions about
the armed forces in Cambodia, Laos, Vietnam, and Europe, on commitments overseas, and arms sales. On three occasions in 1971, the
Senate voted withdrawal schemes for Vietnam and rejected, for the
first time in a quarter century, the bill to authorize military and economic aid abroad. The foreign aid measure nevertheless was revived,

[6] H. J. Res. 1, 92–1.
[7] *The New York Times*, April 18, 1972, p. 1.
[8] *Ibid.*, April 21, 1972, p. 1.

with about as many implied commitments as the Senate professed to be questioning.

These are only a few examples of the congressional assertiveness of recent years. They excite attention. It may be that a new era in congressional influence has dawned since the mid-1960s. Yet, one must turn to the surest guide for perspective on the present. This is the past. Two lessons of history, rooted in constitutional practices, provide some insight.

One is the phenomenon of cycles. Congressional assertiveness is not new. Congressional policy preferences have occasionally been dominant in the past. Congressional agitation drove a reluctant President into a war with Spain in 1898, negated presidential efforts to participate cooperatively with other nations in the League of Nations to curb aggression and promote world order after World War I, and confined the President in the 1930s to a quasi-neutral position in contests between aggressors and victims. From this perspective, the recent assertiveness may, when historians appraise it, emerge as another example of a cycle, a swing of the pendulum, with the new equilibrium never quite the same as before.

The other lesson from history is that the way the Constitution distributes power assures tension in foreign-military matters. The formal allotment of powers between the President and the Congress remains the same as when the Constitution was adopted. They are divided and shared. The allotment compels, and tradition and practice support, congressional participation in defining both the domestic and external purposes of the nation and in achieving the goal of national security always fervently shared by the President and the Congress. Presidential dominance in conducting the external relations of the nation and congressional preoccupation with the domestic tasks of perfecting the Union have represented a rough accommodation to the tensions of the system. National security policy was the sum of their joint and separate efforts. Like freedom or justice, it was a general goal. Only occasionally in the century and a half before World War II did national security matters demand concentrated attention.

Radical changes in the requirements of national security have spurred fresh adjustments to the divided and shared power arrangements of a political system now inextricably drawn into the fantastically complex affairs of every part of the world. New tensions in the respective roles and powers of the executive and legislative branches have been the inevitable result. Imbalances have developed as a consequence of sins of omission and commission by both the President and Congress.

When the equilibrium is upset, the tendency of the President and his associates and of the Congress is to turn to the arguments of lawyers. In essence, the accommodations to the tensions are political. Senator

Stennis in the war powers debate, in which most participants invoked legal arguments, struck the right note. "I do not think . . . that this is primarily a legal question. I think it is a policy or a political question, and I use the term 'political' in the very highest sense." [9]

Politics and policy, rather than legal intricacies, inform the account which follows. Contests over institutional prerogatives and policy directions explain best the congressional roles in foreign affairs. Attention first will be directed to organizational and other characteristics of the Congress.

Organization and Behavior

Other chapters of this volume describe and analyze elements of stability and change in the way Congress is composed, led, and processes its business. These bear as much on its behavior in national security affairs as on its activities in other public policy areas. As a general proposition, national security policy is a blend of all of the nation's policies as they affect the world roles of the United States. It is inseparable from the totality of public policy. While this generalization is accurate, members of Congress perceive certain programs and policies as being more national security oriented than others and display distinctive modes of behavior in reacting to them. This distinctiveness will be examined following brief attention to the particular organizational arrangements through which the Congress deals with foreign-defense business.

FRACTIONS OF INFLUENCE AND POWER

The Congress subdivides and disperses its power and influence. The recipients are committees, subcommittees, leaders, policy specialists, and personalities with media or electoral attractiveness.

In the Ninety-second Congress (1971–72), one could identify 19 permanent (more than half of the total) and 2 joint House-Senate committees which dealt sufficiently with foreign affairs to require the serious, if sometimes episodic, attention of the executive branch. The committees spawned in the neighborhood of 60 subcommittees with titles indicating that their primary duties were in the international realm.

The groups presiding over the major fraction of national security business are familiar—the House and Senate armed services and appropriations committees, the Senate Foreign Relations Committee and the House Committee on Foreign Affairs. Each is equipped with competent, small professional staffs. Foreign Relations, for instance, is supported by ten professionals with extensive experience in public service.

---

[9] *Congressional Record, op. cit.,* March 30, 1972, p. S 5255.

In any Congress, other committees and subcommittees move in and out of the international arena, investigating, overseeing executive performance, or processing legislation about such matters as international finance, export controls, the tariff, import quotas, farm products for foreign policy purposes, international shipping and aviation, and immigration.

The Senate enjoys several advantages over the House. Its smaller size, the few limitations on debate, the greater personal power of a senator and the greater attention accorded by the media to almost any senator over a House member, longer terms of office, and the special powers over treaties and major executive appointments combine to give the Senate more influence and prestige than the House.

Drawing upon the advantages of the Senate, the Foreign Relations Committee towers over the House counterpart. From the 1790s, the Senate committee has assumed that it should be consulted by the executive about significant international matters. A feeling that it has not been adequately and genuinely consulted in recent years has reinforced the tendencies to dissent about aspects of executive-initiated policies and actions.

While also expecting to be consulted rather than simply informed, the House Committee on Foreign Affairs cannot match the Senate committee's historically-rooted expectations for attention. It is a committee deeply concerned about foreign policy and active in many matters, but its main energy in any session focuses on foreign aid. In the 1960s and into the early 1970s it was the part of Congress most responsive to the executive's proposals for foreign aid and, at times, seemed to be about the only friend foreign aid had. From the mid-1960s, as challenges to executive initiatives and proposals in foreign-military matters intensified in the Senate, the House remained highly supportive of the executive.

The congressional choice to disperse its formidable foreign-military powers inhibits and restricts legislative influence in national security matters. Coordinated activity in the face of more unified executive activity is infrequently found. Congress prefers this amorphous situation. For the diffusion of power has its advantages: Congress can evade accountability and responsibility for what occurs in the world relations of the United States. On the other hand, Congress has not been reluctant to share credit for the successes.

Behind the diffusion, in part, is the fact that the nation is divided over many matters. The existence of numerous centers of power and influence permits the divisions to be vented. It is not unusual for sharply conflicting views to surface at about the same time. Thus, within a few days in 1967, a Senate military subgroup urged a wider air war in Vietnam while the head of Foreign Relations, reflecting the dominant sentiments of his group, called for a halt in air attacks on the North. As another example, the House no doubt would be alarmed if its money committee, as it has for a quarter century, did not propose cuts in foreign aid which the House and Senate had authorized. For the House to agree to substantive policy decisions on a few matters as proposed by the funding group, over the objections of the foreign policy specialists, is routine.

CONSTRAINTS

This untidy picture of Congress deferring to its parts, of diffusion, fragmentation, and of speaking with differing voices, is similar for all public policy areas. Yet the Congress displays distinctive modes of behavior in those portions of policy that it senses lie in the realm of national security—events abroad and responses to them, the nation's military posture, foreign aid and foreign economic policy, for example.

Behavioral constraints arise from the attitude of members that in the external realm it is *their* United States as an entity dealing with other nations in a supercharged world environment. This sense, of which elementary patriotism is a part, inspires caution.

In reacting to international matters, the member enjoys greater freedom in expressing himself than is deemed prudent in dealing with much domestic business. Few constituents are likely to mount worrisome challenges about how the congressman reacts to events in India, Africa, Europe, or Japan, or about his attitudes on the price of gold, foreign aid, or the United Nations. For many, less freedom prevails in particulars of the Defense Department's domain, about weapons development and military bases, for instance, policy matters which may bear on the economic health of their districts or states. A few, because of the makeup of their constituencies, must keep their political antennae sensitively tuned to United States policies and programs for particular countries. Generally, the publics the members depend upon for electoral survival are permissive concerning their behavior in the national security realm.

This greater freedom sometimes tempts a few for one reason or another—perhaps mainly for media attention—to behave irresponsibly. The greater freedom, combined with the fact that Congress does have power and responsibilities, also poses dilemmas about appropriate behavior. These have been starkly exposed for many in expressing dissent over Vietnam, with the consequent charge that the dissent may have served to weaken the United States position in negotiations with the North and may have made more difficult executive efforts to extricate the nation from the war. Congress and its members are actors in the international arena. The dilemmas are genuine. The enduring pattern for most members has been caution and restraint regarding the nation's foreign business.

These constraints have become more severe in recent decades because of enhancement of the executive. By a combination of necessity, choice, and neglect, the Congress has acquiesced in executive discretion and predominance in the uses of shared powers and in expansive interpretations of the President's power as Commander-in-Chief. The advantages of the executive are familiar. These include the qualities of the presidential office set out by the writers of *The Federalist* in the 1780s, and especially pertinent in the 1970s—secrecy, always in session, superior information, and the ability to act quickly. Exploiting these qualities in the context of a radically changed world environment, the executive, above all, has the initiative. The President and his associates are the primary, often sole, policy constituency for the Congress in national security matters. Not unexpectedly, the Congress commonly finds itself in the position of responding to policy choices, if any, posed by the executive, to actions taken and commitments made. Congress thus faces the options of being negative or, more typically, of supporting, albeit grudgingly, the executive and legitimizing its policies.

Examples illustrating the enhancement of the executive and the executive advantages in initiation are legion. Several will be developed shortly. In crisis situations, regardless of what subsequent legislative inquiries may reveal, the Congress has hardly any choice but to support the President. The Tonkin Gulf affair of 1964 was not seriously investigated until 1968. President Nixon intervened in Cambodia with American power in 1970 without any consultation with any members of the Congress. Both Presidents Johnson and Nixon bombed in North Vietnam without consulting legislators. Presidents Eisenhower and Kennedy engaged in major clandestine activities in Guatamala and in Cuba, and they and their successors utilized executive agreements, letters, and memoranda for major commitments to many nations. These are a few of the more publicized examples.

The executive advantages and performances in national security policy seemingly lead to the conclusions that congressional power and authority have declined and that the Congress plays insignificant or unimportant roles. The first conclusion should be qualified; the second is false.

As noted, on a few occasions in the past the Congress had the dominant voice in determining the external relationships of the United States. Since the 1940s it has vigorously participated in policy-making. In volume and in quality this participation has increased dramatically over the pre-World War II century and a half. Congressional powers remain intact. What has happened, rather than "decline," has been the phenomenon of an enormous increase in executive stature and performance not matched, in a relative sense, by the Congress. It is lapses in using power, not a general decline from prominence in national security affairs in a rather mythical past, that explains more

satisfactorily the widening gap in influence between the legislative
and executive branches.

More important in assessing congressional influence is that legislative roles have changed in ways that perhaps obscure the vitality
and significance of congressional influence upon the world relationships of the United States. In a word, the Congress has become more
and more a monitor of the executive, as it has more widely than ever
involved itself in consensus-building in the international domain.
Power relationships can never, of course, be neglected. Evidence
mounts that imbalances regarding presidential uses of military power,
for example—uses that might easily unseat the executive in a parliamentary democracy—may be in the process of correction. Politics,
power, and institutional prerogatives are, in any event, joined in the
mosaic of relationships that comprise the American system of divided
and shared powers.

PARTICIPANT IN CONSENSUS-BUILDING

In a broad sense the general role of the Congress in national security
policy is that of participation in processes of consensus-building. What
is involved in consensus-building? [10]

It should first be noted that consensus-building, the search for agreement amid conflicting alternatives and interests, does not always result
in consensus on particular issues between the legislative and executive.
For a spell a policy may rest in a sort of purgatory. Respecting some
matters, presidential uses of the armed forces abroad, for instance, an
uneasy executive-legislative equilibrium may surface temporarily in
the hot crucible of emergency and commitment. The settlement may
reflect no more than a momentary, fragile consensus. With the passage
of time, corrosion of trust and confidence between the executive and
legislative may occur.

Commonly, consensus-building involves many parts of the Congress,
its personalities, and their publics in agreement or competition with
the many voices in the executive branch, the President, and their publics. The publics are general, specific, national, and international. All
participants are actors in international business, seeking acceptable
accommodations that will facilitate the formulation and conduct of
policies and programs.

The abundance of techniques employed in executive-legislative conflict, consensus-building endeavors may be set out in a paragraph.
Drawing upon the words employed in the literature, the houses, their
parts, and their leading personalities prod, modify, amend, check, occasionally veto, occasionally initiate, inhibit, warn, limit, consent, ad-

[10] Roger Hilsman has most completely developed the conflict-consensus framework.
For a recent statement, see his *The Politics of Policy Making in Defense and Foreign
Affairs* (New York: Harper & Row, 1971).

vise, collaborate, query, investigate, bargain, form alliances, appeal to publics, lobby, study, leak information, oversee, liberate, constrain, and communicate.[11] Each of the words could provoke examples. A few brief studies may illuminate the richness of congressional participation. They will, as well, indicate the character of concern and dissent which has recently pervaded the Congress.

Studies in Conflict and Consensus-Building

CHINA

In February 1972, President Nixon spent several days in the People's Republic of China, opening doors closed for more than two decades. He confided in no member of the Congress in the preceding summer when his agent and principal advisor in the whole realm of national security, Mr. Kissinger—who with his staff of more than one hundred was shielded under doctrines of executive privilege from ordinary congressional oversight—secretly negotiated the arrangements for the visit.

The whole show appeared to be presidential. For perspective one must go back more than two decades. The Congress played a significant part both as inhibitor and liberator of the President.

Two decades before, in the early 1950s, Democrats and Republicans joined to freeze China policy in an atmosphere of bitterness and recrimination not matched since, even over Vietnam. The President who visited China in 1972 had in 1952 campaigned successfully as a vicepresidential candidate on a platform which assailed the Democrats for requiring "the National Government of China to surrender Manchuria . . . to the control of Communist Russia," and for substituting "on our Pacific flank a murderous enemy for an ally and friend." [12] He was a senator in the Democratic-controlled Senate which in the years 1950–52 most shaped public attitudes by permitting the proposition to become dominant that State Department ineptness, and perhaps conspiracy by public servants, had resulted in the "loss" of China.

On more than 30 occasions over two decades, the Congress resolved, usually with no dissenting votes, to oppose recognition of the People's Republic, trade with it, and its seating as China in the United Nations.

[11] See Hilsman, *ibid.*; Alton Frye, "Congress: The Virtues of its Vices," *Foreign Policy*, No. 3 (Summer 1971), 108–25; James A. Robinson, *Congress and Foreign Policy-Making* (Homewood, Ill.: Dorsey, rev. ed., 1967); Francis O. Wilcox, *Congress, the Executive, and Foreign Policy*, Council on Foreign Relations Policy Book (New York: Harper & Row, 1971).

[12] Republican Party platform of 1952, in Kirk N. Porter and Donald B. Johnson, eds., *National Party Platforms, 1840–1956* (Urbana: Univ. of Ill. Press, 1956), p. 497.

In the same period a majority of senators and representatives were members of the Committee of One Million, the principal lobby group supporting this position.

Thus, regarding mainland China, the Congress dominated in constraining American policy. Probably only a Republican President, with such impeccable anti-Communist credentials as President Nixon, could have breached these congressional limits. As the Senate Republican floor leader put it, "had the Democratic Presidents moved toward this rapprochement with mainland China, people in this country, led by many Republicans, would still be seeing Communists under the bed and would have raised pluperfect hell." [13]

With hindsight, the Congress helped pave the way for the opening by seriously questioning the propositions it had supported. Frequently, beginning in the mid-1960s, congressional committees and subgroups —the Senate Foreign Relations and Government Operations groups, the House Foreign Affairs Committee, and a subunit of the Joint Economic Committee—questioned the wisdom and appropriateness of these policies regarding one-fourth of the human race. The chairmen of Foreign Relations and Foreign Affairs joined with six congressmen and others composing a commission to recommend Peking's seating in the United Nations. In 1969 the Senate voiced hardly any opposition to a resolution confirming customary practice that recognition of a government "does not of itself imply that the United States approves of the form, ideology, or policy of that foreign government." [14] In other parts of the Congress in the late 1960s and early 1970s, many resolutions were sponsored by members which called for seating the Peking government in the United Nations, while retaining a seat for Taiwan. In 1971 the Congress omitted approving its annual resolution opposing the People's Republic. With no debate, in August 1971, the Senate endorsed the President's "journey for peace" to the People's Republic.[15] Only 54 of the 535 members of the Congress could be induced in the late summer of 1971 to endorse a statement that Peking's admission to the United Nations and the expulsion of Nationalist China might result in a reassessment of American funding and support for the U.N. The few senators supporting this position, however, may have provided the margin, when joined by others disgruntled by the United Nations expulsion of Taiwan, to defeat the foreign aid bill in the fall of 1971.

If one were to identify a key turning point in the development of a fresh consensus about China, it was the televised hearings of the Senate Foreign Relations Committee in 1966. Their purpose was to

[13] Senator Scott, *Congressional Quarterly Weekly Report*, XXIX, No. 40 (Oct. 2, 1971), 2018.

[14] S. Res. 205, 91–1.

[15] S. Con. Res. 38, 92–1.

inform the public about mainland China. Scholars presented their views in a searching inquiry. The Senate group performed on this occasion, as it has on many others, an intellectual-political function, compelling hesitant bureaucrats, the President, and the attentive publics to examine their premises and to move more boldly—which most wanted to do, in any event—to deal with reality. The Senate group made their inclinations respectable.

THE TEST BAN TREATY

On occasion the Congress must squarely face an important policy shift bearing on East-West relations and share responsibility with the President. Such was the case in 1963 when the Senate was asked to consent to ratification of the Test Ban Treaty with the Soviet Union.

In retrospect the consent of the Senate appears almost to have been routine. The principal foreign-military issues in conflict were extensively debated and reconciled within the executive branch before the decision was made to sign the treaty. Within seven weeks of receiving the treaty, the Senate endorsed it by the overwhelming vote of 80 to 19. This deceptively easy triumph for the administration was preceded by rich processes of consensus-building in which the Congress, especially the Senate, played a critical part.

While senators and representatives were usually prepared to comment about disarmament from the late 1940s—questions about fall-out, the United Nations' efforts, and so on were likely to be raised in every home district—the dominant mood was skepticism even about small steps to mitigate the arms race. Over the years, however, a few members specialized in arms control issues and used committees and subcommittees to educate themselves, interested fellow legislators, and various attentive publics. The fall-out hearings of a subcommittee of the Joint Committee on Atomic Energy in the late 1950s and the hearings and reports over several years by the Foreign Relations Subcommittee on Disarmament are examples. They built a public record, a reference library of hearings, reports, and speeches for future use.

Discussions about the prospects and difficulties of arms control gradually spread into other crevices of the Congress. The armed services committees and some of their subcommittees dipped into the issues. The annual requests for authority and funds to sustain the Arms Control and Disarmament Agency, established in 1961, stimulated House and Senate debates. In early 1963, when the prospects for a limited ban seemed brighter, the tempo of the dialogue picked up. The House Republican Conference established a Committee on Nuclear Testing. And in May, as the talks with the Soviet Union continued, 32 senators joined Senators Dodd and Humphrey to introduce a resolution favoring a limited test ban treaty. The resolution provided an optimistic reading of the political temperature of the Senate when the negotiators moved into the final stages of writing a treaty.

Thus, when the Senate received the treaty, most senators had absorbed some general knowledge about arms control and a few were experts on the technical and foreign-military problems of test ban agreements. In the hearings and debates, the Senate drew upon this reservoir of knowledge and competence to explore the proposal thoroughly and to bring an independent stream of judgment to bear.

Because of the overlapping foreign-military issues and the concern of other committees, the Committee on Foreign Relations invited the Armed Services Committee and the Senate members of the Joint Committee on Atomic Energy to attend its hearings and to question witnesses. Such arrangements are rare in the Senate and impossible in the House. Even with this arrangement, the Preparedness Investigating Subcommittee of the Senate Armed Services Committee conducted its own hearings on the military aspects of the treaty. The subgroup monitored discontent and issued a pessimistic report. Its pessimism, while pressuring the executive branch to explain further and to elaborate understandings, was overcome by the dominant *ad hoc* group assembled by Foreign Relations and by its careful examination and blending of foreign and military policy issues.

The political chemistry of developing Senate consent was subtle and intricate. Only a small part of the story has been sketched. While in retrospect the development of consent was essentially bipartisan, the Republican floor leader maintained a studied detachment as he worked with the administration to build agreement. At his suggestion the President sent a letter to the Republican and Democratic floor leaders giving "unqualified and unequivocal assurances" about aspects of future nuclear weapons policy if the treaty were approved.[16]

No President could have carried the Senate, however, in the absence of the continuing disarmament dialogue over the years in the Congress and with elements of the public. In the hearings and debates on the treaty, the Senate served as the final dramatic place in the political system for constructing the national consensus so essential for supporting an important shift in policy. Even Soviet Premier Khrushchev seems to have attended closely to the dialogue and moved at one point to help President Kennedy ease his tasks with the Senate.[17] The Senate promoted public understanding and acceptance of the decision. Throughout the 1960s and into the 1970s, the Senate and House, their committees and members, by hearings, reports, resolutions, and speeches prodded the President to undertake further arms limitations moves, supported him when he did, and vented criticism when he seemed to delay or resist.

[16] *Congressional Record,* 109 (Sept. 11, 1963), p. S 15915.
[17] See Frye, *op. cit.,* pp. 111–12.

CRISES

The rhetoric of crisis is invoked in every session of Congress to spur support for programs. In some circumstances a crisis atmosphere has become almost routine as the leaders work to move bills through a fractured structure that provides so many opportunities to delay, erode, or dilute the recommendations of the executive branch. On other occasions international events of varying magnitude provoke crises to which the Congress reacts.

The frequency of crises and emergencies since World War II has invariably enhanced presidential power. As the nation became vulnerable to military attack, the Congress more willingly conceded extraordinary exercises of executive power. In every emergency, however, lurks the potential of hazardous division and dissension.

On only a few occasions has the President asked the Congress for broad authority in anticipation of a crisis. The risks in asking must be carefully calculated. If the vote is overwhelmingly favorable, potential adversaries are warned that the President has the backing of the nation for whatever he chooses to do. But the debate may be prolonged, division exaggerated, votes close, public confidence shaken, and the backing possibly denied or seriously diluted.

President Eisenhower's request in 1955 for authority to use force, if necessary, to defend Formosa was quickly approved. The resolution was part of a strategy of communicating to Communist China the firm determination of the United States to defend the island stronghold of Nationalist China and vaguely described adjacent areas.

Conveying the unity of the nation and the determination to take risks was evident in resolutions on Berlin and Cuba in 1962. The Berlin resolution expressed the sense of the Congress that the United States was prepared to use any required means to prevent the violation of Allied rights. The Cuba resolution, passed less than a month before the missile crisis of October 1962, warned the Soviet and Cuban governments that the United States was prepared to use any necessary means, including force, to deal with a Soviet buildup of arms in Cuba and Cuban aggression in the hemisphere. The President did not ask for the Cuban and Berlin resolutions. Once initiated in the Congress, he moved to prevent a narrowing of his discretion and succeeded. The Congress provided constitutional legitimacy for virtually any exercise of executive power. When the missile crisis arose, the Congress was not in session, but its resolve to see any crisis through was freshly on record.

The seriousness of the resolutions regarding Formosa and Cuba was underscored in the Senate by joint meetings and reports of the Foreign Relations and Armed Services Committees. All of the resolutions were approved by huge majorities. They expressed a national consensus.

Resolutions in anticipation of crises, whether stimulated by the executive branch or generated within the Congress, entail risks. When President Eisenhower in 1957 asked for approval of his Middle East doctrine, the Congress, under the control of the Democrats, consumed two months to process his proposal. No doubt existed that the Congress would ultimately give him broad authority. The House endorsed the doctrine in only a few hours of debate. Extensive Senate hearings, conducted jointly by Foreign Relations and Armed Services, were followed by twelve days of Senate debate. The President's proposal was thoroughly analyzed and amended. By its debate the Senate again performed an intellectual-political function. It explored alternatives and illuminated areas of doubt. Among other things, the Senate voted for a comprehensive review of Middle East policy and, rather than authorizing the President to use force, simply expressed the view of the Congress that the United States was prepared to use armed force if the President decided that it was necessary. The Senate, in a sense, was preventing the President from diluting his military powers and responsibilities. The House quickly accepted the Senate version.

Resolutions which anticipate crises are rare. More commonly the Congress must react to rapidly moving events. The hazards and strengths of separated and diffused power are quickly exposed.

Acute and sudden crises drastically narrow the range of likely congressional behavior. During the most intense period when the uncertainties are greatest, the Congress normally provides legitimacy for executive responses and reinforces the unity of the nation. As the emergency unfolds and abates, however, elements in the Congress may be tempted to exploit the crisis for partisan advantage. In every crisis the Congress by its behavior affects public confidence in men and institutions. The tests of crises may be illustrated by the Bay of Pigs and Tonkin Gulf affairs.

Congressional reaction to the abortive Bay of Pigs paramilitary operation in April 1961 was extraordinarily passive. Leaders of both political parties firmly backed President Kennedy in his exchanges with the Soviet premier. The Congress provided legitimacy for the operation and conveyed the unity of the nation largely by silence. In the two weeks before the landing the Congress was silent when newspapers reported the training of anti-Castro units in Florida and elsewhere and their movements to forward bases. The President briefed a small bipartisan group of congressional leaders during the three-day period when the invaders were crushed. The leaders were silent. The only member of Congress who had advance knowledge about the CIA scheme was Senator Fulbright. In a session with the President and his principal advisers, the Senator alone opposed the operation. The House and Senate foreign policy committees conducted short, secret hearings two weeks after the event. They did not report. Only in the aftermath, when more information became available about the nature of the invasion and the deep American involvement, were questions raised in the Congress. Even then the criticism was guarded—part of the general stream of debate on what to do about Cuba.

The exceptional congressional restraint may be explained partly by President Kennedy's swift moves to accept responsibility and to form a national front. The President, or a prominent associate, met with former Presidents Eisenhower, Truman, and Hoover, former Vice-President Nixon, General MacArthur, Governor Nelson Rockefeller, and Senator Goldwater. "I would say that the last thing you want is to have a full investigation and lay this on the record," said former President Eisenhower.[18] Republican apprehensions about the extent of the Eisenhower administration's part in planning the affair, fear of war, and, especially, the implication of sensitive agencies, the Joint Chiefs and the Central Intelligence Agency in particular, also contributed to the passivity of the Congress.

The Bay of Pigs affair illustrates the unresolved dilemma of the Congress in performing representative and oversight functions with regard to secret and covert activities by the intelligence agencies, especially the CIA. Most members have no idea where the money for these activities lies hidden in the budget or for what purposes the money is spent. Few want to know.

The Congress has adjusted to mystery by an assumption and by faith in the surveillance conducted in secret by a few of its members. The assumption is that the CIA is a servant of the National Security Council, that it does not make policy, and that the President and his associates are accountable for the agency's operations.

The surveillance is conducted by subcommittees of the House and Senate armed services and appropriations committees. Since 1967, three members of Foreign Relations have been invited to join those sessions when the CIA conducts joint briefings for the Senate subunits, but such sessions are scarce. None occurred in 1971.

Mystery surrounds the oversight activities of the subgroups, but it is likely neither deep nor extensive. Senator Symington, for example, served both as a member of Foreign Relations and of the Armed Services subunit on the CIA. As part of a massive study for Foreign Relations, a subgroup he headed probed extensively into CIA involvements in Laos. From his position he ought to have known what was going on. In a secret Senate session in mid-1971, he conceded major gaps of knowledge which neither he nor the staff could ferret out.[19]

In the quarter century of the CIA's existence, around two hundred

---

[18] *The New York Times*, May 2, 1961.
[19] *Congressional Quarterly Weekly Report*, XXIX, No. 35 (Aug. 28, 1971), 1840–43.

bills have been introduced to bring the CIA and other intelligence operations under closer congressional scrutiny. The common proposal is for a joint or select committee. Only two of the bills ever got out of committee and none was passed. The Congress prefers the *status quo*. While some members are troubled, most are content to let the President and his associates weigh the ethical judgments and take the responsibilities. Most members probably deeply admire the CIA. A more recent development than demands for broader-based oversight, in fact, is the effort to get the CIA to provide analyses for the foreign policy committees on a regular basis. The CIA already enjoys a close relationship on intelligence matters with the Joint Committee on Atomic Energy. Some on Foreign Relations are convinced that the CIA's analyses are superior to those provided by the State and Defense Departments. The revelations of the Pentagon Papers—loaded with CIA memoranda—reinforced this attitude.

Intelligence operations and the bewilderingly complex apparatus of the electronic and communications wizards were involved in the second affair, the Tonkin Bay incidents of 1964. More than three years later, in early 1968, the Foreign Relations Committee probed indecisively into what really happened in Tonkin Gulf in August of 1964. Did one of the attacks by North Vietnam on United States naval ships, for example, really occur? The Senate group may have enjoyed rummaging through stained ship logs, accounts which the communications specialists overheard from the North's military, and the flood of messages to and from Hawaii, Washington, and elsewhere. The inquiry, while perhaps inspiring more caution by the navy in the future, basically reflected an effort to expiate guilt feelings for so readily accepting the Tonkin Gulf resolution by a vote of 502 to 2, as President Johnson often reminded his congressional critics when they backed off from supporting him when the going got rough.

By the resolution the Congress said that it "approves and supports the determination of the President, as Commander in Chief, to take all necessary measures to repel armed attack against the forces of the United States and to prevent further aggression." It supported the proposition that "the United States regards as vital to its national interests and to world peace the maintenance of international peace and security in southeast Asia." [20] A rough outline of a resolution, waiting an event that might justify it, had resided in the State Department's files for some time.

President Johnson's use of the resolution most distressed the Congress. Using it and obligations under the SEATO treaty and the United Nations Charter (all of which the resolution invoked) as partial justification, the President expanded the war, with Congress providing the money required, always by healthy majorities. Twice in 1970, and

[20] P.L. 88–408.

finally with the concurrence of the House in early 1971, the Senate led in repealing the resolution. President Nixon did not object to this first congressional repeal in history of an area resolution. Despite the repeal, area resolutions, if carefully framed and circumscribed, play useful roles in the conduct of foreign relations. Most members of Congress know this. The difficulties arise from perceived executive abuses of the war-making powers and executive assumptions of unwarranted prerogatives, in congressional eyes, in committing the United States by executive agreements and understandings.

DEFENSE BUDGETS, WAR-MAKING POWERS, AND COMMITMENTS

Congressional activity to arrest its decline and to correct executive-legislative imbalances in constitutional powers has focused on three issue-laden areas. They are closely linked, sometimes fused. One target for more than a decade has been funds and authority for the Defense Department. A second involves the President's uses of the war-making powers. The third encompasses United States commitments overseas.

Only reluctantly have elements in the Congress mounted serious questioning and challenges to the executive in these areas. The instincts of majorities have been to support executive initiatives and proposals. A major contribution of the dissidents has been to develop alternatives to the executive-chosen options for their colleagues and publics. The questioning has also, quite importantly, educated all participants about the erosion of congressional power, authority, and influence.

A principal vehicle for closer scrutiny of the defense budgets by the armed services committees became "412," an amendment to a bill which required annual authorization of naval vessels, missiles, and ships beginning in fiscal 1961. Formerly the armed services relied on ongoing authority for these items and thus worked mainly with the money committees. The scope of the 412 prior authorization requirement was expanded over the next decade. By fiscal 1973, about one-third of the defense budget had to survive two extensive yearly inspections, one for authority and one for funds. The double processing by committees, incidentally, was also invoked, beginning in 1972, for the budgets of the State Department and the United States Information Agency.

For months, especially in 1969 and in 1970, the Senate was tied up with such matters as the size of the defense budget, the draft, antiballistics missiles (ABM), chemical-biological warfare, American troop commitments to NATO, Vietnam withdrawal amendments, multi-warhead weapons (MIRV), and cost overruns. In 1969 the Senate debate on military authorizations alone spanned 73 calendar days.

As the United States entered the mid-1970s, the results of these challenges were apparent, if not overly impressive. In showdowns the votes were always there to support the programs and policies of the executive. As in the past, the Congress endorsed a few "add ons," such as for increased ship construction, which the administration had not officially requested. Yet significant changes had occurred.

In 1969, only by a tie vote, 50–50, had the Senate failed to delete entirely authority for deployment of the ABM. At no time in history had the Congress so vigorously challenged a basic strategic decision. A proposal in 1970 for modest extension of ABM sites survived Senate defeat by a vote of 47–52. To avert defeat in both years the adminis-tration and the armed services committees retreated from more am-bitious ABM deployment plans. Restrictions were placed on the use of funds and forces in Cambodia, Laos, and Thailand. The Joint Eco-nomic Committee, the House and Senate foreign policy groups, and the House Government Operations Committee probed more exten-sively than ever before into military matters. From the mid-1960s on, individual members and coalitions, often drawing upon non-govern-mental expertise, contested what had become virtually sacred assump-tions. To preserve their effectiveness in the Congress, the normally pro-Pentagon armed services committees were stirred to unusual ac-tivity.

The debates over Defense Department funds and authority often were commingled with disputes over war-making powers and com-mitments. The Congress moved more warily in these areas because of doubts about constitutional powers and a sense of guilt that it had directly or indirectly sanctioned policies it was now questioning.

Since President Washington pursued the Whiskey Rebels in the 1790s, ambiguity has marked executive-legislative war-making powers. In the 1970s, scholars could consult a huge library of hearings, reports, and staff studies about them.[21] The uncertain relationships stem from interpretations and uses of the President's powers as commander-in-chief and the formidable authority of Congress over military matters, including the power to declare war and the power to implement its war powers by "necessary and proper" means.

Expansive executive use of war-making powers in Southeast Asia provoked the questioning from the mid-1960s. To this recent concern were added memories of the uses of power in Korea in the early 1950s, in Lebanon in 1958, and in the Dominican Republic in 1965. To many in the Congress the executive branch in the 1970s seemed to be

---

[21] For a sample, see the report on the War Powers Bill, S. Rept. 92-606; *Congress, the President and the War Powers*, Hearings before the Subcommittee on National Security Policy and Scientific Developments, Committee on Foreign Affairs, House, 91-2 (Washington, 1970); *War Powers Legislation*, Hearings, *ibid.*, 92-1 (Washing-ton, 1971); *War Powers Legislation*, Hearings before the Committee on Foreign Relations, Senate, 92-1 (Washington, 1972).

saying that the nation's armed might could be disposed as the President directed, with the Congress, like the public, retaining only a right to be informed. While the arguments in studies and hearings piled up, the Congress moved only timidly to assert what it perceived as its prerogatives and powers. The Congress does have an ultimate weapon in the power of the purse. It was used mildly, as noted, to curb some uses of funds and forces in Southeast Asia. Senate passage of the War Powers Bill in 1972, noted at the beginning of the chapter, represents another effort to clarify executive-legislative war powers, "to confirm and codify the intent of the framers of the Constitution," as the Foreign Relations group put it. It "must be perceived as necessary legislation which should not have been necessary. It would not have been necessary if Congress had defended and exercised its responsibility in matters of war and peace and so prevented the Executive from expanding its power. . . ."[22]

The theme of congressional lapses runs through the conflicts between the executive and legislative branches and efforts at consensus-building over commitments abroad. The ongoing dialogue has also engaged various publics as the Congress and the President have been searching for a consensus on the nation's vital interests in a new era.

The word "commitments" fuses the concerns over military matters and war-making powers. What are the obligations of the United States to other nations? Either directly or by neglect, the Congress has sanctioned most of the accumulated obligations. It has added some of its own, regarding Israel and Rhodesia, for instance. The executive, by ingenious legal and political arguments, has moved to span and fill in the gaps left by the Congress. Thus the NATO and SEATO treaties, and accumulated resolutions, bills, and appropriations by the Congress, have provided a quasi-legal basis for thousands of executive pronouncements, letters, memoranda, and executive agreements to "fill in details." Secrecy, assumed prerogatives, executive privilege, and congressional silence have been invoked to hide the character of some obligations. In 1971, for instance, the President pledged more than $400 million in economic aid to Portugal by an executive agreement in return for favors about bases in the Azores. Less than a quarter century before a request by the President for about the same amount of money for Greece and Turkey had to survive intensive congressional questioning before approval.

The challenges of elements in the Congress to this state of affairs have resulted in three overlapping efforts. The common theme has been pursuit of concepts of executive-legislative "jointness" in com-

---

[22] S. Rept. 92–606, pp. 21–22.

mitments. This theme, while ostensibly accepted by the executive, in reality has been resisted by the executive's burgeoning expertise and by the President himself.

One effort, incubating for about two years, won Senate approval in 1969, by a 70–16 vote, of a resolution which asserted "that a national commitment for the purpose of this resolution means the use of armed forces on foreign territory, or a promise to assist a foreign country, government or people by the use of the armed forces or financial resources of the United States, either immediately or upon the happening of certain events. . . ." [23] A treaty, statute, or resolution should specifically provide "for such commitment." Even the staunchest critics of the Tonkin Gulf resolution concede that it would have been acceptable in satisfying the criteria of the Senate's commitments resolution if the 1964 resolve had been more precise and limited in time. To many in Congress, President Nixon's intervention in Cambodia in 1970 and in Laos in 1971 appeared to defy the Senate's resolution.

A second effort has been investigation. A subunit of Foreign Relations probed intensively in 1969 and in 1970 into a whole array of commitments abroad. It sent its own investigators into the field in an effort to lift the veil of secrecy about such matters as involvements in Laos. It questioned reluctant officials about agreements on military bases and the deployment of tactical nuclear weapons abroad.[24]

The third, and overlapping, effort has focused on attempts to get the executive branch to keep Congress informed, and to consult the Senate Foreign Relations Committee particularly, about executive and other international agreements. The Senate group explored the legal and political problems. In early 1972, by a vote of 81–0, the Senate approved a bill which called for submission to appropriate congressional groups, with security safeguards, of all international agreements.[25] At this writing, the conflicts had not been resolved, and the Senate's activities appeared to have had only a slight impact on executive behavior.

The Present and the Future

These sketches reveal only fragments of the immersion of the Congress in conflicts and consensus-building in the nation's world

[23] S. Res. 85, 91–1.

[24] See the sanitized hearings of Senator Symington's subunit, *United States Security Agreements and Commitments Abroad*, 2 vols., Hearings before the Subcommittee of the Committee on Foreign Relations, Senate, 92–1 (Washington, 1971), and the report based on these, *ibid.*, pp. 2415–42.

[25] S. 596, 92–2. For a sample of hearings, see *Transmittal of Executive Agreements to Congress*, Hearings before the Committee on Foreign Relations, 92–1 (Washington, 1971), and *Executive Agreements with Portugal and Bahrain, ibid.*, 92–2 (Washington, 1972).

relationships. A more comprehensive account would display the members and parts at work on such matters as foreign aid, dollar and trade issues, farm products for foreign policy purposes, cultural exchanges, arms sales, atomic energy, and outer space. It would give attention to extensive travel by members abroad, to their participation in international conferences, to the roles of the media, and to staffs. The international actor roles of members would be appraised in a longer study. One would note how individual legislators both help and hinder the shaping and conduct of policy by floating ideas to probe their receptivity, by vigorously criticizing a foreign regime, or by unusual attention to foreign personalities and causes. One would observe, for instance, how some legislators helped to foster a friendly image for the United States when the executive branch, in late 1971, "tilted" toward Pakistan in that nation's efforts to quell an uprising in its eastern half and in the India-Pakistan war.

This has been a picture of the Congress at work, of Congress as it is. The scene sometimes is tangled and turbulent, in a word, messy. Despite current stresses and strains, the Congress richly and constructively participates in the democratic search for agreements about the nation's international business. Recent and current uneasiness stems, as noted, from worries about executive gains and legislative lapses in the interpretation and uses of shared powers. Above all its source is division in the nation which Congress inescapably reflects. Publics pressing for policy changes naturally zero in on the President, the Congress, or both, and call for reform.

In these circumstances the essay should end on a theme of prescription. As Francis O. Wilcox observes, "strengthening the congressional role is likely to result in a more viable foreign policy, if for no other reason than that it will command broader public support, based on a broader national consensus." [26] The Congress understands its problems of organization, behavior, and performance. Scarcely an idea can be proposed that has not been advocated in hearings, reports, or staff studies. A few committees have conducted imaginative experiments. Three general areas in which the Congress might enhance its legislative roles can be briefly identified.

The first involves the tension over war powers and commitments. Wiser and more prudent presidential and congressional action would have averted exacerbation of tensions over institutional prerogatives and shared powers and responsibilities. Wisdom and prudence did not prevail. Distortions of proper executive-legislative balances have occurred, and the courts will not resolve the disputes. Politics will eventually provide a tolerable equilibrium and restore the only basis

for continuing, livable arrangements—mutual trust and confidence
between the legislative and executive branches and with their publics.
Meanwhile, legislation which explicitly defines war powers and the
uses of executive and other agreements may be necessary.

A second requirement is for Congress to sharpen its tools for questioning, testing, and oversight of the executive. A few of a multitude
of possibilities—all pressed or tried—may be suggested. One should
be the constant quest for executive-developed information and diag-
noses. Means are available to preserve required secrecy. Second, greater
emphasis should be placed on independent testing of policies and
proposals. A few committees and groups of members have demonstrated these possibilities by calling upon nongovernmental expertise
and by sending out their own staff members to ferret out information.
Examples are the performances of the coalition contesting the ABM
in drawing upon nongovernmental expertise and the Symington subcommittee's uses of staff for field investigations in the commitments
study. A third route for promoting legislative effectiveness in moni-
toring and testing is for the committees and their subgroups more
commonly to anticipate issues and focus intensively on a few vital
ones in their efforts to affect policy in its formative stage. Such endeavors may also be used to highlight critical problems which seem to
have gotten out of hand. The China hearings and studies, long before
pandas and ping pong became chic, the arms control studies, and the
inquiries into war powers by House and Senate groups are examples.

Third, to confront a united executive on more equal terms, the
Congress must discover means by which to coordinate and unify its
own elements. A strong Congress is more than the sum of its parts.
Fragmentation and diffusion erode its power. An occasional assembly
of congressional leaders, called to inform them of what they have already heard, serves more to stultify than to edify. What seems to be
required is a willingness to experiment with new forms of congressional control. In three policy areas—atomic energy, economic policy,
and taxation—the Congress has partially come to terms with its fis-
siparous tendencies through the creation of joint committees. Suggestions for promoting congressional coherence in national security
affairs include the creation of party executive committees, a joint
congressional or joint congressional-executive committee on national
security policy, and an arrangement for both houses to question top
executives.[27]

To sum up the case for heightened congressional involvement, consider the argument of the Foreign Relations Committee in its report
on the War Powers Bill:

[27] For a perceptive analysis of these and other suggestions, see *ibid.*, esp. pp. 78–81
and pp. 155–60.

... The processes through which the President reaches decisions are largely personal and private, beyond the reach of direct institutional accountability. Congress, on the other hand, makes its decisions almost entirely in the open and under public scrutiny. The President is subject to quadrennial plebiscite, but Congress provides the American people with points of access through which they can hold their Government to day-to-day account and thereby participate in it. Inefficient and shortsighted though it sometimes is, Congress provides the only feasible means under the American constitutional system of drawing the President, at least indirectly, into the adversary processes of democracy. The executive branch is endowed with organizational discipline and legions of experts, but Congressmen and Senators have a unique asset when it comes to playing an effective, democratic role in the making of foreign policy: the power to speak and act freely from an independent political base.[28]

The nature of Congress makes it improbable that it can ever dominate the foreign policy-making process, setting the nation's goals in international politics and prescribing the conditions of international relationships and commitments. No one, in fact, seriously sponsors this notion of congressional hegemony. But Congress can enhance its roles in shaping national security policy. The means by which to restore a measure of equilibrium between the branches are clearly at hand. Now lacking, it would seem, is a critical element: the political will to do so.

[28] S. Rept. 92–606, p. 22.

David B. Truman

8

The Prospects for Change

Any deliberate change in a key institution, if it has consequences that are not merely trivial, may be regarded as a reform. But the effects of such changes do not necessarily move in the same direction. That is, they may affect the distribution of power—within the institution or between it and other segments of the government—in differing or contradictory ways. To take an obvious example, if an attempt were made to limit the capacity of the Rules Committee to keep bills from the floor of the House, a time limit could be placed on Rules consideration of bills, like the one in force during the Eighty-first Congress (1949–1951) and the Eighty-ninth Congress (1965–1967). But if the authority to call up such blockaded bills were given to the chairmen of the standing committees that originally handled them, the effect would be further to enhance the power now dispersed among committee chairmen. The same authority granted to the Speaker, however, would be a step in the direction of centralization, since it would strengthen his hand against the standing committees.

Three Problems

PROBABLE EFFECTS

An initial problem, then, in examining any proposed change is to estimate the character and direction of its effects. Relatively few proposals, however, are so simple and so uni-dimensional in their consequences that one can predict their effects with a high degree of confidence. Especially if they are part of an omnibus or composite proposal, the problem of estimating *net* consequences seriously complicates the assignment. This may be one reason, as Huitt implies (chapter 4), why few if any observers predicted that the Lafollette-

Monroney bill, which in amended form became the Legislative Reorganization Act of 1946, would result primarily in weakening central leadership in Congress to the advantage of the standing committees and their proliferous subcommittees. The provisions that had this effect were associated with others that conceivably could have operated in the other direction—the legislative budget, party policy committees, and regulation of lobbies—but the latter either failed to work or were dropped from the measure in the process of enactment.

BASIC FUNCTIONS

An attempt at anticipating effects is nevertheless essential, even though estimates are difficult and their reliability uncertain. When the attempt achieves some clarity, however, a second and more fundamental set of questions will confront a reflective observer: what are the *needs* of the Congress? What, more fundamentally, are the distinctive functions it is to perform in the governmental scheme? A representative assembly, as Huntington has pointed out (chapter 1), can be a significant component of government without being in a strict sense a legislature, that is, an agency that assumes the chief role in both preparing and enacting statutes. If it is to be more completely a legislature in this sense, the needs of the Congress are not the same in most respects as they are if it is to be primarily a delaying and legitimating body or if it is to act chiefly as critic and modifier of administrative policies.

The problem of basic function is important not for the reason that it is in fact possible to make a formal and official choice among the alternatives. Institutions are rarely created by fiat or by a single conscious choice. It is important rather because incremental choices will lead by steps toward one alternative or another, and both realism and satisfaction are likely to be served if these fundamental questions are kept in view.

FEASIBILITIES

The Congress today is more nearly a legislature in the strict sense than is the national assembly in any other major country of the world. One may, however, question whether it is in any realistic sense possible, under the technical conditions of an industrialized and interdependent society, for the Congress more fully to exercise the legislative function. The point is raised not in order to propose an answer but rather to introduce the third problem to be confronted in assessing proposals for change, the problem of feasibility: can it be done?

Discussions of reform frequently are carried on with the unstated assumption that anything is possible, that the question of feasibility is essentially irrelevant. Yet proposals for change that would require major alterations in the Constitution almost certainly are beyond the bounds of feasibility. They may have utility as means of agitation and criticism, but they lack more than a toehold on reality. It is well to remember that in nearly two centuries the nation has not returned to Philadelphia and that the document written there displaced a system that had been in effect less than a decade. Even there the question of feasibility was paramount. It is no disservice to the achievement of that assembly of notables to say that they were not free to adopt any arrangements they chose, that they were obliged to take account of existing distributions of power and to reckon with continuities of practice and of expectation.

The most significant changes, written and unwritten, in the Constitution of the United States came in the wake of desperate crises: the Civil War, the Great Depression, and World War II. Crises of these proportions almost certainly would place the whole nation in jeopardy. Reforms contingent upon such upheavals, therefore, cannot be regarded realistically as feasible.

The constraints of feasibility apply equally, however, to less sweeping proposals. For adoption and accomplished effect depend upon the convergence of existing power as the fulcrum of change. The authors of the preceding chapters are not of one mind on the changes that might be made in the Congress, but none would dissent from Ralph Huitt's trenchant observation (chapter 4), that "a successful reform is a demonstration of effective massing and use of power, not a prelude to it."

Current Proposals and the Dispersion of Power

One thread that runs through all of these essays is the dispersion of power, in the past half-century apparently an increasing dispersion, within and between the houses of Congress. Nearly ten years ago, in the first edition of this collection, I observed: "Almost regardless of what may be taken, explicitly or implicitly, as the appropriate basic functions of the Congress, restraints upon this dispersion are likely to be at the focus of controversy in the days ahead." This prediction was not in error; attempts have been made to strengthen the central organs of power in House and Senate, but they have been defeated in almost every case. The problem of dispersion of power remains at least as central as it was a decade ago, and there even are some indications that changes made in recent years have rendered the problem more acute. The committee authorizations that led up to the Legislative Reorganization Act of 1970, for example, specifically excluded from consideration the bastions of dispersed power. A number of the provisions adopted in the otherwise innocuous legislation, moreover, tended to cut into the power of committee chairmen but at the same time and in consequence further dispersed power in both houses.

These would include the requirement for more open meetings of committees, for public disclosure of votes in committee, the recording of teller votes in the House, and allowing a committee majority to call a meeting over the objections of the chairman, among others. In the opposite direction, other actions have placed some limits on the chairman of the House Rules Committee and have slightly increased the discretionary authority of the Speaker and of the Senate floor leaders, but such alterations have not been of significant consequence.

The problem of dispersion of power in the Congress remains central and is likely to appear on agendas in one form or another for some time ahead. It is useful, therefore, to draw these observations to a close by reviewing some of the current and recurrent proposals for change in relation to their probable effects on dispersion.

NEUTRAL EFFECTS

Many suggestions for revision, of course, would have no appreciable effect on dispersion, whatever else they might accomplish. In turn, a number of these could be adopted without major difficulty simply because they do not significantly affect the power structure or the political risks of the individual members. In this category would fall most of the suggestions for altering the "workload" of the Congress, such as providing separate days for committee and floor work, delegating to some special tribunal the handling of additional private bills —since 1946 chiefly bills dealing with the immigration and naturalization problems of individuals—and adding to the personal staffs of representatives and senators. They might well lighten the burdens of members, but none of them would touch the power structure at all closely. Some of them would, of course, promote efficiency in the sense that they would save time, but "waste" is after all a relative term, to be measured by what might have been done with what was saved. What appears as a "waste" of time, moreover, may, in a chamber in which power is diffused, be a source of some control by leaders, as the adjournment rush in most legislatures demonstrates.

Also in the neutral category probably should be placed proposals that Congress divest itself of the somewhat anachronistic duty of being the legislature for the District of Columbia. The change would reduce the power and perquisites of two committees; and it would be least a symbolic loss for those who fear self-government in a city in which white citizens are not a majority, but the effects on Congress would be slight. Equally nominal, for the Congress, would be a requirement of joint hearings by House and Senate committees. If the change could be made, which is doubtful, some time of administration witnesses would be saved, which would be a gain, but the congressional effects would be insubstantial. Unless it were given power over revenue and appropriations, the creation of a joint committee on fiscal policy would likely go the way of the 1946 reorganization's legislative budget or at best become a vehicle for instruction, such as the Joint Economic Committee. (If it were given such power, which is unlikely, it would become a formidable rival to any other points of control in the Congress.)

Finally, it seems likely that proposals in the realm of congressional "ethics"—chiefly conflict-of-interest, "moonlighting" activities, and income "disclosure" proposals—would have a neutral effect as long as they went no farther than disclosure. They might reduce the utility of some Congressmen to outside interests, and they would tend to increase public respect for the Congress—clearly an advantage, especially if they resulted in eliminating the double standard for the legislative and executive branches—but their power implications would otherwise be slight.

REINFORCING DISPERSION

A considerable number of suggestions, especially some that are urged in the name of "democratizing" the House or Senate, would have the effect of further weakening the power of the central "elective" leadership, the Speaker and the floor leaders. Thus the suggestion, recurrent over the years, that the number of signatures required in the House to make effective a petition discharging a committee from further consideration of a bill be reduced from the present 218 to something like 150 would transfer control from one minority to another (and shifting) one equally inaccessible to control by the elective leaders. Similarly, as noted earlier, under a 21-day rule for calling a bill out of the House Rules Committee in which authority so to act were granted to the standing committees, the effect would be to weaken the Speaker's control of the agenda if he "owned" the Rules Committee. In any case it would in this form enhance the powers of the chairmen of the legislative committees. (The version of this rule that was in operation in 1965 and 1966 gave discretionary authority to the Speaker.)

In both House and Senate several proposed modifications of the seniority rule, however unlikely of adoption, would tend toward further dispersion. For example, caucus election of committee chairmen by secret ballot or the choice of chairmen by majority vote of the committee members, both of which were debated and rejected in the Ninety-first Congress (1970), would at best give nothing additional to the central leadership and at worst would strengthen the autonomy of chairmen, especially if an incumbent were regularly reelected.

Further increasing the professional staffs of the standing committees, as the Legislative Reorganization Act of 1970 did, whatever its benefits in other respects, tends to strengthen committee autonomy.

Similarly, the elimination of remaining jurisdictional ambiguities among committees would, as did the "reforms" of 1946, reduce further the discretion of the elective leaders in both houses. Finally, the introduction of electronic voting equipment, frequently recommended by outsiders and defended by members as a time-saver, especially in the House, would strengthen minority control by facilitating snap votes. Further, it probably would take from the central leadership the time it now has during a long roll call to muster maximum support from the waverers or the negotiators.

STRENGTHENING CENTRAL LEADERSHIP FROM INSIDE

A great many devices can be imagined that would directly increase central control from within the House and Senate or do so indirectly by reducing the opportunities for a minority to block or seriously to delay congressional action. These would in varying degrees assault the collective powers of the present oligarchy, and their prospects are therefore correspondingly limited. In a body where risks are individual and localized, decentralized authority is likely to have a broad base of support, especially among those who have been re-elected at least once. Such decentralization puts within a member's reach the means of helping himself politically—an entirely worthy motive—and it is the more attractive because he cannot clearly see the capacity of any central leadership, in or out of Congress, to do the equivalent for him. A successful assault, therefore, would require a crisis severe enough to isolate the members of the oligarchy and to solidify the rank and file around central leaders willing to spear-head a serious shake-up.

The most promising, though not necessarily feasible, means all would have one feature in common, namely, increased leadership control of the timetable, not only in the chambers, but also in the committees. In the Senate a simpler and more easily invoked rule for limiting debate than the present two-thirds of those present and voting would control the most serious and most notorious threat to the timetable in that chamber, the filibuster. In the House a reinstituted 21-day rule, one that placed the authority to call up a bill blockaded by the Rules Committee in the hands of the Speaker or the majority leader, would strengthen the position of at least the Democratic leaders in the chamber. Some minor steps in this direction were taken in 1970 by increasing the Speaker's control of dilatory actions in the House and his ability in some circumstances to bypass committee chairmen in bringing a measure to the floor and by slightly augmenting the joint powers of the Senate majority and minority leaders to influence committee timetables.

In both houses some alternatives to or modifications in the seniority rule would aid the leaders in relation to the committees and in the chambers generally. The slight changes approved by the Republican and Democratic caucuses in the House in 1971, to give some formal caucus control of nominations to committee positions and to permit committees on committees not to follow seniority, are too recent to permit confident evaluation, but they do not seem likely to produce any startling reversals of pattern. A return to the practice under which the Speaker designated committee chairmen in the House and a granting of comparable power to the majority leader in the Senate would of course contribute to centralized control. The circumstances that would have to exist in order to make such a change possible, moreover, would assume use of the power, at least for several years. The less drastic proposal for caucus election of chairmen from among the three most senior members of a committee would have the same tendency only if the Speaker and majority leader were able and willing to make their preferences prevail. If they were not, the result would be a reinforcement of dispersion.

STRENGTHENING CENTRAL LEADERSHIP FROM OUTSIDE

A striking fact about the Congress in this century is that most, if not all, of those developments that have tended toward reducing or restraining the dispersion of power in the separate houses and in the Congress as a whole have come from outside the legislature and chiefly from the White House. In some instances the Congress has been formally a partner in the changes, where legislation has provided the occasion for them, and in some instances not. But in either case the antidispersion effects have been secondary, and largely unintended, consequences of lines of action taken by the President primarily to discharge his own responsibilities and to meet the needs of his role.

Thus the Budget and Accounting Act of 1921, which established the executive budget in pursuit of the goal of fiscal efficiency, created for the first time a government-wide fiscal program and gave the President responsibility for its formulation and, equally important, its public presentation. The act did not achieve quite the integration of the appropriating and revenue activities in the Congress that some sponsors hoped for, but it did lead to the setting of rational, if not inflexible, proportions in expenditure. In the course of time, moreover, it created something of a counterbalance to the agency-committee relation that could be useful in as well as outside the Congress. The Employment Act of 1946, though it created no comparable operating functions, placed on the President the responsibility for developing and pronouncing the requirements of the economy as a whole and the government's part in meeting them. Although little more than an agenda-setting device, it is at least that and as such is a check on complete committee freedom in setting the congressional program, which, as

Mansfield's essay (chapter 6) clearly shows, would make coherent and integrated policy determination completely impossible.

Alongside and reinforcing these formal and legislatively created activities, at least three less conspicuous practices have developed since the 1930s. In the first place, the President's legislative program, as Neustadt has demonstrated (chapter 5), developed from the needs of a succession of chief executives, but it acquired vigor and, in all probability, permanence because it also met the needs of others—the agencies and, more important, the Congress, including its committees. It has provided the latter with not merely a "laundry-list" but a set of priorities. Its priority-setting qualities, moreover, have been strengthened in consequence of the increased and continuing prominence of foreign policy-national security problems. Presidential priorities are not coincident with congressional ones, but in these areas limits have grown up around committee autonomy and hence around congressional disjunction, limits that have been strained but not abandoned in consequence of the controversies surrounding the war in Southeast Asia. (See Carroll, chapter 7.)

In the second place, as a likely consequence of the President's stake in his program, the growth of a White House staff specialized in legislative liaison has introduced an element of coherence and coordination into congressional deliberations, especially at the committee stage. Again, although it has been little studied, one suspects that its viability depends not merely on presidential desire but also on its utility *in general,* and not necessarily for identical reasons, to committee chairmen, to elective leaders, and even to some agencies. It clearly is not and cannot be a legislative high command, but it seems to have acquired informational and secondary influence capabilities that are centripetal in tendency. These are only capabilities, however. Neglected or badly used, they can aggravate conflicts between Congress and the White House and can undermine the efforts of legislative leaders to promote coherence.

Thirdly, the now well-established practice of regular presidential consultation with his party's principal elective leaders in the Congress works in the same direction. Like the two developments already mentioned, it was initially an outgrowth of presidential needs, but apparently it also has utility for elective leaders, especially if they head a nominal majority in Congress. Particularly if these leaders in name see themselves potentially as leaders in fact—and they need not do so —their relations with the President seem useful. The President's program and priorities are not necessarily theirs, and they do not, if they are prudent, attempt to operate simply as his lieutenants. But they may share with him the handicaps of power dispersion in the Congress, and their collaboration with him may—again if they see themselves as more than the servants of the congressional oligarchy—place limits on its effects, to their joint advantage.

A possible implication of these developments for the further restriction of dispersion is that they may offer something of a pattern for the future. Needs in the Presidency, if they are at least consistent with needs in Congress and among its central leaders, may lead to new practices whose consequence, in all likelihood unintended, could be some further limit on the dispersion of power. One such need, as yet not clearly felt, is suggested by Neustadt (chapter 5) in his discussion of the common stakes of elective politicians against career officials. This may yet prove to be the most critical factor in resolving the complex problem of coherence and accountability in a divided system that invites a dispersion of power.

A next step, though it also would be a long and difficult one, might be, as Walter Lippmann and Huntington (chapter 1) have suggested, toward a commitment in Congress to bring to a vote, at least by mid-session, any legislation carrying top priority from the administration. The prospect of such a commitment would require more care in the construction of the President's program, since some means would be needed explicitly to distinguish urgent needs from trial balloons, and the invidious judgments that this would require might be too costly politically. It also would require a collegial commitment from the congressional oligarchy that might prove impossible of achievement. But the attempt would at least follow logically from the trends of several decades.

Prospects of strengthening central leadership through jointly acceptable leverage from outside Congress have at least the semblance of feasibility, and not only because of the developments already identified. Evidence suggests that reforms that would rest largely on the initiative or conscious concurrence of the Congress itself do not command requisite majorities. A random sample of the House in 1963 found a majority supporting only 14 of 32 specific proposals of reform. Of the proposals enjoying such support, only 2 were ones likely to be of major consequence—reinstatement of the 21-day rule and a four-year term for representatives (which senators certainly would not favor). The remainder, including most of those discussed in these pages, appealed only to a minority.[1] Subsequent action in Congress, including the Legislative Reorganization Act of 1970, fully confirmed the validity of this estimate.

Whether or not outside leverage leads to a reduction in dispersion, the examples discussed here underscore a central point: the Congress and its power structure cannot profitably be viewed as something

---

[1] Michael O'Leary, ed., *Congressional Reorganization: Problems and Prospects* (Hanover, N.H.: Dartmouth College, 1964), pp. 18–21, 58–63.

separate and isolable from the remainder of the government and the society. They affect and are affected by needs and changes in the society and in the government as a whole. They must, therefore, be looked at within this context. From this context, moreover, will come the pressures for change, such as they may be, in the structure of congressional power. Congress alone, it is clear, cannot deal constructively with the problem of dispersed power in Congress.

Index

The American Assembly
COLUMBIA UNIVERSITY

About The American Assembly

The American Assembly was established by Dwight D. Eisenhower at Columbia University in 1950. It holds nonpartisan meetings and publishes authoritative books to illuminate issues of United States policy.

An affiliate of Columbia, with offices in the Graduate School of Business, the Assembly is a national educational institution incorporated in the State of New York.

The Assembly seeks to provide information, stimulate discussion, and evoke independent conclusions in matters of vital public interest.

AMERICAN ASSEMBLY SESSIONS

At least two national programs are initiated each year. Authorities are retained to write background papers presenting essential data and defining the main issues in each subject.

About sixty men and women representing a broad range of experience, competence, and American leadership meet for several days to discuss the Assembly topic and consider alternatives for national policy.

All Assemblies follow the same procedure. The background papers are sent to participants in advance of the Assembly. The Assembly meets in small groups for four or five lengthy periods. All groups use the same agenda. At the close of these informal sessions, participants adopt in plenary session a final report of findings and recommendations.

Regional, state, and local Assemblies are held following the national session at Arden House. Assemblies have also been held in England, Switzerland, Malaysia, Canada, the Caribbean, South America, Central America, the Philippines, and Japan. Over one hundred institutions have co-sponsored one or more Assemblies.

ARDEN HOUSE

Home of The American Assembly and scene of the national sessions is Arden House, which was given to Columbia University in 1950 by W. Averell Harriman. E. Roland Harriman joined his brother in contributing toward adaptation of the property for conference purposes. The buildings surrounding the land, known as the Harriman Campus of Columbia University, are fifty miles north of New York City.

Arden house is a distinguished conference center. It is self-supporting and operates throughout the year for use by organizations with educational objectives.

AMERICAN ASSEMBLY BOOKS

The background papers for each Assembly program are published in cloth and paperbound editions for use by individuals, libraries, businesses, public agencies, nongovernmental organizations, educational institutions, discussion and service groups. In this way the deliberations of Assembly sessions are continued and extended.

The subjects of Assembly programs to date are:

1951——United States–Western Europe Relationships
1952——Inflation
1953——Economic Security for Americans
1954——The United States' Stake in the United Nations
——The Federal Government Service
1955——United States Agriculture
——The Forty-Eight States
1956——The Representation of the United States Abroad
——The United States and the Far East
1957——International Stability and Progress
——Atoms for Power
1958——The United States and Africa
——United States Monetary Policy
1959——Wages, Prices, Profits, and Productivity
——The United States and Latin America
1960——The Federal Government and Higher Education
——The Secretary of State
——Goals for Americans
1961——Arms Control: Issues for the Public
——Outer Space: Prospects for Man and Society
1962——Automation and Technological Change
——Cultural Affairs and Foreign Relations
1963——The Population Dilemma
——The United States and the Middle East
1964——The United States and Canada
——The Congress and America's Future
1965——The Courts, the Public, and the Law Explosion
——The United States and Japan
1966——State Legislatures in American Politics
——A World of Nuclear Powers?
——The United States and the Philippines
——Challenges to Collective Bargaining
1967——The United States and Eastern Europe
——Ombudsmen for American Government?
1968——Uses of the Seas
——Law in a Changing America
——Overcoming World Hunger
1969——Black Economic Development
——The States and the Urban Crisis

1970——The Health of Americans
    ——The United States and the Caribbean
1971——The Future of American Transportation
    ——Collective Bargaining in American Government
1972——The Future of Foundations
    ——Corrections

Second Editions, Revised:
1962——The United States and the Far East
1963——The United States and Latin America
    ——The United States and Africa
1964——United States Monetary Policy
1965——The Federal Government Service
    ——The Representation of the United States Abroad
1968——Cultural Affairs and Foreign Relations
    ——Outer Space: Prospects for Man and Society
1969——The Population Dilemma
1972——The Congress and America's Future